HOT, HOT
CHICKEN

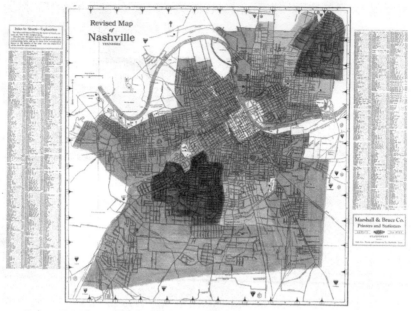

Robert K. Nelson, LaDale Winling, Richard Marciano, Nathan Connolly, et al.,
"Mapping Inequality," *American Panorama*, edited by Robert K. Nelson and
Edward L. Ayers.

HOT, HOT CHICKEN

A NASHVILLE STORY

RACHEL LOUISE MARTIN

VANDERBILT UNIVERSITY PRESS

NASHVILLE, TENNESSEE

Library of Congress Cataloging-in-Publication Data

Names: Martin, Rachel Louise, 1980– author.
Title: Hot, hot chicken : a Nashville story / Rachel Louise Martin.
Description: Nashville : Vanderbilt University Press, [2021] | Includes
    bibliographical references and index. | Summary: "The history of
    Nashville's Black communities through the story of its hot chicken
    scene, from the Civil War through the tornado in March 2020" —Provided
    by publisher.
Identifiers: LCCN 2020046179 | ISBN 9780826501769 (paperback) | ISBN
    9780826501776 (epub) | ISBN 9780826501783 (pdf)
Subjects: LCSH: Prince's Hot Chicken (Restaurant)—History. | Fried
    chicken—Tennessee—Nashville—History. | African
    Americans—Tennessee—Nashville—Social life and customs. | African
    Americans—Tennessee—Nashville—History. | Prince family.
Classification: LCC TX945.5.P687 M37 2021 | DDC 647.95768/55—dc23
LC record available at https://lccn.loc.gov/2020046179

To my parents.

Contents

Acknowledgments

This book could not exist without the hot chicken makers whose lives and experiences I've attempted to reconstruct. I am especially grateful to two in particular. Back in 2015, André Prince Jeffries, current owner of Prince's Hot Chicken, sat down with me for several hours in the midst of a busy service to explain how race and hot chicken had intertwined in Nashville's history. Her insights into the city's past and present helped me clarify the ways this story was unique to Nashville and the ways it was true of cities across the nation. And then when it came time for me to write the book, Dollye Matthews, co-owner of Bolton's Hot Chicken and Fish, shared how her family's experiences both mirrored and diverged from the Prince family's stories. I am grateful to both of you for sharing your memories and your perspectives with me.

Thank you also to the other Nashvillians whose voices contributed to this book: Keel Hunt, Bill Purcell, Learotha Williams Jr., and Steve Younes. I appreciated your willingness to share your thoughts and memories. And thank you to Franklin historian Thelma Battle, who helped me fill out the Prince family's pre-Nashville story. Her decades of research into the Black experience in Williamson County has created an invaluable archive for anyone wanting to know about the lives of those omitted from other records.

I cannot overlook Chuck Reece at *The Bitter Southerner*. When I pitched "How Hot Chicken Really Happened" to him back in 2015, I was a historian who wanted to write, but I only had a couple of clips in my portfolio. He gambled on me. Then he led me through the process of turning my research into an essay other people would want to read. His edits were some of the best writing classes I've had.

I am grateful to the team at Vanderbilt University Press for the opportunity to transform my essay into a book. Zack Gresham, my editor, stayed committed to this project even when my early drafts should have scared him off. Thank you for giving me the space to see where my research might lead me and the deadlines that kept me focused on the key questions of the narrative. And thanks also to Betsy Phillips, a fellow writer and a marketing guru, who knew just when I needed a cheerleader.

Thanks to Sam Warlick, who pulled some marathon reading sessions, double-checking my understanding of Nashville's development and helping me cull some of the research that had blinded me to the bigger storyline. And to the rest of my friends who listened to me worry about missing city directory entries and suggested where I might find lost divorce records and let me interrupt our conversations to spurt random facts about Nashville, thank you. I only have one more favor to ask. Next time I say I'm going to research and write a book in less than six months, tell me no.

And in everything I write, I owe a debt to Jacquelyn Dowd Hall, my graduate school advisor, who taught me how to search for and listen to the voices purged from the official records.

Finally, I am grateful my parents who listened and explored and distracted and believed and asked and brainstormed and read and fed and laughed and loved me through this project and all the others I've undertaken. Thank you seems inadequate.

Set It Up

A Tennessean's Take on *Mise en Place*

A smallish man putters behind the warped glass storefront. Surprised to see signs of life inside the damaged strip mall restaurant, I park my Prius and watch him work his way around a jumble of white ladder-back chairs cantilevered against the middle window. The man grabs a five-gallon bucket, one of those pails that could hold anything from paint to Quickrete to roof sealer, and lugs it past a stack of fire-proof insulation. I lose sight of him when he heads toward the back of the building where the kitchen used to be.

Driving by, I hadn't noticed how much had changed in the fourteen months since the accident that shut down this location, but now that I've stopped, I catalogue the differences. Inside, an unfamiliar trio of booths faces the far wall. These aren't the six historic white wooden booths that André Prince Jeffries had trucked along with her when she moved the family business here to East Nashville. Those benches had heft. They curled and curved like high-back church pews. And like all good church pews, they were unpadded, a guarantee that if the food's afterburn didn't sober up Jeffries' late-night crowd, the seats would get them out the front door before they decided to sleep off their weekend pleasures. But the booths in the left-hand window today have no such stately heritage; they are the same patchwork of blue and red vinyl that appears in every nameless pizza joint.

From what I can see, just about everything in the restaurant has been altered. Prince's was multi-colored—cream walls, slate ordering window, turquoise restroom hallway. And all of it was covered in family memorabilia and community notices and autographed headshots and Christmas lights. The new restaurant wears a uniform navy peacoat blue. Someone has switched out the sign; "Prince's Hot Chicken Shack" is now labeled "Café 1-2-3," the name of a long-defunct Nashville restaurant.

Even the front windows are washed clean of paint, wiped clear of the cartoon drawing of a red-shirted Thornton Prince III wearing a crown and hoisting a monster-sized steaming leg of fried chicken over his head. Only the hours remain, stuck to the door in peeling vinyl decals:

TUESDAY – THURSDAY
11:00 am – 11:00 pm
FRIDAY
11:00 am – 4:00 am
SATURDAY
2:00 pm – 4:00 am

Gone too is the press of regulars, celebrities, and tourists who had visited this East Nashville strip mall. The last time I was here, customers pushed through the door and lined up along the turquoise wall, inching toward the woman ringing up orders. A few were like me, occasional visitors needing a quick hit of spice. Most were friends. They chatted with each other, with the staff, with André Jeffries, with the cooks hidden in the kitchen. Then everything paused when the woman in the window yelled a number. A customer would shove forward to grab their brown paper bag of food. That early on a Thursday, they would be taking their meal to go. The chicken's grease and sauce would quickly saturate the paper, so they'd wrap their bundle in a white plastic bag plucked off a nearby counter.

All that ended on December 28, 2018, when an unnamed someone rammed a stolen SUV into the tobacco shop at the end of the strip mall.

The only other person on site was a Prince's employee who was deep in the restaurant's bowels preparing for a marathon pre-New Year's Eve Friday night. "I heard big bangs, 'Boom-boom, boom-boom!' " he told a reporter for the *Tennessean*. "It was like the police knocking on your door." When he came outside, no one was there.[1]

Police arrived at 4:33 that morning and found the vehicle on fire, igniting the building around it. The SUV was empty, a brick on its accelerator. The driver was gone, and no witnesses had seen him/her/them escape.[2] Rumors swirled through Nashville. Was the crash an insurance job by the building's owner or another shopkeeper? A plot by a guy who'd planned to open a convenience store nearby? An over-blown smash-and-grab? With no suspects, police declined to speculate.

The first estimates said the restaurant would reopen within two weeks. Then the building's owner discovered the accident had cracked the rafters. Months passed. The damage remained. Early in July 2019, André Jeffries gave up. She sent her team to take down the sign above the door, and she announced she wouldn't be reopening in East Nashville.[3]

The driver of that SUV had destroyed a Nashville institution. Sure, the East Nashville site wasn't where the original chicken shack had been located, but the business had been there for twenty-nine years, which was about as long as it had settled anywhere. Luckily, Jeffries already had a new spot on Nolensville Road up and going, but the South Nashville outpost wasn't supposed to replace this East Nashville one. After a decade of watching so many other hot chicken joints franchise and grow, South Nashville was to be where Jeffries finally took her shot and expanded her family business. How many of the East Nashville regulars made the seventeen-mile drive south to the new location? This forced relocation marked the end of an era.

And as with every other move the Princes' business had made, it tracked with changes happening in Nashville itself. But before we jump too far ahead, I guess we should go back and talk about the hot chicken origin story.

Hot chicken's creation has become part of Nashville's mythology, the sort of tale locals can recount with practiced pauses and wry chuckles. It happened like this:

Back in the 1930s—or maybe it was the 1920s or perhaps as late as the 1940s or even the 1950s—well, anyway, there was once a man named

Thornton Prince III. He was a handsome man, tall and good looking, fine as a peacock. "Beautiful, wavy hair," said his great-niece André Prince Jeffries. Debonair, with a dashing sense of style and a touch of Tennessee twang (or so I assume). Women loved him, and he loved them right back. "He was totally a ladies' man," Jeffries laughed. "He sure had plenty of women."[4]

So this one Sunday morning back sometime before most of us were born, Thornton Prince III came in from a long night of catting around, and he told his woman—wife? girlfriend? does it matter?—to make him breakfast. Well, this woman, wife or girlfriend or whatever, she was fed up with his philandering ways.

What could she do with a serial cheater like this? Some women look the other way. Others walk out. A few get even. This one, though, she wanted retribution. She started out by playing it sweet. That morning, just like all their other morning-afters, she got up before him. And she didn't make him dry toast or gruel. Oh, no, she made him his favorite. She made him fried chicken. After all, Sunday morning was that time of the week when families across the South woke up expecting to enjoy some popping-hot fried chicken for breakfast. This woman wasn't making her chicken with love, however.

I like to think she went out and wrung the neck of the skinniest, stringiest yard bird she could find. No plump church chicken for this sorry son-of-a-gun, no sir. Then, she added the spiciest items she had in her kitchen. Dried pepper flakes? Maybe. Fresh chilies plucked from her garden with all their seeds? Perhaps. Half a bottle of Tabasco sauce? Could be. "She couldn't run to the grocery store to get something," Jeffries said. Nobody knows what went into that first hot chicken as she layered on whatever she had on hand. Whatever she added, by the time the bird was cooked, Thornton Prince III's woman was sure she had spiced it up beyond edibility.[5]

As Thornton Prince III took his first bite, she must have braced herself for his reaction. Would he curse? Whimper? Stomp out? And where was she while he ate? Maybe she was in the kitchen, scraping and seasoning her skillet, or perhaps she'd fled back to the bedroom, ready to scamper if he made a big fuss. I like to think she was sitting right there at the table with him, cutting into her own chicken—unpeppered, of course—ready to push the charade as far as she could.

But her plan for revenge backfired. Thornton Prince III loved that over-spiced poultry. He took it to his brothers. They loved it also.

Soon enough, the woman disappeared from his life, but her hot chicken lived on. The Prince brothers turned her idea into the BBQ Chicken Shack, the business André Jeffries renamed Prince's Hot Chicken Shack when she took it over.[6] "We don't know who the lady was that was trying," Jeffries said. "All the old heads are gone. Gone on. But hey, we're still profiting from it." She paused. "So women are very important."[7]

These days, that angry woman's dish is all the rage. It's on the list of "must-try" Southern foods in *Esquire*, *USA Today*, *Southern Living*, *Men's Health*, *Forbes*, *Travel and Leisure*, and *Thrillist*. It's been written about in the *New Yorker* and the *Ringer*. Restaurants in New York, Detroit, Denver, and even Australia advertise that they fry their chicken Nashville-style. Upward of ten thousand people attend the annual Hot Chicken Festival, held every July 4. In 2013 the James Beard Foundation gave Prince's Hot Chicken Shack an American Classic Award for inventing the dish, and celebrity chefs make pilgrimages to Nashville to eat it on camera.

Why has this woman's chicken become such a cultural phenomenon? Hot chicken aficionados and purveyors have offered different explanations for the food's popularity, for why it seems to grab ahold of certain people's taste buds, embedding itself in their guts and drawing them back time and again.

André Prince Jeffries had an easy explanation for it. "My mother said, if you know people are gonna talk, give them something to talk about," she explained. "This chicken is not boring. You're gonna talk about this chicken."[8]

Spicy food appeals to people who are "more emotional—more fired up about everything they do," another hot chicken purveyor mused. "If you are a very sensitive person and emotionally hooked to what you are eating, it's got to give you a little more, like a drug."[9]

Others suggest hot chicken is popular because it is excellent hangover food, something generations of BBQ/Prince's Hot Chicken Shack eaters have known. Nashville may be the buckle of the Bible belt, but it's also Music City, USA, fully stocked with musicians and misfits who drink hard and live late into the night. "In Nashville, at least among the drinking class, folks appreciate the kind of heat that compels you to grab a first-aid manual, thumbing wildly for a passage that differentiates between second- and third-degree burns," food historian John T. Edge wrote.[10] This was a reason Thornton Prince III kept his joint open until the wee hours on the weekends, and that's the reason why André Jeffries continues to do so today.[11]

"I think it's popular in Nashville because there are a lot of people living today that had ancestors stuck on pepper," Dollye Matthews of Bolton's Spicy Chicken and Fish told an interviewer for the Southern Foodways Alliance. "Maybe they had hypertension and couldn't use salt, so they used pepper instead. . . . A couple of generations like that, and you know, you just got the clientele for hot and spicy chicken."[12]

But although hot chicken has long had a loyal following, its widespread popularity is new, even among much of Nashville. My Nashville roots go three generations deep, but I had never eaten hot chicken—or even heard of it—growing up. I moved away for graduate school in 2005. I came back eight years later to a new Nashville where everyone hung out in neighborhoods that had been called "blighted" when I left. Folks said a hundred people a day were moving to the city, and all the transplants ate Nashville-style hot chicken. This local dish I didn't know had become internationally famous.

Embarrassed I didn't even recognize this dish everyone else loved, I turned to Google hoping an image search would jiggle loose a memory. The web was full of photographs of fried chicken slathered in hot sauce a stomach-curdling shade of orange, served on a slice of Bunny white bread and topped by a crinkled dill pickle slice. None of it looked familiar.

I asked my dad if he had ever eaten it. "Nope," he said. But he taught school in the 1970s, and he remembered that some of the Black teachers carried their own bottles of hot sauce. Sometimes they'd prank him by spiking his cafeteria lunch.

This was not the answer I wanted. Was hot chicken a part of the city's history that had been invisible to me as a white woman? I asked Denise, an older African American woman in my church who was raised in the city, what she thought. "Of course you didn't eat hot chicken," she said, shaking her head. "Hot chicken's what we ate in the neighborhood."

Still hoping I was wrong, I went to the downtown public library to do a very unscientific survey of what they had on hand. I sat in their second-floor reading room, surrounded by stacks of cookbooks published by the Junior League and the extension agency and local restauranteurs, searching for a recipe proving that in Nashville we didn't choose our chicken style based on race. I walked away with several new ways to fry a chicken. One of them added some black pepper. Several of them mentioned serving chicken while it was still hot. None of them showed me how to make my chicken spicy enough to ignite the interest of foodies and hipsters.

Denise was right. For almost seventy years, hot chicken had been made and sold primarily in Nashville's Black neighborhoods. Most of that time, it was sold exclusively at Prince's.

Since I've come back, I've learned to see multiple different Nashvilles. My city chooses which face it shows each person. There have been moments when we've tried to unify ourselves, but our efforts usually end in failure because we've built our divisions into our government, our schools, our food, our very landscape.

Not all Southern history dates from the Civil War, but that's where this story begins. The Civil War was Nashville's first urban planning initiative, ad hoc and piecemeal though it was, and it created the neighborhoods where hot chicken incubated for perhaps half a century, vastly popular among Black Nashville but unnoticed by all but a handful of white eaters. Since the Civil War a hundred and fifty years ago, Nashville has weathered five more waves of change. The projects have had different names—slum clearance, urban renewal, Model Cities, Enterprise Zones, gentrification—but each one has had the same goal, to unwind the independence that planted itself in the spaces the refugees claimed when they stole themselves away from slavery and declared their freedom. Today, new Nashville is spreading those divisions even further apart.

And while this is a tale about Nashville history and Nashville food, this is also the story of the nation. The same forces, the same policies, and the same motivations played out in cities across America in roughly a similar way, from Atlanta to Los Angeles, from New York to Seattle, from Chicago to Houston.

This is that story, told through the history of a piece of chicken and the family who made it famous.

Sunday, February 23, 2020
Nashville, Tennessee

CHAPTER 1

Brine with Hot Sauce

The Princes Move to Nashville, 1860–1924

A scrum of new neighborhoods have been carved into the farmland that once lined Split Log Road. The other developers had done their best at the naming game: Cromwell and Northumberland and Cross Pointe and Inglehame Farms and the Laurels and Tuscany Hills. The employee who came up with Taramore, however, what with its nod to a mythical *Gone with the Wind*–like lifestyle of moonlight and magnolias, deserved a raise.

I drove through the enclave, hoping to see a hint of the life the Prince family had led there in the aftermath of the Civil War as they negotiated what freedom and citizenship would mean for a Black farming family in Middle Tennessee. But when the builders for Pulte Homes created Taramore, they had bulldozed the acreage into a series of two-hundred-some-odd gently sloped, sodded yards, perfectly groomed settings for the McMansions erected in the center of each plat. The developer even cut down most of the mature trees, and the spindly saplings residents had put in to replace the lost woodland still needed decades to reach maturity.

FIGURE 1.1. The Sayers' home, Wood Park, today stands in the center of the Tara-more subdivision. The window to Ann Currine's kitchen is peeking from behind the large tree on the right. Photo: Rachel Louise Martin

Only Wood Park remained. The red-brick, columned Greek revival house had once anchored life on the property. Erected in 1845 and built from bricks cast on site by John J. Sayers' enslaved laborers, the home was once a showpiece of Williamson County. Now it had been restored and remodeled into the community's clubhouse. The renovations to the building were carefully considered. I pressed my nose against the windows. An elegant stairway still curved through the tall foyer, and appropriate antiques graced the front rooms. The only obvious alter-ation to the historic structure was a sunroom/meeting space framed out in the breezeway that once separated the house from the kitchen. The grounds, however, had been refitted to the community's desires. Out back where once the enslaved cook probably had tended a kitchen garden, the developer had laid a couple of tennis courts and dug a swimming pool complete with a twisting green-and-white waterslide.[1]

Behind the pool, I discovered a bike path. Back when the Princes and the Sayers lived here, Wood Park had been known for its five "everlast-ing springs."[2] Those springs had created a series of meandering stone creeks that carved deep valleys transecting the property. The builders of Taramore hadn't been able to conquer the landscape or the waterways, so they had platted a greenway along them. They left the land around the paved route lined with the choking sort of undergrowth that encroaches on natural areas across Tennessee.

Maybe half a mile down the path, I saw a rusted metal eave peeking through a tangle of cedar trees and honeysuckle. Hiking up my skirts, I tried to plow my way through the brush, but I was blocked by a blackberry bramble wrapped in poison ivy. I tried another angle but again hit a thorny jumble. Surrendering, I retreated to the trail. A little ways on, I looked to my right and realized the tumbled pile of rocks beside me was the remnants of a dry-stack stone fence, a bit of landscape architecture known locally as a "slave wall."

Were these stones laid by some of the Prince family? Perhaps. The first definite reference to any of the Thornton Princes is found in the 1880 census. That year, Thornton Prince II—this would be the father of the man who inspired hot chicken's creation—was a thirteen-year-old farm laborer on the Sayers' property. He was living with his brothers Billie and Austin (who may have been his twin), and he was under the care of the Sayers' forty-five-year-old cook, a woman named Ann Currine who was probably his mother.*

Currine would've worked in the two-story brick kitchen the Sayers ordered their builders to construct fifteen feet or so from the main house. The outbuilding was just close enough that the food cooked there might reach the dining room while still warm, but it was far

---

* Here's what I know: according to later records, Thornton Prince II's mother was a woman named Ann, and in 1877, a woman named Ann Prince had married a man named Winsor Currin. That's almost enough evidence to make a plausible story line connecting Thornton Prince II to the cook, but it's just scant enough to mean it may be completely untrue. 1880 US Census, Williamson County, Tennessee, population schedule, p. 240-41 (stamped), dwelling 135, family 136, R.B. Sayers, digital image, Ancestry.com, accessed September 25, 2019, http://ancestry.com; 1900 US Census, Williamson County, Tennessee, population schedule, p. 0344 (written), dwelling 15, family 15, Thornton Prince, digital image, Ancestry.com, accessed September 25, 2019, http://ancestry.com; Davidson County, Tennessee, Death certificate no. 60-03141 (1960), Thornton Prince, Tennessee Department of Public Health, Nashville; Williamson County, Tennessee, Marriage Bond, p. unknown (1877), Currin-Prince, Tennessee County Marriages 1790-1950, Nashville.

enough away that there was a chance of saving the house if the kitchen caught fire. The distance also ensured that the smells of the kitchen wouldn't fill the house when Currine singed off chickens' feathers or chopped raw onions.[3]

But is this where the Princes lived before the Civil War? I don't know. The records never mention them, an unsurprising development since one of the best ways to deny a people citizenship and even humanity is to refuse to record their names and hence their existences. In 1860, when the Civil War began, Ann Prince/Currine would have been an enslaved woman in her mid-twenties. That year, the United States Census Bureau created a slave schedule, or census, for Williamson County. The document recorded no names, but it did list sex and age. Was Currine one of the two twenty-three-year-old Black women living on the Sayers' farm? Possibly. And where had she been living in 1850? In the schedule made that year, the Sayers' entry has faded away. Was Ann's information one of those lost lines?[4]

Wherever she was in 1860, Ann Currine had already begun her training as a cook. She may have even been in charge of the Sayers' kitchen. Currine would have created all the food the white family ate, whether the Sayers wanted a quick snack or a celebratory feast. Hospitality was how families like the Sayers established their social standing. From intimate dinner parties to summertime picnics to lavish balls, they depended on their cook to create dishes that would impress their neighbors.[5] "Plantation cooks were highly skilled, trained, and professional," Kelley Fano Deetz wrote in *Bound to the Fire*, a study of enslaved chefs in Virginia. "[White] Southern hospitality relied almost exclusively on enslaved domestic labor."[6]

Ann Currine could probably craft delicate pastries, butcher hogs, whip up frothy crème anglaise, and pound out beaten biscuits that didn't taste like hard tack. She would have known the favorite dishes of each of Wood Park's white residents, and she would have avoided the foods they hated. And in an era before electric stoves and oven timers, she would have done most of this over an open flame, and she would have been able to judge a dish's doneness through smell, sight, experience, and intuition. When she made a mistake, serving an undercooked roast or a charred bit of toast, the fault and the punishment would have fallen to her. Enslaved chefs were under the constant scrutiny of the slaveholders who claimed the right to punish the enslaved for even the smallest infraction. Long after slavery ended, stories lingered of cooks who were whipped for burning the day's bread, for making meals that didn't suit one of the family members, even for being suspected of eating some of the food they had cooked.[7] But when the family and their guests enjoyed the meal, they would have praised the mistress of the house, not Currine.[8]

The enslaved chefs were highly skilled workers, but their jobs were physically taxing. Culinary historian Michael W. Twitty set out to re-create the labor his ancestors had done in plantation kitchens in Georgia and Virginia by cooking in those same spaces, using period tools and techniques. Hefting the iron cooking pots on and off the fire left his arms sore, and chopping wood for the fire put calluses on his hands. Working over an open flame singed the hair off Twitty's arms, and he was always aware of how flammable his cotton and flax clothing was near the hearth. Even thirty-six hours after he'd left the kitchen, the scent memory of the meal he had prepared would linger. "The smell of the burning wood becomes the smell of your clothes and your body," he wrote. "It gets down to the root of your hair follicles. Your sweat marries with the smokiness." Just as exhausting was the condescension or disdain or confusion of the white tourists who saw him at work.[9]

Enslaved cooks straddled the worlds of the enslaved and the free, "living and laboring in their enslavers' homes, under their watchful eyes, yet belonging to the larger enslaved community who resided in field quarters away from the main house," Deetz wrote. "These cooks occupied this liminal space and used this axis to manipulate their existence in the brutal culture of chattel slavery."[10]

The enslaved chefs—especially, though not only, the female chefs— also had to fear sexual violence. Their work in the kitchen kept them near the white family where their enslavers could have easy access to their bodies and where they were separated from most of the other enslaved laborers on the property. The kitchen's separate building also meant that when the cooks were attacked, the slaveholding family could claim to have heard and seen nothing. Alice Randall and Caroline Randall Williams, a mother and daughter writing duo, set out to use food to re-create the lives of five generations of women in their family, a journey that became their book *Soul Food Love*. "Until we started working together on this volume, we knew the kitchen was a difficult territory for some Black women," they wrote in the book's introduction, "but we had never contemplated the significance of kitchen rape—an event we discovered was sufficiently common in our family history as to merit the coining of a phrase so the atrocity might be better mourned."[11] Was this part of Ann Currine's experience? She at least lived with the fear and the threat of it.

And what about Thornton Prince I? His life was even sketchier in the records than Ann's was. All that's certain is that he was from Mississippi, and by 1880 he was no longer living with his family in Williamson County. Had he been sold away from them before the Civil War? Been killed during the conflict? Left them voluntarily? All of those are possibilities.

Slavery wrought chaos on the lives of those trapped within its system. No matter how "good" a white owner supposedly was, the slave system was an economic one. The humanity of those trapped within it could never matter as much as the price they might bring on the auction block. Marriages and other familial bonds were not formally recognized by the legal system, thus denying the ties that bound the enslaved people together. And families lived with the constant threat of sale. Parents, children, siblings, cousins, and spouses were sold whenever the white owner decided. Even running away—the act of stealing one's person out of slavery—destroyed families. Successful escape meant never again seeing the friends and family left behind.

Black families faced further upheaval during the Civil War and the violence that swept the South during the war's aftermath. At the beginning of the war, the United States still embraced slavery. The federal troops sent south to fight the Confederate forces were instructed not to aid and abet the escaping enslaved peoples. In fact, because the Fugitive Slave Law was still in effect, the white soldiers were supposed to return the refugees to their captors. Then in late May 1861, three enslaved people—Shepard Mallory, Frank Baker, and James Townsend—escaped into Union general Benjamin Butler's camp near Hampton, Virginia. Butler suddenly changed the rules. He did not contact their white owners. He put them to work instead, arguing that these humans were "contraband of war." If he found an abandoned wagon or a rogue mule, he wouldn't send it back to its owner to work for the enemy. He would confiscate it for the federal troops. Why shouldn't these men be analogous to any other bit of moveable property? Since he didn't believe the escaped people were free, Butler wrote a receipt for them, a promise he would return them to captivity when the war ended.[12]

Then half a million enslaved people ran away from bondage and into the Union camps in Tennessee and across the rest of the South. "All of them knew that if freedom was to come during the Civil War, it was not going to come directly to them," wrote historian Amy Murrell Taylor in *Embattled Freedom*. "Freedom had to be searched for and found." Union commanders, however, continued calling the escaped people "contrabands" and they called the Black settlements "contraband camps," perhaps to remind themselves, their troops, the public, and the refugees that slavery lived on.[13] But the slave system had begun to collapse. Suddenly the war was no longer about the right of the federal government to regulate slavery; it had become a fight to end it.

These enclaves of refugees sprouted up anywhere the military went. Many were temporary migrant communities following the soldiers as they campaigned. Others were permanent settlements where residents platted streets, built wood cabins, and organized churches. In Nashville, three camps perched near the military installations on the eastern, western, and southern borders of the city. Another one north of town was a farming community. One south of town ran a supply depot for the army.[14] It's tempting to imagine the Prince family living in one of these camps, joining the mass of people who had walked away from bondage, moving into Nashville and shepherding their growing flock of children toward freedom. Was that where Thornton Prince II was born and spent his earliest childhood days?

If the Princes were in the Nashville camps, their early experiences of freedom were not halcyon, idyllic, or secure. Former slaveholders swept into the enclaves to reclaim the people they saw as their property, and some Federal commanders allowed them to do so. Slave catchers and patrollers abducted people and dragged them back into forced labor. Confederate soldiers raided the camps, killing, maiming, and kidnapping the refugees; on one Nashville raid, the refugees fought off their invaders using nothing but their construction tools. And the freedpeople were sexually assaulted by white soldiers and civilians on both sides of the conflict.[15]

The Army made no provisions for housing, feeding, clothing, or training the refugees, so the freedpeople made do with outworn boots, remade clothing, and half-rotten food. In one of the Nashville camps, the refugees lived in leftover tents from a military hospital. The requisitions officer who passed the tents along made no effort to repair their rips, wash away the blood, or clean up the contagion splattered across their walls. Sanitation was nonexistent, and epidemics spread. Smallpox, dysentery, pneumonia, typhoid, yellow fever, tuberculosis, and cholera swept through the clusters of freedpeople. One rainy winter when the mud ran six inches deep in the camps, one-sixth of Nashville's refugees died.[16] A Union officer stationed at Chattanooga wrote to his commander to complain about the situation in Nashville. He'd heard thirty freedpeople died every day, and he believed it. That very morning, he'd seen a couple of children rescued from the city. "They are nearly starved, their limbs are frozen," he wrote, "—one of them is likely to lose both feet, —Their mother died in the camp." The local undertaker who oversaw burials in the area estimated that he and his assistant had buried 12,561 federal soldiers; eight thousand Confederate soldiers and ten thousand freedpeople.[17]

But the people who lived in Nashville's refugee camps had gained something they'd never had before: freedom. And they made what they could of their new circumstances, seizing every opportunity to construct better lives. They established schools and churches. They worked jobs and were paid for their labor (though they had little recourse if a boss refused to hand over their wages). They married, able for the first time to solemnize legally recognized unions. In 1864 they held a shadow presidential election to show white politicians that they were ready for the vote.[18]

When the Civil War ended, the people living in Nashville's refugee camps had choices: return to where they lived before the conflict, hoping to negotiate labor contracts with the white people who once claimed to own them; strike out for somewhere new, gambling they would find more opportunity elsewhere; or stay in Nashville, building a new life in the growing city. Many chose to remain. Between 1860 and 1870, African Americans grew from being 23 to 38 percent of the local population. But if the Prince family had been living in Nashville, they were among those who went back home, heading south to neighboring Williamson county.

For the first few decades after freedom came, things seemed to go well for the family. They settled onto (or back into or remained at) Wood Park. In 1889, Thornton Prince II married Mary Maury (or perhaps Murray, the two are pronounced just about the same in rural Middle Tennessee). The new couple started having babies, first John and then Fannie, then Thornton III and Ida and Bessie and Maggie and Boyd. By the time Mary gave birth to her youngest son, James, in 1912, she'd had twelve children, ten of whom were living, a remarkable feat. But Middle Tennessee was an increasingly challenging place to raise a young Black family.[19]

Reconstruction had seemed to offer African Americans new opportunities. Black men got the vote, and a handful were elected. Schools opened, educating children and adults alike. People worked toward land ownership and lobbied for fair wages.

The loss of hope didn't happen at once. In the 1870s, abandonment and apathy by the federal government and violent opposition by groups such as the Ku Klux Klan let white Southerners "redeem" their communities. Lynchings, riots, rapes, and other attacks terrorized Black communities. Jim Crow laws hardened the divisions between Black Tennesseans and their white neighbors, making inequality part of the legal code.

For a while, the Princes resisted all of these forces that tried to keep them entrapped, building economic independence for themselves through hard work. In 1891, Thornton Prince II even registered to vote, a bold move in the segregated, white supremacist South. The family eventually bought their own portion of the Sayer plantation, everyone pitching in to make it happen. Mary took in laundry. Some of the boys picked up odd jobs on neighboring farms. One of the girls became a hairdresser. As a boy, Thornton Prince III probably assumed that he would inherit a part of this farm his family was laboring together to build, that he was witnessing the beginnings of the generational wealth white families had always been free to accumulate.[20]

But the Princes' plans fell apart. By 1920, Thornton and Mary were living in a rented house in Franklin, the county seat. Though Thornton Prince II was somewhere around sixty-five years old, he was still working, having taken a job as a laborer with the railroad. Perhaps these disappointments were why Mary and Thornton Prince II sent so many of their children to Nashville during this decade. Maybe they were hoping their kids would find a better life in the capital city.[21]

Nashville, however, offered little more opportunity than the Prince children had found in Williamson County. The freedom and equality and citizenship the refugees had claimed during the Civil War had largely disappeared. Nashville had become a segregated city, a place where there were white neighborhoods and Black neighborhoods and very little shared space between them.

As the second oldest son, Thornton Prince III was one of the first of the kids to strike out on his own, though he began with a misfire. On the day after Christmas 1910, he applied for a marriage certificate. His intended was Jennie May Patton, an eighteen-year-old girl raised on a neighboring farm. Was this a whirlwind romance or something both families had always expected to happen? Did the young couple rush to the courthouse heady and in love after a Christmas proposal or had they been plotting their marriage for some time? The marriage license gave no clue. Here's what it did say: They both signed the declaration. Thornton's signature is bold and certain as though he bore down upon the tip of the fountain pen's nib, thickening each downstroke. Jennie May's signature is lighter and slightly smaller, tilting upward toward the end. Someone has come back after the fact and added a "col" above each line, lest the couple forget their race.[22]

But Thornton and Jennie May never took their vows. They returned their unexecuted marriage license to the Williamson County clerk some three months later.[23] Was Jennie May Patton the first hot chicken cook? Had Thornton Prince III jilted her at the altar? Maybe, but if so, they both recovered quickly. Less than a year after the marriage certificate

FIGURE 1.2. Arthur Rostein, "Girl at Gee's Bend, Alabama" (1937). Collection of the Smithsonian National Museum of African American History and Culture, object no. 2012.107.34

had wended its way back to the county clerk's office, Jennie May was married to someone else.*

Thornton Prince was also ready to try again, and quickly. He wedded fourteen-year-old Gertrude Claybrook on July 28, 1912.[24] Claybrook was

---

* On February 5, 1911, Jennie May Patton married Walker Holt, a twenty-nine-year-old boarder and hired farm laborer living on another nearby property. Jennie May and Walter had one son together, Walker Holt Jr., but theirs was neither a happy nor a lasting marriage. In 1920, Jennie May was divorced and working as the live-in servant for a white family in Nashville. She'd left her son with his grandparents in Williamson County. Walker died on New Year's Eve 1925, and Jennie May Patton married again. She died a short three years later of a kidney disease; Williamson County, Tennessee, Marriage certificate no. 1432 (1911), Holt-Patton, Tennessee Division of Vital Statistics, Nashville; 1920 United States Census, Davidson County, p. 245; 1920 United States Census, Williamson County, Tennessee, p. 242; Davidson County, Tennessee, death certificate no. 443 (1925), Walker Holt, Tennessee Department of Public Health, Nashville; Davidson County, Tennessee, death certificate no. 2890 (1928), Jennie May Raun Lane, Tennessee Department of Public Health, Nashville; "Lane," Nashville Tennessean, February 20, 1928.

another local girl, born and raised in Williamson County, but her short life had been an unstable one. The second youngest of ten children, her mother had died when she was a toddler. Soon, her father sent her to live with two of her older sisters, Lourena and Bulah. Lourena was a widow with two young children who worked as a domestic servant in the home of a nearby white family, a job with long and unpredictable hours. Bulah, who also had two children, took in laundry. Gertrude probably helped her older sisters about the house, and in return, they would have given her a last little bit of parenting.[25]

The jobs Gertrude's sisters had found were two of the most common for Black women of this era. Almost all married white women were able to fulfill the Victorian ideal for womanhood and settle into their homes as housewives and mothers, but Black women did not have that luxury. Only about three percent of working Black women found jobs as teachers, the most prestigious positions available to them. About the same number worked as seamstresses or skilled workers. The rest labored as either laundresses or domestics, just like the Claybrook sisters did.[26]

Each of these jobs came with its own disadvantages. Lourena probably earned more money, but because she worked within a white household, she was in a position that mimicked the enslaved service of her ancestors. She did not control her hours or her work environment. She had very limited time with her children. And she was vulnerable to sexual violence. Bulah's work as a laundress was harder on her physically and it paid less, but it happened in her own house and on her own time, giving a degree of dignity to the labor. Plus, she was home and able to raise her children as well as Lourena's and Gertrude.[27]

By marrying the relatively prosperous Thornton Prince III, Gertrude Claybrook was striving toward a different and a better future for herself, but at fourteen, she was an extremely young bride, even for that time. She was six years his junior, a significant difference at their ages.

Gertrude and Thornton Prince III settled into married life, and they soon started expanding their family. Dorothy Lee Prince was born to the couple on December 6, 1914.[28] Three years later, Gertrude gave birth to Thomas Edward Prince on December 27, 1917.

But those were not the only children born to Thornton Prince III during these years. On August 4, 1916, Mattie Lizzie Crutcher—another

FIGURE 1.3. Department of Agriculture Extension Service, "Negro Family Budget of Canned Fruits and Vegetables: Mr. and Mrs. J. F. Bryan Expert Canners in Their Community" (1928). National Archives, photo no. 5729293

young woman born and raised in Williamson County—gave birth to a son named Jasper Lee Prince. Born between Gertrude's two children, Jasper, not Gertrude's Thomas, was Thornton Prince III's oldest son.[29]

Did Gertrude Prince know about Jasper? Maybe not. Maybe she was buried so deeply in her own young, growing family she didn't notice her husband's distraction. Or maybe the couple had a falling out sometime after Dorothy's birth. Perhaps Thornton and Gertrude even separated. Maybe he had moved out. Maybe he'd been so lonely that he had turned an old friendship into a poorly chosen fling. Perhaps when the couple reunited, Gertrude's family and his conspired to protect Gertrude from what had happened, shielding her from the gossip.

Or maybe Gertrude Prince knew it all. Perhaps she demanded Thornton make a clean break and give them a fresh start. I suspect that might have been the case. By 1917, Gertrude and Thornton Prince III were on their own, living some five miles northeast of Nashville and a good twenty-five miles from where they'd grown up. Today, that's just a quick whip around the city, but in 1917, it would have been a full day on horseback. Gertrude Prince had tucked her family—her husband—away, far from Mattie Crutcher and Jennie May Patton Holt and any other woman he may have once courted.[30]

The acreage the Princes had rented north of Nashville was too large for them to handle alone, so Thornton's younger brother Boyd joined them, bringing with him his new wife Clara. Soon they had two children of their own.[31]

The Prince brothers had found themselves a stretch of rolling, fertile land ready for crops. The land provided other foodstuffs as well. Its fencerows were full of blackberries, and the Prince children could forage persimmons and walnuts from the woods. A nearby creek was stocked with fish ready to feed hungry bellies, and the men could hunt for deer and squirrels and raccoons and doves.[32]

Family lore says that Thornton Prince III ran a pig farm. This could have meant a variety of things in 1917. Poor Southern farming families of all races had long relied on pork to fill out their nutritional needs. Hogs were cheap—or even free—to feed. Farmers left them to nose out their own food from the fields and woods. Come cold weather, subsistence farmers across the region would put aside their other chores for a few days while they butchered and salted and smoked meat for the coming year.[33] This was true snout to tail eating. The families needed every bit of protein and fat the animal could provide, the root of the Southern penchant for things like fried chitterlings, pickled hooves, and fatback in collard greens. So maybe Thornton and Boyd Prince were running a subsistence farm that included a few hogs.[34]

Or maybe the Prince brothers were trying to join a new agricultural movement. Large scale industrial hog raising wouldn't take off until the 1950s, but its earliest iterations were already appearing. Mechanization, World War I, and increasing levels of racial violence across rural America were driving waves of Southerners into American cities. These new city dwellers who had formerly raised their own foodstuffs now had to buy their groceries. Commercial swine production arose. "A heavy July run of packing sows tells its own story," a reporter for the *Breeder's Gazette* wrote in 1922. "The country planned a substantial increase in

FIGURE 1.4. Willow Street today. Gertrude, Thornton, and the children lived about where the Maersk trailers are in the center of the image. Photo: Rachel Louise Martin

swine production last year, and females held for breeding purposes . . . are now being rushed to market to take advantage of prevailing prices."[35]

The Prince brothers' farming venture, however, was a short-lived. Nashville was growing, expanding ever outward toward Thornton, Gertrude, Dorothy, and Thomas. In 1917, the Princes were the only people left in the neighborhood who still farmed their land. Their neighbors were white dentists and businessmen and musicians who commuted to the city and back every day. A developer soon bought the land Thornton Prince III had rented, and the new owner subdivided it. The real estate speculator built a small strip of businesses anchored by a grocery store and a pharmacy. But the young Prince family had been driven off before any of these amenities came out from town.[36]

When Gertrude, Thornton, and the kids left the farm, they moved to South Nashville, joining one of the Black communities that had arisen where years earlier a refugee camp had been. Their home at 82 Willow Street is long gone, just a flattened patchwork of concrete on one corner of the current TCW Distribution's parking lot, an anonymous fraction of a narrow industrial park tucked between the interstate and a tangle of railroad tracks.

About all the Princes might recognize in this place is a brick freight depot that has become the Tennessee Central Railway Museum. Maybe that's appropriate. The railroad might have been what drew them here in 1922.[37] The Tennessee Central was supposed to connect the mountains of Tennessee to the Mississippi River, but it never became the major artery its founder intended. At some moments in its history, it threatened to shake up the infrastructure of the Southeast. Other times, it was a vanity line for businessmen who wanted to access East Tennessee's coal fields. By the time the Princes had moved onto Willow Street, the railway had abandoned all passenger services, but it still hauled coal and timber off the Cumberland Plateau and into the city.[38]

Austin Prince, an uncle who was possibly Thornton Prince II's twin, was the first Prince to move there. He and his wife Fannie bought a home at 63 Willow Street, and Austin took a job as a dry goods porter. Boyd came next, leaving the farm Thornton and Gertrude had rented and setting up house a few doors down from Austin and Fannie. He became a porter for Holbrook and McClellan, "jobbers of country meats and lard." The firm had stores in Nashville, but they also sent their processed meats to other cities, quite possibly via the Tennessee Central. Thornton and Gertrude Prince moved in next door to Boyd in 1922. Thornton picked up odd jobs, whatever he could find.[39]

The Princes were one of many African-American families on the move during this era, an exodus we now call the Great Migration. Between World War I and World War II, millions of Black farmers left the rural South for Southern cities and the urban North. Their reasons were many: the dangerous, violent white supremacy practiced unfettered across the Southern countryside; the educational opportunities for children in the cities; the wages to be found in urban areas; the dream of finding something better somewhere else. Then the boll weevil destroyed acres of cotton, and the bottom fell out of the agricultural market. And then mechanization reached the farms, and suddenly a single white landowner could plant and till and harvest land that had previously been rented out to Black families. The Great Depression— which came to the agricultural South years before the 1929 stock market crash—caused more individuals and families to pack it in, determined to try their luck off the farm.[40]

The cultural reverberations of the Great Migration are still felt today. It was the cauldron for the Harlem Renaissance in New York City, and it put Bessie Smith and her blues in a Chicago Recording Studio. But the Great Migration didn't only take rural Black Southerners beyond their regional homeland. It also took them into Southern cities, especially the cities of the upper South like Nashville. For some of the migrants, Nashville was a way station, a stopping off point on their journey north. For others like Thornton Prince III and his family, the city was the destination. These families crowded into slapdash housing, hoping for a better life for themselves and for their children. But these homes were never built to last.[41]

The Princes' residences on Willow Street have been destroyed either by time or by the city's changing economic landscape. Disappointed by how little of the Princes' world remained, I turned my Prius toward the railroad, sliding under the narrow one-lane overpass. I paused underneath, opened my window and looked up at the thick, creosote-coated timbers holding up the tracks. The weathered lumber had begun to splinter with the strain of generations of trains rumbling overhead. Was this something Gertrude and Thornton saw? Now I was grasping for any connection to their lives.

Just past the overpass, the road dead-ended at the Cumberland River, and I realized the Princes had been living in Nashville's flood plain. There has only been one major flood in my lifetime. In May 2010, thirteen inches of rain fell in thirty-six hours, running off already-saturated soil, filling every low-lying intersection, cascading through feeder streams into our rivers, and overwhelming the water management system that usually protects Nashville from the worst of our weather.

Willow Street must have been affected by that incident. I parked and pulled up an aerial image from the weekend on my phone. Sure enough, only the roofs of the warehouses peaked above the flood. Everything else—the parking lots, the trucks, the railroad lines—was submerged under murky water the color of rotten pickles. And today we have a complicated series of locks and dams to control the water that runs through the Cumberland River. In Thornton and Gertrude's day, the spring flooding would have been a seasonal event. Some years worse, some years better, but every year the water would have come.[42]

The flooding was just one of the forces that would've made the Princes' lives on Willow Street hard. For many children, Willow Street was deadly. They died of pneumonia, convulsions, and congestion of the brain. They contracted malaria. They suffered from whooping cough. They died of cholera. They drank poisoned milk.[43]

Adults didn't fare much better. Some of them contracted consumption, also known as tuberculosis. Others caught—and died—of smallpox some two hundred years after the development of a reliable vaccine. They suffered from an unnamed debilitating paralysis that eventually stopped their lungs. They died from intestinal obstructions. They got into violent fights and died of their injuries. Willow Street and other impoverished places also had the highest murder rates in the city, a concerning statistic since the United States was "the most murderous country in the world," and Nashville was the seventh most murderous city in the nation. Most of Nashville's white residents would have blamed Willow Street's violence on some innate moral, intellectual, emotional, or spiritual failing of its inhabitants, ignoring the way the economic, political, judicial, and educational systems hadn't mitigated the turmoil there. And sometimes the residents passed of old age when they should have still been in the prime of their lives.[44]

The afternoon I drove around Willow Street, I'd set my GPS to avoid the interstates, so instead of shuttling me out of the neighborhood, my phone directed me under the I-24 overpass. Suddenly, I knew where I was. Willow Street in 2020 felt like an isolated outpost, but in the 1920s, it was part of a sprawling network of Black communities in South Nashville. That was before urban renewal's supporters used the infrastructure boom of the 1950s and 1960s to hack apart neighborhoods, razing houses and turning byways into dead-end roads.

The Willow Street that Gertrude and Thornton Prince III had known may have been paved over, but I'd found a cache of homes that had survived. Most of them were small frame houses just about large enough to be called "tiny house living." Southerners would call them shotgun shacks because according to tradition if you stand in the front door, you can shoot straight out the back.

I pulled over to admire a restored peacock blue house. It checked all the architectural style boxes for homes of the shotgun type: one room wide, probably three rooms deep, a solitary front window, and an off-set front door. This gem of a home was between two vacant lots, but then came two more shotguns. Both of these had been painted clean shades of cream. Someone had tacked a lean-to kitchen addition to the third home. Two more vacant lots, and then I passed a brick building that could have once been just about anything from a garage to a masonic lodge.

Most of Nashville's shotgun houses, including this little cluster, were built between 1880 and World War II. Landlords loved them. They were cheap to construct and easy to rent to the working class, and in the early days, they were used to house both white and Black families.[45]

As charming as the houses looked on this sunny spring day in 2020, a century ago they would have been part of miles of underdeveloped neighborhoods. Back then, most of the houses in this district lacked running water. Few streets had sidewalks. Paving was sporadic. Poverty was rampant. The city had few social services and no minimum wage, so local residents often worked multiple jobs and still had to rely on charitable organizations to help them meet their basic needs. In a nearby site, forty-nine people shared one outdoor spigot. On another street, six families shared a one-pit privy. The city's failure to provide basic infrastructure and sanitation was part of the reason for the neighborhood's high rates of premature and preventable deaths.[46]

As the twentieth century progressed, white workers' wages grew faster than those earned by Black laborers, and the white families had easier access to housing loans. The racial housing restrictions that trapped African Americans did not affect white residents, and real estate agents were more willing to show them a wider variety of options. White workers moved into better housing. By World War II, most shotgun houses were rented by African Americans.[47]

Despite the terrible conditions that existed on Willow Street, as a working-class Black couple in the early 1920s South, Gertrude and

Thornton Prince's choices were limited. At least here they had family around them. Their community soon fell apart, however. Boyd and Clara were the first to go. Then Austin and Fannie moved. By 1926, Gertrude and Thornton had left Willow Street as well, but they did not leave together. After fourteen years, their marriage was over.

What happened to their relationship? It could've been because of the age difference between them, though that should have felt much smaller by now. Or maybe it was caused by the money trouble they surely had to have had. Or perhaps they had disagreements over how to raise the children.

Here's one important clue: James Thomas Prince, Thornton's third son, was born in Louisville, Kentucky, on December 4, 1924. His birth certificate is not yet public record, so I am not positive who his mother was, but he was born when Gertrude was still living in Nashville.[48]

Let's put Gertrude Claybrook Prince on the list of possible hot chicken inventors.

CHAPTER 2

Toss to Coat

Forgotten Promises, the Origins of Urban Renewal, and the Cost of Erasure, 1925–1940

Today 436 5th Avenue North is an exit ramp for Nashville's downtown bus station, but in 1926, it was the headquarters of the city's Black YWCA. The organization was housed in a nineteen-room, three-story Capitol Hill house originally built for the town's white gentry. It was a gracious structure. White stone columns framed the house's tall glass front door, and its generous front porch was lined by a squat neo-Egyptian limestone balustrade. The ladies of the YW stacked the house's railing with petunias and geraniums in clay pots, a mosaic of color to greet their visitors.[1]

The Black branch of Nashville's YWCA was less than five years old. The group's leaders, who met rolling bandages for World War I, had wanted the home to be a shelter for the many rural Black women who were moving into Nashville, a place that would provide the ladies with "a true compass needle that will, when they set-sail for a new city port, safely guide them." The woman who calibrated that compass was the former head librarian for the Carnegie Library's Black division. Under her guidance, the young women who lived at the home attended lectures, took classes, received employment advice, and socialized with other "respectable" ladies.[2]

In 1926, one of those lodgers was Gertrude Claybrook Prince. She probably hadn't had many other places to go when her marriage crumbled. Her immediate family had dispersed, most of them leaving Tennessee altogether. The two sisters she'd lived with before her marriage to Thornton Prince III had both died, Lourena in 1915 and Bulah in 1918. For Gertrude, the YWCA would have been a much-needed opportunity to start her adulthood anew. Here, Prince would have had a single room with space only for herself, no children and no husband allowed. And she would have been surrounded by other young women, mostly single girls newly arrived in the city, but maybe there were a few others who were, like her, fleeing husbands and hoping to find better lives for themselves. But the YW did not put its lodgers up for free. The organization was training the women to be the sort of independent professionals who could stand on their own two feet. Every one of them was urged to get a respectable job and start paying her own way. Gertrude Prince found a position—perhaps with the help of the YWCA—as a cashier for a life insurance company.[3]

Though the YWCA aspired to teach the young women to be thoroughly middle class, the area around it was a hodgepodge, a neighborhood in transition, heading in a direction that appalled many of the city's leaders. Historically, some of the wealthiest white families in the city had lived on Capitol Hill, erecting their urban castles next to the state legislature. Their columned mansions followed the ridges running from the state house toward Nashville's business districts.

In the days after the Civil War, recently freed African Americans set up a refugee camp in the shadows of the state capital. Slowly a new neighborhood emerged and grew, expanding until its edges rubbed against the town's mansions. Within it, the new residents started their own churches and shops and schools. They laid out streets and built lives for themselves. Their white civic leaders, however, did nothing to help, leaving the newcomers to cobble together their buildings as best

FIGURE 2.1. George N. Barnard, "Nashville, Tennessee, View from the Capitol, 1864" (1862–1864). National Archives, photo no. 533376

they could despite having been left cash poor after Emancipation and the failed dream of Reconstruction. And the white families living up the slope from the freedpeople treated them with contempt.[4]

Then at the turn of the twentieth century, white residents began to leave Capitol Hill. Recently laid streetcar lines and the growing availability of the automobile meant wealthy Nashvillians could abandon urban living. They moved into the suburbs sprouting in the newly shorn fields and forests around the city, claiming a bit of space and privacy. Their departure aligned with the beginning of the Great Migration. The incoming Black residents needed somewhere to stay, so landlords—many of them slumlords—hacked and carved away at the old mansions, transforming them into apartments.

One of these mutilated mansions was a two-story Italianate brick home that sat at the corner of 6th and Gay Street, right in the heart of the Capitol Hill community. I squinted at the grainy newsprint, trying to draw out its details. The picture hinted at a daylight basement that could have held a kitchen and possibly servant housing. A double-landing staircase led to the front entrance. Curtains hung in the windows. Were they lace? What roof was left was nothing but lumber. I wondered what it had been: slate? Red tile? The home had been reduced to a hovel.[5]

"Violence and weather bent the ornate iron fences; the cornices crumbled, the stained-glass windows shattered, the weathervanes rusted, and tall weeds grew in unkept yards," one former resident remembered. "It was all over for the houses on Capitol Hill."[6]

The city's disinterest left the area vulnerable to trouble. Soon Capitol Hill was known for saloons, prostitution, and other vices. Nashville's white society—many of whom visited Capitol Hill's licentious and illegal enterprises—chose to forget that the neighborhood had some of Nashville's oldest Black churches, most prosperous Black businesses, and most established Black schools. They chose to forget that they had permitted—or even created—the unsanitary conditions there, that they had patronized—or even invested in—the area's illicit businesses. They renamed the neighborhood Hell's Half Acre, accusing the residents of leading and promoting sinful lifestyles.[7]

Though that assessment had obvious racial and class prejudices behind it, the neighborhood did need help. Like Willow Street, most of Hell's Half Acre had unpaved streets and no sewer system, no electricity, and no running water. By the 1920s, Hell's Half Acre and other neighborhoods like it across the city needed a dramatic intervention to remake them into safe, sanitary places where people could live and work and thrive. Nashville's government, however, didn't have the funds necessary for an urban renovation project on that scale.

Then the Great Depression crashed the American economy. When President Franklin Delano Roosevelt came to power in 1933, he pushed through a series of programs designed to jumpstart the economy by providing Americans with jobs, cities with projects, and the nation with an improved infrastructure system, one that was finally ready to handle the pressure and opportunities offered by the twentieth century.

Slum clearance was one of Roosevelt's New Deal programs. He saw it as something that would benefit everyone: impoverished people would have better housing; unemployed laborers would have work; cities, states, and federal agencies would gain larger tax bases. The federal slum clearance program proposed covering up to ninety percent of the rehabilitation and renewal costs, which should have made it irresistible, but Nashville's officials and Tennessee's politicians balked and dallied despite their obvious needs.[8]

Nashville's housing reformers lobbied and campaigned, trying to increase public pressure on state and local politicians. The editor of the *Tennessean* picked up his pen to bash the "rugged individualism" that kept Nashville from becoming a place where every home had "sufficient sunlight, sufficient air, sufficient privacy, sufficient sanitary arrangements and sufficient room for the number of persons who live in it." He announced, "a nation . . . cannot take just pride in its accomplishments until there is sufficient and proper housing for every one of its citizens." Still the politicians dawdled.[9]

In September 1932, one full month after the *Tennessean* editorial, the federal government promised New York City one hundred million dollars in aid, its largest grant to that point. Nashville still didn't apply. Over the coming year, local slum clearance advocates watched the federal budget dwindle further as other states and municipalities joined the New Deal's rehabilitation efforts.[10]

Fed up, on November 1, 1933, a group of Nashville businessmen met with Gerald Gimre, the city's first zoning and planning engineer. It was a fateful meeting, perhaps one of the most formative of Nashville's second century, though likely none of the men involved realized it at the time. And it surely should have merited more than the eighth of a column the *Tennessean*'s editors gave it, tucked away on page twelve of a Thursday morning paper alongside the stock prices and an announcement for a farm rally in Alabama. By the time the meeting ended, the men had formed a committee. Their purpose was straightforward: they would force the city to join the slum clearance movement by campaigning for the construction of Nashville's first public housing projects, one white and one Black. And with the creation of that unnamed committee, urban renewal in Nashville began.[11]

Gerald Gimre was the perfect choice to head up this new housing movement. An Iowan born and raised, Gimre's background was as all-American as the cornfields that had surrounded Marshalltown, his hometown. He'd been the sort of teenager who probably loved high school. No, he hadn't been a star athlete—he quit the basketball team after just one year—but he'd been active in student government and a member of the glee club, a winning debater, and a gifted baritone who sang solos for the Ladies' Aid Society fundraisers, earned multiple encores at a local music festival, and sang the opening number at the city's 1915 Memorial Day celebration. He was even the star of his senior class play, and he "handled his long part perfectly," a local reporter wrote in a review of the production.[12]

His portrait in his senior yearbook showed a kid with one of those Midwestern faces that was remarkable only because it was so everyday handsome. He had blue eyes and brown hair and was of medium height and medium build. His features were reasonably even, without any one being noticeably stronger or weaker than average. He looked at the camera, not discombobulated by its gaze but without any charisma to draw his viewer. He looked competent and prepared and forgettable.[13]

Gerald Gimre's family was comfortably middle class. His father, a Norwegian immigrant who came to the United States as a toddler, sold farm equipment for the local supply store. He appeared to have raised Gerald with a strong sense of civic responsibility, a belief that was reinforced at the local YMCA where Gimre was one of the teen leaders. There, he heard about the debt he owed to the men who "gave their time and money" so he "could enjoy clean and helpful recreation and sports." He heard that boys "whose habits and life were clean" were more likely to find good jobs. And when they had found those jobs, they could pay back the debt they owned the older generation by helping the next generation "grow to be men."[14]

After graduating from high school in 1916, Gerald Gimre went to the University of Illinois and entered the College of Agriculture where he majored in landscape architecture. His choice of major wouldn't have surprised anyone back in Marshalltown; his high school capstone essay was "The Carnation," after all, dedicated to that popular plant, though landscape architecture in this era was about more than gardens, encompassing roads and buildings as well.[15]

World War I briefly interrupted Gimre's plans. In September 1918, he headed to basic training at Camp Dodge instead of back to university for his junior year. He applied for officers' training school, was accepted, and transferred to Camp Pike in Arkansas. But the war was too short for this prospective officer to complete his training. Gerald Gimre was mustered out at Camp Pike on December 8, 1918.[16]

His brief stint as a soldier behind him, Gerald Gimre returned to the University of Illinois and picked his studies back up. He joined the University Landscape Architects' Society, one of only two students to win a spot after ranking highly in a departmental competition. He was also inducted into Scarab, a professional architectural fraternity, and became the assistant editor of the *Reptonian*, the Landscape Club's annual publication. He participated in the Cosmopolitan Club, an organization that encouraged cross-cultural, international friendships and travel, and he discovered a talent for art, exhibiting watercolors of various French and English gardens in a campus gallery. He graduated in 1920 with honors. The year after he graduated, his department exhibited "Moorish Garden" and "A City Home," two of his plasticine models, in the main corridor of the College of Agriculture.[17]

After graduation, Gerald Gimre worked briefly with the Detroit city planning commission and then moved to Ohio to be a city engineer. During his decade in Ohio, he fought to improve local zoning codes, a battle that would occupy much of his first years in Nashville. These ordinances, he argued, would "provide for the public health, morals, safety, and general welfare. . . . They foster pride in the citizens of the city; they promote happiness and contentment; they stabilize the use and value of the property and promote the peace, tranquility and good order."[18]

Nashville appointed its first City Zoning and Planning Commission in 1932 (after an almost decade-long fight by local boosters and businessmen),[19] and on June 30, 1932, the city hired Gerald Gimre to help launch the program. Development in Nashville up until that point had been a matter of luck, negotiation, and neighborhood covenants. Gimre's job was to change that, creating a predictable, systemic process of growth that would benefit developers, politicians, and residents.[20]

When Gerald Gimre got to town, he rented a unit in the newly constructed Gainsboro Apartments, a luxury building on Nashville's upscale West End Avenue that included amenities like a marble lobby, electric refrigerators, and in-unit garbage incinerators. He joined the Chamber of Commerce's Safety Board to help tackle traffic safety and fire prevention in the city. And he started crafting Nashville's first zoning code.[21]

And then the fight for zoning ordinances became personal for Gerald Gimre. Local real estate developer Benjamin Haiman had wanted to build a block of businesses on West End Avenue in the heart of its burgeoning residential district and just about kitty corner from Gimre's swanky new digs. But Haiman wasn't talking about opening up a tea shop or shoe store. He specialized in filling stations and machine shops and other such ventures.* Thirty-five neighborhood residents showed up to protest his plans.† This crew of wealthy Nashvillians were willing to do just about anything to protect their homes. The last time someone threatened to build in their neighborhood, they had pooled their money to buy the land—fourteen acres in total—and turned it into a city park. This time, however, they had Gerald Gimre on their side. The debate required two meetings of the new zoning and planning commission, but Haiman lost.[22]

A zoning code for Nashville laid out on clearly labeled zoning maps would let the Haimans of the world know whether they'd be able to build what they wanted where they wanted. Gerald Gimre and his new team began a survey of the city, going building by building. They would use the information they generated as the basis for their proposed regulations.[23]

The new zoning ordinance they created was straightforward enough. "Residence A" blocks allowed for white single family dwellings and duplexes.

---

* Benjamin Haiman, a Jewish immigrant from Russia, lived with his wife Rosa and their six children less than a block away from where he wanted to build his new businesses. The fact he was a neighbor, however, did not endear him to the protestors.

† This wasn't the first of this sort of trouble Haiman had had. A couple of years earlier, he had bought some land a bit farther out West End. The property was under restrictive covenants. Today, these covenants are most notorious for the ways they enforced racial segregation across the city, but in the days before zoning codes, residential developers could also use them to force a neighborhood to remain a residential district. The deed for the land Haiman purchased stipulated that "no shop, store, factory, saloon or business house of any kind, no hospital, asylum, or institution of like or kindred nature, and no charitable institution shall be erected and maintained on the premises hereby agreed to be conveyed." When Haiman bought the land, he either did not know or did not care about the rules. He had set his pumps and poured a concrete pad, but he had not started constructing the building. The case wound its way through the court system, eventually landing before the Supreme Court of Tennessee who sided with the neighbor, releasing their judgement on March 26, 1932; *Ridley v. Haiman*, 164 Tenn. 239 (Tenn. 1932), https://casetext.com/case/ridley-v-haiman.

Only "carefully restricted" non-residential use would be permitted, like schools, churches, and parks. "Residence B" districts allowed up to four white families per building, and the areas could also include boutique businesses, cemeteries, and fraternity houses. "Residence C" blocks would be for white multi-family dwellings of any size, and they could include hotels and newsstands and restaurants. If twenty percent of a block was used for business, then it was zoned as one of the city's "Commercial Districts," and these could include any type of residence as well as retail businesses and light manufacturing. "Industrial Zones" were for larger plants and "businesses which are considered objectionable." And "District D" blocks were anywhere African Americans lived and worked.[24]

Gimre presented his new zoning maps on January 26, 1933. He tacked two oversized citywide maps—each one was six feet by seven feet—up on the walls and then scattered a series of smaller sectional maps around them. One of the wall maps showed every building in the city, color-coded according to use. The other outlined the proposed new zoning districts. The council passed the new zoning code on July 19, 1933.[25]

Nine days earlier on July 10, 1933, Thornton Prince III had made the front page of the *Nashville Tennessean*. This was almost the first definite record of him since he'd left Willow Street, and his reappearance was worthy of a front page story. Prince, who was working as a chauffeur, had parked his car on the street in front of his building. Early that Sunday morning, two guys from his neighborhood had stolen it. The theft was bold. They hadn't bothered with a getaway plan before driving it away from its parking spot. The thieves didn't even go on a country excursion, leaving town for a few days until people forgot who had driven what. They just cruised.[26]

A few hours later, Prince saw them pull up to the corner of his block still driving his car. He apprehended them, placed them under a citizen's arrest, and turned them over to a passing police officer who charged them with grand larceny and petit larceny.[27]

But where had Thornton Prince III been during the nine years since his split from Gertrude? The evidence is shaky, almost titillating. And the absence of a definite, reconstructable narrative is just another way Black lives were written out of American history.

FIGURE 2.2. The condominiums being constructed here sit on the corner where Thornton was living when he reappeared in Nashville and recaptured his car. Photo: Rachel Louise Martin

In 1924, Prince's son James had been born in Louisville. According to the Louisville city directory, Thornton was not living there at that time. That works, since Thornton and Gertrude were still together, living with their children on Willow Street.[28] A year later, when Thornton disappeared from Nashville, a new Prince moved to Louisville, which is also convenient. But this Prince didn't go by Thornton (though that's a concrete clue I wish I could give you); this new Kentucky-based Prince called himself James.

Seems an impossible leap, right? But let me lay this out.

First, Thornton Prince III had just named his son James. Second, Thornton Prince II had died in 1924, and when his father died, Thornton Prince III began signing official documents under a variety of different names: Thornton Prince, Thornton J. Prince, J. Thornton Prince, and James T. Prince. And over the next several decades, he would appear in the Nashville city directory and in the newspapers as both Thornton and James (and one time, John). When this happens in Nashville, other clues identify him—his wives' names and his addresses and his jobs. The Louisville directories do not list significant others and I don't have a job or an address to use as a starting point, making identification much less certain.

If Thornton Prince III and James Prince are the same person, then he moved to Louisville in 1925 and found work as a day laborer. Two years later, this same James Prince took a new job at Crutchers Garage Company as a car washer. Could those Crutchers possibly have been related to Mattie Crutcher, the mother of Jasper Lee Prince? That would be almost too good to be true. Whoever the Kentucky Crutchers were, they thought James Prince was a good employee, and after a year's employment, they promoted him to being a serviceman.[29]

Thornton Prince III reappeared in Nashville on December 24, 1928, to marry a woman named Mattie Hicks. Then both of them disappear. Had he and Mattie returned to Louisville after their marriage? James Prince still lived there. Then in 1930, James Prince left Louisville. Three years later, Thornton was in back Nashville and working as a chauffeur.[30]

So it may be that Thornton Prince III moved to Kentucky, changed his name, spent time with his new son, learned to drive and maintain a car, and came back to Nashville with a new profession. Maybe. Or maybe he went home to Williamson County or perhaps he rented another farm out northeast of Nashville. The records simply do not say.

And his marriage to Mattie Hicks? The answer to that is similarly besmirched. By 1933 when Thornton was back in Nashville, Mattie had disappeared. As with everything else about this decade of Thornton Prince's life, she is largely a mystery. She may have been born and raised in Murfreesboro, a small town some forty miles south of Nashville. She may have moved to Nashville in 1922, just about the same time Thornton and Gertrude relocated to Willow Street. If she did, then she spent the next six years working as a maid in various white households around town before marrying Thornton in 1928. Here's one clue that suggests this might be the right Mattie: this Mattie Hicks disappeared from the city directory in 1928, the year of Mattie and Thornton's marriage. She resurfaced three years later, again as a Hicks and again as a domestic.[31]

Whoever Mattie Hicks Prince was, she was well-respected and well-connected. The officiant at her marriage to Thornton was the Reverend G. B. Taylor, one of the most powerful Black men in Nashville. He had founded Second Baptist Church and the Industrial School for Negro Boys. He'd been the chairman of the National Baptist Sunday School Congress and of the National Baptist Publishing Board. He was a busy man who could have easily pawned the couple off on a junior clergyman. Since wherever Thornton Prince III was, it seems unlikely the two men had a close relationship, the pastor's decision to solemnize the marriage spoke highly of who Mattie Hicks was and how much her community respected her.[32]

Did Mattie and Thornton Prince have any children together? Again, that's unknown. Thornton had a daughter born sometime around this time period, but birth certificates do not become available until a century has passed. Was she Mattie Hicks' daughter? Maybe.

So, here's what we know: Mattie Hicks' marriage to Thornton Prince III was so brief that her name should join the list of women who may have invented hot chicken.

Gerald Gimre had a fight on his hands during these years while Thornton and Mattie Prince fell in love and then fell apart. He was full of idealistic visions for how he would remake the Depression-riddled city, a process that would require more than a shiny set of zoning laws. He probably expected widespread support for anything that would improve life in Nashville. Slums ribboned out from the city center. Neighborhoods were filled with disease and filth. Many residents lacked any of the amenities that improved modern urban life, and they lived in homes constructed of shoddy, substandard materials that had been left unmaintained by irresponsible landlords.[33]

To build Gimre's case, the City Zoning and Planning Commission issued a new housing survey. In it, the researchers concluded that 13,500 of the city's forty thousand families needed new housing. Eighty percent of the families living in poor white neighborhoods were without electricity, over 30 percent had no running water, close to a quarter of them were overcrowded. Black neighborhoods were even more dire. There, almost half of the houses were already condemned and 83 percent had no running water. "We hold our noses when we think about the slums of New York and Chicago, and the sharecroppers' shacks in the Mississippi delta," the commission's spokesperson concluded, "but we can't dodge conditions as bad or worse right here in Nashville."[34]

The City Health Officer tacked on his own report. Nashville was losing over one million dollars a year in food, products, and property damage to its rats, he claimed. That number did not include the public health crisis the rat infestation caused. For instance, typhus—an infection carried by fleas common to rats—was in the city for the first time in Nashville's history.[35]

But Gerald Gimre saw reason to hope Nashville could heal itself, if its leaders would just take advantage of the New Deal programs. He and his allies on the Zoning and Planning Commission created the Citizens Advisory Committee on Housing. Under his guidance, the new commission reached out to the federal government for help constructing Nashville's first public housing.[36]

They proposed to create two new housing projects. Cheatham Place, the white project, would be a series of brick townhouses constructed on the edge of Germantown, a white neighborhood that was also known as Butchertown because of the meat processing warehouses located there. The African American housing project would be Andréw Jackson Courts, built just off Fisk University's campus.[37]

But Nashville had moved too slowly. By the time Gimre pitched the projects to the federal authorities, most of the federal slum clearance funds had already been allocated to other cities. The federal government offered the city two million dollars, or enough money for the city to buy up the designated land and put out a call for architectural plans. Undaunted, Gimre moved the projects forward. He negotiated for the city to buy the land for Cheatham Place outright without using either condemnation or eminent domain. Every single property owner agreed to a price the city could pay, the last time the city would complete a project like this without resorting to the courts. One reason that happened may have been that most of the dwellings were owned by absentee landowners. No one thought to consult the neighborhood's soon-to-be displaced residents.[38]

Gerald's vision for Cheatham Place sounded idyllic, spacious, even beautiful: 352 row houses, broken into smaller complexes and clustered around common courts. Every unit was fireproofed, built of brick with reinforced concrete floors. Each unit also had central heat, running water, electrical plugs in every room, an electric stove, and an electric refrigerator, as well as copper screens for every window and every door. The roofs were edged with copper gutters. The community house would have a fellowship hall, a professional kitchen, a medical clinic, and offices. And the city would only use a quarter of the acreage for the houses. The rest would be left green, and families were free to plant gardens.[39]

In May 1935, the feds promised the city another three and a half million dollars, enough to cover most of the construction. Then Congress grew wishy-washy about its appropriations. Publicly mandated slum clearance and publicly funded low-rent housing smacked of socialism, Roosevelt's critics claimed. Gerald Gimre and his team heard that all the money they had been promised was gone, but he told his team to keep working. His faith paid off. A few weeks later, the funds were restored.[40]

The construction laborers poured the first Cheatham Place foundations on February 18, 1936. They started pouring foundations at Andréw Jackson Courts a few months later.[41]

The theory behind the New Deal worked. Nashville's construction industry restarted. "Think of the money being paid to Nashville's builders—money for furniture, for children's education, for automo-

FIGURE 2.3. Kenneth Space. "Fisk University, Social Science Class" (1937–1938) National Archives, photo no. 26174813

biles, for the repair of their own homes and other things neglected during the recent lean years," the editor of the *Tennessean* wrote. "All Nashville enterprises are benefitting from the dollars being released for construction."[42]

But after Cheatham Place had been started yet before the first wall went up for Andréw Jackson Courts, the federal administrators overseeing Nashville's two projects started doing the math. Andréw Jackson Courts was supposed to have many of the same amenities going into Cheatham Place, but the administrators decided that the bids for the project were too high, that it "could no longer be termed low-cost housing." They axed Jackson Courts' central heating units and ordered another round of bids. The second bid failed as well. On the third bid, the Works Progress Administrators finally awarded the project to a contractor out of Dallas. He promised to build 398 units for half a million less than Cheatham Place was going to cost.[43]

Their concern may have been justified. Nat Caldwell, a reporter for the *Tennessean*, profiled a Mrs. James Patrick Murphy, a white mother of three displaced from "the line of three-room wooden shacks" that had stood on the land that was becoming Cheatham Place. She hated her new home, but she couldn't afford Cheatham Place, where the smallest two-room unit rented for $17.75 a month, or about three times what she could pay. The construction manager at Cheatham Place tried to redefine the housing project's purpose. "Officially we refer to this job as a slum clearance project," he said. "But what we actually are trying to do is to provide good homes at moderate prices."[44]

Even the cuts made to Andréw Jackson Courts weren't enough. Though many African Americans in Nashville were desperate for better housing, the units failed to rent, proof of the predictions that the projects were just too expensive for the people who needed them most.[45]

So Mrs. Murphy and her former neighbors and the people displaced by Andréw Jackson Courts moved into other slums around Nashville, shoving into any spare room available, worsening their overcrowding and giving Gerald Gimre new projects to plan.[46]

In 1938, the federal government changed the rules. Nashville would receive no more money until the city turned its ad hoc housing committee into the Nashville Housing Authority (NHA), a new branch of the mayor's office. The city attorney called the mandate unconstitutional. City Council members hedged and stalled. The mayor's staff turned to shenanigans, twice "losing" the paperwork needed to create the new commission.[47]

The federal government stopped sending money, and soon the city's funds ran out. On Thursday, October 27, 1939, Gerald Gimre requested an indefinite leave of absence from his job because the city could no longer afford his salary. The planning commission praised Gimre for being "the outstanding planning engineer in the United States" and then appointed his assistant Charles Hawkins as his acting successor. While he waited for them to cobble together more funds, Gimre became a consultant for the United States Housing Authority, the National Resources

Commission, the Tennessee Zoning and Planning Commission, and the Mississippi Zoning and Planning Commission.[48]

Two weeks later, the city caved and created the NHA. Though Gerald would have been a logical director for the new office, the committee did not immediately hire him. "We'll use him if we need him," the chairman told a local reporter.[49] The new commission rushed two representatives to Washington to request twelve million dollars for slum clearance and low-rent housing.[50]

Nashville was again too late. The entire eight hundred million had already been promised to other cities. "There's no good reason why Nashville should be so egregiously the old cow's tail—last over the fence in any progressive endeavor," the *Tennessean's* editor railed. "Yesterday the plain lack of initiative and business sense on the part of our city administration cost us five million dollars and our hopes of improving the living conditions of our poorly housed anywhere in the future. That is expensive remissness."[51]

Charges of graft and incompetency soon dogged the new NHA, and the entire board resigned en masse. The new new Nashville Housing Authority was more willing to work with Gerald Gimre. They hired him to draw up an application for a three million dollar grant that would help fund two new housing projects—one white and one Black.[52]

But the federal housing authority raised another roadblock. As of January 1939, sixty-five of Jackson Court's units were still unleased. A government representative said he couldn't see "any justification for allocating more money." Then Gimre and the NHA convinced the federal authority to transfer control of Andrew Jackson Courts to the city; they lowered the rents and filled the units. In June 1939, the NHA board made Gerald Gimre the organization's new executive director, and in return, the federal agency scrounged together three million dollars, enough for the city to start their projects. Back-channel rumors suggested that soon the administration had even more money for Nashville.[53]

Then momentum stopped. Congress killed the bill that would have funded a new six million dollar grant for the city. Perhaps that was for the best, some Nashvillians murmured, hearing the rumors that the United States would soon be embroiled in the conflict developing in Europe and Asia.[54]

At least Gerald Gimre still had three million to spend. The city placed the African American project in Thornton and Gertrude's old South Nashville neighborhood and named it after J. C. Napier, a prominent Black Nashville banker. The new white project was first called Bosco-bel Heights, but today's Nashvillians—and many National Public Radio fans—would know the complex as the James A. Cayce Homes.[55]

The housing projects have "added new average value to our real estate" across the city and have had "a toning effect on the sections they serve," one man wrote the *Tennessean*. City leaders couldn't stop now, he argued. The most serious problems in the city had yet to be addressed. "We have a section immediately north of our fine state capi-tol which is a menace to health, an eye sore from the L&N Railroad," he continued. He was talking about Hell's Half Acre. "A housing proj-ect on this site can clean up an old eye sore, a cesspool of crime and a harbinger of disease," he continued.[56]

"Your capitol is a perfect example of wanton indifference to the beauty of a storied past," an anonymous editorialist agreed. "Surely there are some citizens in this state who can . . . help save this fast rot-ting carcass of a by-gone age."[57]

Gerald Gimre concurred with their assessment. The area "had the appearance," he said, "of a gentleman attired in a resplendent dress suit coat, shirt and tie, but with muddy shoes and tattered, filthy trousers."[58]

It was time, everyone seemed to agree, to tackle Hell's Half Acre.

The plans Gimre's team had started to draw up would affect the Black YWCA but not Gertrude Claybrook Prince. She had left that neighbor-hood years before. At first, it had seemed the YW's intervention in her life had worked. Her job at the insurance company got her back on her feet. After a couple of years, she was able to move out and rent space in a two-story Folk Victorian–style house in South Nashville. There was a guest house on the property, and I want to imagine that she was liv-ing there with her two children, Dorothy and Thomas.[59]

She wasn't able to maintain her new, stable lifestyle, however. She lost or left her job at the insurance agency and had to go to work as a house-keeper. That meant moving out of the pretty Victorian. Life became too hard. On November 14, 1933, Gertrude Claybrook Prince died of alcohol poisoning in the room she was renting near Jefferson Street.[60]

Her daughter Dorothy was only seventeen, a year too young to fill out her death certificate, and most of the Claybrooks had either died or moved away. Perhaps that's why the responsibility fell to another woman, not a relative but a friend. This friend knew only a sketch of Prince's life, the sort of surface details most of us know about the people we see socially. She found Prince's marital history particularly confusing. She first wrote that Gertrude Prince was widowed. She scratched that out and squeezed "Divorced" in above the line. And the friend learned Gertrude had married one of the Prince brothers a few years back, but she thought the ex was Thornton's brother Will. And Gertrude Prince's mother's name? The friend had no idea.[61]

Someone—maybe the friend, maybe the local burial society—bought a plot for Gertrude Claybrook Prince in Mt. Ararat Cemetery, the oldest African American cemetery in Nashville. No one, however, purchased a headstone for her. Today she lies somewhere in the rolling acreage of the graveyard, her unmarked body resting in anonymity beside generations of other Black Nashvillians.[62]

Was this the end of the woman who invented hot chicken, a quiet, unremarkable death in a rented room on a Nashville side street? When restaurants around the world from Hong Kong to Buenos Aires serve a style of fried chicken they call "Nashville hot," are they unknowingly paying tribute to a short life that ended with a scratched-out certificate in a county courthouse?

And how much did Dorothy Prince know of her mother's life? Hot chicken mythology holds that a girlfriend invented the dish, but maybe a Prince daughter should be added to the list of possible candidates.

FIGURE 2.4. The lawn of Mt. Ararat Cemetery where Gertrude Claybrook Prince lies in an unmarked grave, with the Nashville skyline in the distance. Photo: Rachel Louise Martin

CHAPTER 3

Shake That Dredge

The Redevelopment of Hell's Half Acre
and the Destruction of Thornton Prince III's
First Restaurant, 1941–1952

One hundred forty limestone steps curved up Capitol Hill's steep grade. Below them Victory Park was beginning to green for spring. I stared at the emptied space, trying to imagine the chaotic press of people who once shopped and ate and worked and worshipped and celebrated and lived here. Of all the urban renewal efforts undertaken in Nashville, the Capitol Hill Redevelopment Project, the endeavor that did away with Hell's Half Acre and one of the signature projects of Gerald Gimre's career, is one of the urban renewal initiatives that troubles me the most.

Thinking a visual aid would help me conjure the destroyed neighborhood, I pulled out a copy of a photograph a long-ago train passenger had snapped of this same lawn, back before the bulldozer came. In the image, the state's white limestone Greek revival legislative building reflected the sun so brightly, perched as it was at the top of the hill, that it bleached out the sky around it. Though the image was black and

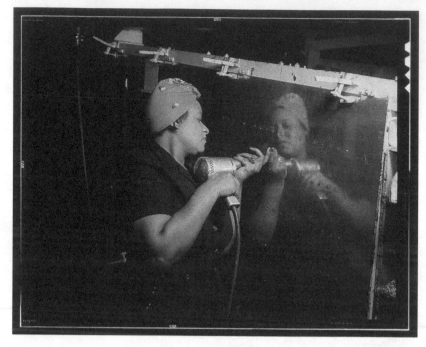

FIGURE 3.1. Alfred T. Palmer, "Operating a hand drill at Vultee-Nashville, woman is working on a 'Vengeance' dive bomber, Tennessee" (February 1943). Library of Congress, object no. LC-DIG-fsac-1a35371

white, the sky seemed to glow with the brilliant azure of a Tennessee sky in April. Below it, the hill was covered in a jumble of roofs and walls, chimneys and telephone poles. Every structure had a dingy smudginess about it as though the soot left by a century of passing trains had built up a layer of grime no amount of scrubbing could remove. It was "a picture of almost unrelieved depression," a local journalist had written of the photograph. "Crumbling buildings in the last stages of dilapidation press close together; windows and doors sagging dejectedly. . . . A deadening film of gray covers buildings, trees, and inhabitants alike."[1]

At first glance, maybe, but just past the railroad tracks I could see a single-story whitewashed brick building. Its façade had the two pilastered windows typical of small-town shops across Middle Tennessee. A couple of blocks away, a sizeable church rose. Looking closer, I counted four more steeples in the frame.[2] Allegations regarding Hell's Half Acre and its misbehaving residents erased the people who lived on Capitol Hill long before they were moved out.

Gerald Gimre's fight to raze Hell's Half Acre took considerably longer than he hoped it would thanks to international events and ongoing municipal apathy. At the beginning of 1941, though official United States policy maintained America would stay out of the burgeoning conflicts in Europe, Africa, and Asia, the federal government pulled its funding for slum clearance and reallocated the monies to build housing for defense workers. Then Pearl Harbor happened. Men (and women) rushed to enlist. Politicians ramped up their patriotic rhetoric. Civilians across the country donated rubber and bought war bonds.[3]

Nashville's city leaders managed to make the earliest days of the war something of a lark. In September 1942, the Belle Meade Theater hosted a war bond auction, and in one night, they raised $788,000. Mayor Thomas Cummings bid fifty thousand dollars to win a gold-painted mock peanut the size of a football. Another man spent a hundred thousand on an American flag. A Tennessee ham went for eleven thousand. When the items for auction started running low, the theater's manager wrangled a feral cat that lived in the alley. Winning bid for the animal, four hundred dollars (the fleas were thrown in for free). The bent and useless hangers from the coat room? A thousand dollars each. Gerald Gimre also got in on the action. He spent fourteen thousand dollars for a purse actress Laraine Day had left behind.[4]

But Gerald Gimre's commitment to his nation went beyond silly patriotic gestures. Though he was forty-five, he re-enlisted, choosing to enter the Navy for this world war, the second of his life. Doing so took some extra paperwork because he had never been issued a birth certificate. That oversight remedied, Gimre joined up as an aviation officer. When he left town, the push to remake and rebuild Nashville ground to a halt. Gimre served until close to the end of the war. After his discharge in 1945, he returned from active service but remained a reserve officer.[5]

Gerald Gimre came back to Nashville, and he stepped back into all of his old responsibilities, a list that stretched beyond urban renewal. He was literally a Boy Scout. The Boy Scouts fit his vision of how well-meaning, well-educated white men could set about changing Nash-ville for the better.

Gerald had first volunteered to be a Scout master in 1933, a scant year after arriving in town, and he assumed responsibility for the youngest troop at the Tennessee Industrial School, an institution that housed, educated, and protected white children who were orphaned, abused, unhoused, or at risk. The children did almost everything on campus until they aged out at eighteen: school, recreation, dining, medical care, scouting. They offset the cost of their living expenses by working on the school's farm.[6]

Gimre apparently invested himself in his young charges, and they responded by earning merit badges and other accolades at a notable clip. "The enthusiasm and advancement record being made by this troop is putting the rest of us to a test," the school's Scout scribe reported to the *Nashville Tennessean*.

"We like Mr. Gimre so well that he could talk about arithmetic and geography or digging potatoes and we would like it," another boy wrote to the paper a few months later. "Mr. Gimre says he is proud of us," the boy reported. "That tickled us all over."[7]

As the boys grew, Gerald Gimre aged up with them, staying with his boys and advancing with them as they matured. The troop was loyal to him in return. Many months, they wrote to the *Tennessean* to brag about their one hundred percent attendance rate, and in 1937, the troop won the attendance cup. Gerald Gimre was rising up the list of Scout leaders as well. By 1938, he was on the executive board of directors for the Nashville Council of the Boy Scouts of America.[8]

The Boy Scouts preached much the same message Gerald had heard at his hometown YMCA back when he'd been a teen leader. "Every generation has to be civilized, humanized, culturized, and Christian-ized," one local pastor told Gimre and the other adults affiliated with the Nashville Area Council in 1947. "When we call a boy delinquent, we say we have not taken him through these processes." Gerald Gimre had appreciated the men who had trained him to be a responsible civic-minded citizen. The Boy Scouts let him pass those lessons along.[9]

When Gerald Gimre returned from the Navy, he didn't go back to his troop, perhaps because his Scouts would have aged out of the Tennessee

Industrial School by then, but he did return to the greater Boy Scouts organization within weeks of his homecoming, rejoining the executive council. The energy he had previously invested in one troop now went into the regional Scouting campaign. In 1951, he would become the chairman of the council's organization and extension committee, overseeing 2,300 Scout leaders and almost seven thousand boys. He would stay on the executive council through at least the mid-1950s.[10]

The Boy Scouts also indirectly set Gerald Gimre up with his post-war housing. In 1945, he did not return to his apartment on West End. Instead, he moved into one of Leslie G. Boxwell's gracious Belle Meade homes. Leslie Boxwell had been the first chair of the Nashville Council's first camping committee, and to this day, the local Boy Scout camp is called Camp Boxwell. In 1927, Boxwell was elected the Nashville Council's president, and he held that post until 1947.[11] Though Leslie Boxwell and Gerald Gimre probably met through the Scouts, they also traveled in many of the same social circles and shared many interests. And before Boxwell was a Scout leader, he had been involved in Nashville's urban development.

Boxwell had come to town in 1909 for a sales job. As his career took off, he began joining in the civic activities that defined responsible citizenship for white men of his class. In 1913, he was part of the group of local leaders who organized the Tennessee Highway Association, a good roads movement which led to the founding of the first highway department and the paving of roads across the state. Good roads weren't just about making travel easier. They would bring "more money, better farms, better homes," Boxwell wrote in 1914, and because of them, Tennesseans would "live longer and happier, be better citizens, better husbands and wives." During World War I, Boxwell raised money for war bonds. Then he helped found the Nashville Board of Trade, which would become today's Chamber of Commerce. He was an active supporter of the Tennessee Valley Authority's work (and his company was one of their contractors). And he joined the Rotary Club in 1917. Boxwell and Gimre made a powerful political team.[12] Leslie and Jeanette, or Nettie, his wife of thirty-five years, spent about half the year at their home in Baton Rouge. But whenever they were in Nashville, they and Gerald Gimre were housemates. Nettie died in 1947, but still Gimre stayed on in the Boxwell home.[13]

His personal life resettled, Gerald Gimre got back to work on the Capitol Hill Redevelopment Project. He rallied the politicians and journalists who supported slum clearance, urging them to relaunch their lobbying for remaking Nashville.

"Our Athens of the South has the only full-scale faithful reproduction of the Parthenon in the world," the editor of the *Tennessean* wrote in November 1945. "Did you know also that half of the houses within its limits do not have running water or toilet facilities? And that at least one-fourth of its 48,000 dwellings are in need of major repairs? And did you know that the population is steadily moving out of the city, leaving a widening circle of blighted property around the business and industrial areas?" After listing more of Nashville's needs—resurfaced streets, more traffic signals, more public services—the editor urged the city's residents not to piddle away the next few years, hoping someone would come to renew their town. "An intelligent city does not just sit by and watch itself falling into dilapidation," he continued. The people who were living without electricity and running water faced the same sanitary conditions as the workers who had built that first Parthenon some twenty-five hundred years ago. That was unacceptable. It was time for Nashville to "overtake the standards of our own times."[14]

What neither Gerald Gimre nor the editorialist had mentioned was how racism had structured growing, segregated Nashville, especially in their plans for places like Hell's Half Acre.

Thornton Prince III may have opened the first BBQ Chicken Shack in 1945—that's what some Prince family tradition holds. Or the business may have already been going for a decade by then, operated out of Prince's private kitchen on Jefferson Street. "Well, sure," Dollye Matthews, one of the proprietors of Bolton's Hot Chicken and Fish said. "I mean, when I was going to college, there was a lady on Jefferson Street who ran a cafeteria line through her dining room."[15]

Still hoping I could find a solid timeline for the BBQ Chicken Shack, I combed Nashville's newspapers. I found my first possible reference: on September 11, 1936, a man was shot in a restaurant called the Chicken Shack. The article called the business a "lunch joint," but the man had been shot on a Friday night. Clearly the business didn't close at 2 p.m. So far, I thought, so good. Then the story took a turn. The police arrested the owner, a twenty-four-year-old man named George Hall. So this couldn't be Thornton Prince III's BBQ Chicken Shack.[16]

Another possibility popped up. On May 3, 1940, the *Nashville Globe* published a list of the city's Black businesses. And there it was, the final entry in the "Restaurants" section: The Chicken Shack at 1305 Jefferson Street. Six months later, a reporter for the *Tennessean* wrote about a break-in at a restaurant of the same name where "burglars entering through a window got thirty-two dollars from two electric phonographs."[17] The only obvious problem was that the two addresses didn't align, but the restaurant could have moved or a reporter may have been sloppy in their notetaking. I checked the city directory, but it didn't list the restaurant at all, not surprising since the directory in that era did a horrible job of including Black businesses. For instance, of the forty-one Black restaurants included in the *Globe's* 1940 round up, only seven appeared in the directory's listing of "Restaurants and Lunch Rooms."[18]

I went back to the newspapers only to hit a new snag. On January 17, 1941, a man named Roscoe Springer was shot five times in the chest in the Chicken Shack, the restaurant he operated. He died on the way to Hubbard Hospital. And he had no connection to the Prince family. Well, he did have a sister named Mrs. Annie Hicks, but it would be a stretch to transform her into the mysterious and missing Mattie. This wasn't the right chicken joint either.[19]

Segregation and official refusal to recognize Black economic ingenuity and entrepreneurship makes the date of the first BBQ Chicken Shack almost impossible to know. Banking practices, real estate conventions, and a host of different laws forced many Black businesses into an unofficial existence. As of 1940, families like the Princes faced a new hurdle when looking for homes to buy or storefronts to rent. Nashville was redlined. A system created by the Home Owners' Loan Corporation, redlining helped real estate agents and lenders sort America's cities at a glance. Think of it as a simplified version of Gerald Gimre's 1933 zoning maps.

In 1940, the Marshall-Bruce printers (the same company that printed the annual city directory) released the Nashville map. All of the places the Princes had lived and would live—Willow Street in South Nashville, Jefferson Street, East Nashville by the Cumberland River—all these places had all been scribbled over with a red highlighter. This marked them as D areas, or neighborhoods "characterized by detrimental influences in a pronounced degree, undesirable population or an infiltration of it." In other words, D areas were where Black Nashvillians lived. Banks and mortgage companies would refuse to lend to anyone buying in the red zones. Lenders would automatically refuse business loan applications from people who lived there and would not fund new businesses there.* The red "hazardous" warning covered forty-three percent of the city.[20]

Then I became distracted from my search for the BBQ Chicken Shack. On August 4, 1944, the *Nashville Globe* reported in its society pages that Jasper Lee Prince had spent a week visiting with his newly wed sister Dorothy Prince Wright in her South Nashville home, and he'd been "highly entertained."[21]

So many of the unstated details in that story intrigued me. First, Dorothy and Jasper weren't full siblings. Dorothy was Gertrude Prince's daughter and Jasper's mother was Mattie Crutcher. The half siblings apparently had a close relationship despite the resentment that had surely colored their mothers' interactions. Second, why would Jasper have stayed with her for a week? Or even overnight? Though he'd been born in Franklin, Jasper had been in Nashville since 1931, living in a home his grandfather had rented in a nearby South Nashville neighborhood.

---

*   The blocks surrounding the Prince's neighborhoods were tagged with a dingy mustard, the thirteen percent of the city designated "definitely declining" because of either "obsolescence" or "infiltration of lower grade population." This meant that the Black neighborhoods were beginning to grow beyond their borders, pushing onto streets that had once belonged to white residents only; a few loan officers would take that gamble. Beyond that was a ring of navy blue, the fourteen percent of the city that bankers, realtors and white purchasers would find "still desirable." Here, mortgage companies were advised to lend up to sixty-five percent of a property's appraised value. And then came the one solid aqua-colored block of homes and neighborhoods in West Nashville were Gerald Gimre lived, the wealthy white suburbs officially labeled "best." Lenders could invest there without concern; Robert K. Nelson, LaDale Winling, Richard Marciano, Nathan Connolly, et al., "Mapping Inequality," *American Panorama,* ed. Robert K. Nelson and Edward L. Ayers, accessed March 20, 2020, https://dsl.richmond.edu/panorama/redlining/#loc=12/36.151/-86.888&city=nashville-tn.

When he married in 1934, he and his new wife had moved in with his family; five years later, Jasper had bought the property.[22]

Sure enough, Jasper's visit to Dorothy may not have been simply a chance for two half-siblings to catch up. He may have been there to recuperate from an unacknowledged illness. Three years later, Jasper Lee Prince was dead of tuberculosis. He was thirty years, two months and twenty-five days old. His mother filled out his death certificate.[23]

According to Mattie Crutcher, Jasper had only known he had the disease for the past ten months, but he was probably ill for far longer than that. When he'd been drafted in 1943, he hadn't gone to boot camp because the recruiters had rated him as a 4-F. Was he showing symptoms even then? Was that part of the reason he'd left his family home in 1944 to visit with his half-sister who lived just a few streets over? His rapid decline after his January 1946 diagnosis suggested that was true. Tuberculosis usually takes two to five years to kill. He'd entered the Davidson County Tuberculosis Hospital on July 4, 1946, and died on October 29, 1946, probably passing away from multiple organ failure or a massive lung hemorrhage.[24]

I combed the institution's minute book for clues to Jasper's life there. The doctor who directed the hospital did not use patients' names, but he did categorize them by sex and race, sorting out their treatments, recoveries, and declines into stark tables and figures. In July 1946 when Jasper Prince entered the institution, the hospital housed eighty-two white women, sixty white men, twenty-two Black women, and twenty-one Black men. That month, two white women, one Black man, and one white man had arrested tuberculosis, which meant doctors found no detectable levels of bacilli in their systems for the past six months. They were ready for release. At the other end of the table, four white men and one Black man had died in in the past thirty-one days.[25] Which of the numbers catalogued over the next three months represented Jasper's decline? Had he been the one patient given a lobectomy in August? One of the three to receive an intra-pleural pneumonolysis in September?

Only one of the anonymous numbers was definitely attached to Jasper Prince: he was the only Black man to die in October, perishing alongside one Black woman, three white men, and four white women. That same month, only thirty people were discharged from the hospital. Did that mean the institution had a thirty percent death rate?[26]

As bleak as those numbers sound, tuberculosis in 1946 was significantly more survivable than it ever had been before. In 1940, it had killed half as many people as it had in 1920. By 1945, mortality had declined by another fifteen percent. "This may not sound impressive in a nation where 55,000 people annually die of this disease," admitted the editors of the *Nashville Globe*, nor could they give much comfort to the 1,770 families in Tennessee who lost loved ones in 1945, but for new patients, the tuberculosis diagnosis was no longer the death sentence it once had been.[27]

Part of the reason for the decline in death rates was that tuberculosis was increasingly easy to diagnose. No longer did doctors wait until patients began coughing up bloody sputum. In April 1930, the state of Tennessee had purchased a portable x-ray machine, and the health department hired a radiologist to run it. Early diagnosis meant early intervention, which helped improve patients' chances. It also lowered infection rates. Since tuberculosis wasn't usually contracted with brief contact but required extended exposure, patients could be separated from their families and communities before the contagion spread.[28]

But the improved outcomes were not shared equally by all Nashvillians. Black Americans were still twice as likely to die from tuberculosis as white Americans were. In Nashville, the disease was even more deadly for people of color. Here they died at three and a half times the national rate. Because of this, a rumor started up that African Americans were carriers of the disease, responsible for keeping the contagion alive. For once, public health officials intervened. Black Nashvillians were not the carriers of the illness, the analysts said. White and Black residents had similar infection rates. The trouble was access to doctors. "Many Negroes discover their tuberculosis only after it has reached serious proportions, when little can be done to stop the infection," the *Nashville Globe* reported. The problem was the inequalities built into the medical systems and into the local housing and into the economic situations of the infected.[29]

Gerald Gimre used public health studies like these to further bolster support for his slum clearance projects, especially his plans for Capitol Hill. Federal funding initiatives had floundered, however. In August 1945, a trio of powerful senators had proposed a new housing bill that would underwrite the construction of 1.5 million new dwellings every year for ten years. President Harry S. Truman loved it. Congress didn't. No housing bill passed Congress until July 1948 when the legislators voted through a new GI Bill. Truman blasted it, calling it a "'teeny-weeny' bill" and "a piece of slipshod legislation that failed miserably to meet long-range housing needs." Republicans accused the president of having "the same socialistic tendencies we have been fighting since 1935." The Cold War was on, and anything that smacked of Roosevelt's New Deal didn't have a prayer.[30]

A few months later, a housing reform proponent in Washington, DC, convinced five senators to tour a blighted neighborhood that existed within sight of their offices. The stench inside one house was so foul that a senator vomited. The men rushed back to the Congressional washrooms to scrub themselves before their committee meetings. "The only trouble with that," one of them said, is "you can't scrub out your soul." But still the federal housing bill languished.[31]

Rather than waiting for the feds to get their act together, Gerald Gimre decided to rally Nashville to the cause. He teamed up with the Nashville Planning Commission and Parent-Teacher Associations across the city to do a community-wide housing survey. He warned Nashvillians that since the town had undertaken almost no slum clearance and created little new public housing in a decade, the results of the new survey would probably be of "disgraceful proportions."[32]

The city's leaders thought they knew the perfect first project to rally community support: they'd clear a handful of acres along the border of the Hell's Half Acre neighborhood for a municipal auditorium. They proposed making it the sort of venue they thought every modern city should have, complete with a ten-thousand-seat arena for sporting events, a smaller theater for the symphony and the ballet, and a convention center to draw in new tourist dollars.[33]

The auditorium went on the 1946 ballot. It failed.

Since the federal government wouldn't move and the city of Nashville had failed to make progress, the State of Tennessee stepped in. The governor ordered the state property administrator to buy the fifty pieces of property nearest the Capitol building for state redevelopment. He then expanded the purchase order to seventy plots.[34]

One of those seventy doomed plots was a restaurant run by Thornton Prince III. But it wasn't the BBQ Chicken Shack.

As was true for so many of the chapters in Thornton Prince III's story, this new venture had started with a woman. On August 23, 1944, Prince had tried again to nail down true love. Or perhaps love had tried to pin him. Anyway, on that day, he had wed a woman named Caroline Bridges.[35]

The couple moved into the home Caroline Bridges Prince had occupied since the mid-1920s, a nicely sized bungalow just two blocks from the heart of the Jefferson Street business district. She'd bought the home with Samuel Bridges, her first husband, and she'd stayed there after he died of kidney disease in 1934. Thornton Prince III, however, wasn't her first attempt at remarriage. In 1940 she had wed Thomas Boleyjack, a beer distributor. But by 1942, Caroline was a Bridges again, and Boleyjack had moved out of her house. Their relationship, however, was not over. In 1943, the couple took out a loan against her house, and a short time later, the reason for the mortgage became clear. Boleyjack had converted his beer distributorship into a restaurant, an upgrade that would have required funds not only for remodeling but also for new permits. Then Boleyjack defaulted on the loan, and both he and his business disappeared. Caroline Bridges' home was set to be auctioned off on August 28, 1944, but somehow, she redeemed it, perhaps with Thornton Prince's help.[36]

In 1946, Thornton and Caroline Prince took over the management of the Hilltop Inn, a three-story brick apartment complex near Belmont University that still houses students today. A year later, they had added the Hilltop Restaurant on a piece of land kitty-corner from the state capitol building. The couple divided control of their businesses between them: Caroline oversaw the apartments while Thornton ran the restaurant.[37]

I'd love to know what dishes Thornton Prince III served at the Hilltop Restaurant. Had he already been given his hot chicken breakfast? Was this its public debut? Was this a stagger-step on his way to creating the BBQ Chicken Shack? Or the Hilltop might have had nothing to do with chicken. Maybe it was just another one of Nashville's many meat-and-threes, nicknamed because patrons chose a meat and three sides. Or maybe it was a deli or a burger joint.

Whatever the Hilltop Restaurant was, thanks to the state's involvement in the looming Capitol Hill Redevelopment Project, the Hilltop

Restaurant's days were brief. According to the governor's orders, it would be torn down along with the Black YMCA, the headquarters for the *Nashville Globe* and dozens of homes. The only building slated to be spared was St. Mary's Catholic Church, a white congregation.[38]

As more details about the state's project emerged, many Black Nashvillians were frustrated by the shape it was taking. They recognized the needs within their communities. They wanted homes that connected to city water and sewer services. They called for better sanitation and more frequent trash collection in their neighborhoods, and they supported proposals to improve segregated schools, regulate substandard housing, and police illegal gambling dens. But they also recognized that what the city and state were now proposing on Capitol Hill wasn't a plan being made with their betterment in mind. It was simply a plan to evict them. "Although Negroes of Nashville compose better than twenty-eight percent of the population of Nashville and pay millions of dollars in direct and 'hidden' taxes for the city's upkeep, they seldom or never are consulted with regard to city planning," the editor of the *Nashville Globe* wrote in protest. "The whole plan has been announced with the plain implication that nothing beautiful can be planned for Nashville unless all Negroes are moved out of sight."[39]

White Nashvillians weren't much more excited about the project, though unlike Black residents, most of their concerns were about how high their taxes would go. Trying to drum up support, the mayor's administration resurrected the downtown municipal auditorium, and he accused his opponents of being allied with slum lords and of being those "who stand in the path of any progress."[40]

This time, Nashville voters bought in. In May 1949, they approved a series of bonds to raze and rebuild Hell's Half Acre: five million for the new auditorium; one million for a new municipal building that would house the fire department, the police department, and the city jail; one million for a new cloverleaf at the base of one of the Cumberland River bridges. Gerald Gimre promised that these proposals were only the beginning of what he had planned downtown.[41]

A month later the US House of Representatives finally passed Truman's housing bill, setting aside one and a half billion dollars for a revitalized slum clearance program. That afternoon, Gerald Gimre

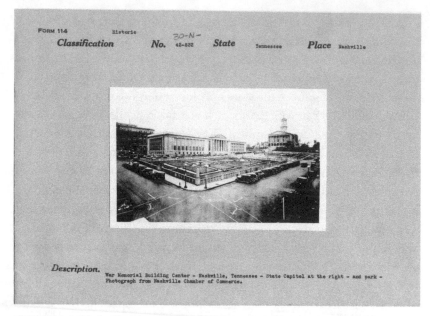

FORM 114   Historic

Classification   No. 30-N-42-532   *State*   Tennessee   *Place*   Nashville

Description.

War Memorial Building Center - Nashville, Tennessee - State Capitol at the right - and park -
Photograph from Nashville Chamber of Commerce.

FIGURE 3.2. Nashville Chamber of Commerce, "War Memorial Building Center—Nashville, Tennessee, 1949–1967." National Archives, photo no. 135804238

FIGURE 3.3. *(facing page)* Theater advertisements in the *Nashville Globe* (February 23, 1917). Digital Initiatives, James E. Walker Library, Middle Tennessee State University

and the other planners unfurled the architectural renderings they'd commissioned for a revamped downtown district. "The Nashville of the future—a marble, steel and glossy-glass architectural dream come true—began taking form yesterday with virtual assurance of federal aid for a slum clearance and redevelopment program," the *Tennessean's* editor wrote. In addition to the razed slums, the new governmental buildings, and the new municipal auditorium, the NHA had platted "bright ribbons" of highways, expanded parking facilities, and widened boulevards across Nashville's central cityscape.[42]

There was only one wrinkle: President Truman's administration would no longer fund any project that furthered segregation. A representative for the NHA reassured white Nashvillians that the new ruling wouldn't affect the city's plans for Capitol Hill. Yes, most of the people to be displaced were Black. Yes, Nashville's public housing—the places the NHA expected to rehouse most of Hell's Half Acre's former residents—were segregated. But that wasn't what Truman meant, the representative claimed. Sure enough, a month later, the Federal Housing and Home Agency announced that Nashville would be given six million dollars toward the Capitol Hill Redevelopment Project, an announcement that included no caveat regarding the city's segregated places.[43]

The governor's efforts continued apace. By the end of March 1950, the state of Tennessee owned seventy-one pieces of land, including the Hilltop Restaurant. The final plot purchased belonged to Hattie Jackson, a single Black woman who owned a two-story brick house worth nine thousand dollars, about double what the median home value was in the state in 1950.[44]

As Hattie Jackson's home showed, the area officials called a "slum" was not as uniformly handed over to blight and vice as the mayor and Gerald Gimre liked to pretend. The Capitol Hill Redevelopment Project wouldn't only take out the shacks and hovels that teetered on the hill. It would also destroy the many homes that were not slum property. It would devastate the thriving businesses that served the community. It would tear down the headquarters for the Southern Coach Lines, and it would dismantle the Black Masonic lodge that Black Nashvillians had first organized in 1865. It would raze the Bijou Theater, the fifteen-hundred-seat flagship venue for a regional African American theater chain and one of the only houses that showed first-run movies to Black audiences. The Bijou was where Black Nashville had gathered to celebrate the end of World War I, and it was where they'd cheered for Bessie Smith, Ethel Waters, and Count Basie.[45]

And the city officials intended to do it all without consulting the people who had built their lives in the shadow of the state capitol. They didn't have to. Gimre and the mayor's office had become powerful allies in the game of urban renewal. They worked together to get most white residents behind their plans, and they even had the support of Nashville's two major, politically dueling white newspapers, the *Nashville Tennessean* and the *Nashville Banner*. Gerald Gimre and the municipal government created a regulatory and funding system that did not require them to reach out to voters for comments or feedback. According to a scholar who analyzed the project after the fact, Gimre and the city officials built so much political muscle that they even pressured the state into going further than the governor wanted to go. In short, the Capitol Hill Redevelopment Project "presented a classic example of an urban renewal program conducted by a well-established public housing authority, operating in a legal environment in which few formal planning restraints were imposed," the scholar explained.[46]

There was "a view that Nashville had held for some time that suggested that one of the major problems with downtowns was people," former Mayor Bill Purcell explained to me one afternoon as we looked out the window of his high-rise downtown law office. "That if you could eliminate the people, then the city would be successful. . . . They banned vices, they banned activities that they felt were detrimental to civic life, and they banned residential living."[47]

Capitol Hill's residents, however, did not go quietly. The Bijou's owners, the Masons, the head of the Southern Coach Lines, and a handful of other business owners in the area fought back. They brought a series of court cases against the city, and they launched a massive public relations campaign, trying to save their buildings. They slowed the project by a couple of years, but ultimately, they lost their fight.[48]

On July 17, 1957, a white man driving a bulldozer pulled up in front of the Bijou Theater. A reporter snapped a picture of it, the image a study in contrasts. The street was already reduced to piles of dirt, but the glass-encased signs out front of the building protected posters advertising Walt Disney's *Littlest Outlaw* and Jack Webb in the first feature-length production of *Dragnet*. The placard under the ticket stand still invited patrons to "Come inside for a Tasty SNACK." The man on the bulldozer had turned his machine toward the Bijou's electrical pole, but the lightbulbs lining the theater's tiled entrance were lit and the neon-rimmed BIJOU above its marquee was intact, ready to flicker on. Two Black men stood in the venue's open front doors watching, hips cocked and arms akimbo; the man on the bulldozer hid behind his sunglasses and pretended he could not see them. Hell's Half Acre was imploding.[49]

The Hilltop Restaurant was long closed by then. It had probably shut down about the time the state started tearing down properties in 1950. That was also about the time Thornton and Caroline Prince's marriage disintegrated.

Their short marriage had faced a number of challenges. Hilltop's closing had to have been a blow. Then Thornton Prince III lost a second child, his second son, in a tragic moment of violence. On Sunday, June 26, 1949, Thomas Edward Prince, his son with Gertrude, was stabbed in the chest by an ice-pick-wielding housemate. Thomas was rushed to the hospital, but the doctors couldn't save him.[50] He lingered for six hours and ten minutes before dying of his wounds. The housemate told the authorities that the attack was in self-defense, that Thomas had "advanced on her with a knife."[51] The jury didn't buy it. In March 1950, she was found guilty and sentenced to two years in the state prison.[52]

Whatever had happened between Thornton and Caroline Prince, by 1951 Caroline Bridges was living alone in her house, and she'd gone back to calling herself Samuel's widow. On February 10, 1953, the court granted Caroline a divorce from Thornton.[53] Because he had failed to keep up with his temporary alimony, the court ordered that he immediately pay her $562.50 and hand over his 1948 Chevrolet sedan.[54]

Maybe Caroline Bridges Prince was the woman who sashayed in with that first piece of hot chicken.

Caroline and Samuel Bridges' home still stands, but it's changed dramatically in the intervening decades. Its back alley is now the y-interchange where I-40 and I-65 meet. A later owner added a two-story apartment block to the back of the bungalow. Or was it Caroline's addition? Had she enjoyed her time at the Hilltop Inn so much she decided to use her home to earn a living?

But then someone else bought Caroline Bridges' home and desecrated it. They renamed it Ann's Hacienda Hotel, and they painted the home's wood—though not its brick, thank heavens—in something that

FIGURE 3.4. The front of Ann's Hacienda Hotel, the brick bungalow that belonged to Caroline Bridges Prince. Photo: Rachel Louise Martin

has faded to a particularly unfortunate shade of Slushee blue. They let the building become rundown, and then they stopped maintaining the landscaping. Eventually, they abandoned the home altogether. These days it stands empty, its doors and windows boarded over.

CHAPTER 4

Let It Rest

The Barbecue Chicken Shack,
Culinary Nostalgia, and the Death of
Thornton Prince III, 1952–1960

And here it is at last. The first definite, irrefutable, unmistakable, unequivocal reference to the business that we now know as Prince's Hot Chicken Shack. It's right there in the 1953 Nashville city directory: the Chicken Shack restaurant at 1711½ Charlotte Avenue. Yes, this is absolutely the right Chicken Shack, even though there was still no BBQ or Barbecue or Bar-B-Q included in its name. We can know this because the directory tells us its manager was Thornton Prince. Well, actually, the directory calls him John, but he's living at the right address. So this is it, the first time hot chicken entered the official landscape of Nashville.[1]

The building that housed this, the first known BBQ Chicken Shack, is long gone, replaced by a Krystal's parking lot, but the makeup of this stretch of Charlotte Avenue otherwise is much as it was in 1953, a hodgepodge of businesses and houses, churches and offices, restaurants and factories. The Krystal is surrounded by the Alive Hospice Cen-

FIGURE 4.1. The Krystal sign marking the spot where the BBQ Chicken Shack used to be. Photo: Rachel Louise Martin

ter, the Fattoush Café, Foundation Building Materials, and Jiffy Lube. The BBQ Chicken Shack's neighbors were the Bailey Toil Restaurant, a couple of private homes, the Clarksville Ice and Coal Plant, a contractor's office, and a beer shop. Another similar characteristic of this block then and now is that most of the customers and the folks living nearby were and are people of color.[2]

By 1953, Chicken Shacks were an established part of the Southern restaurant industry, so widespread they were almost cliché. Hattie Mosely Austin had started Hattie's Chicken Shack in Sarasota, Florida, in 1938. Open twenty-four hours a day, the business catered to working stiffs who needed a fast lunch, families looking for a filling meal, and jazz musicians unwinding after shows. Just about the same time, down in Baton Rouge, Tommy Delpit abandoned his ice cream parlor and transformed it into the Chicken Shack. Up in Chicago, Harold Pierce "noticed that the fast-food industry avoided . . . the Black community," so he and his wife launched Harold's Chicken Shack in 1950. And there were other chicken shacks in New York City; and Luverne, Alabama; and Los Angeles, California; and Clinton, Tennessee. Of course, there had also been at least two previous Nashville restaurants of that name. Thornton Prince III's spicy chicken gave him a chance to be outstanding in this crowded field.[3]

Today, fried chicken—hot or not—is one of those defining dishes of Southern food and soul food, right up there with collard greens and cornbread and buttermilk biscuits. In this era of modern industrial food production and genetically engineered poultry, chicken is the cheap meat. But until the mid-twentieth century, for the Prince family and many other families in the South both white and Black, chicken was a celebratory dish. Weekday meals were filled with smoked pork and salted ham hocks and bacon. Chicken was for Sundays and birthdays and when the preacher or the teacher came for a visit. And the very best fried chicken was a seasonal dish. "Like many other things of that day, frying chickens were produced only once a year in late spring through early summer," African American cookbook author Edna Lewis wrote in her classic *The Taste of Country Cooking*. "They were hand-raised and specially fed. . . . The first fried chickens were served at Sunday morning breakfast when the outside work was finished."[4]

FIGURE 4.2. "A Chicken for Every Pot," political ad in the *New York Times* (October 30, 1928). National Archives, photo no. 187095

That's why "in the hard-times election of 1932, the Republican Party's campaign slogan was 'a chicken in every pot,'" John Egerton wrote in *Southern Food*. It was a promise that hearkened back to King Henry IV. "The fact that neither the party nor the king could deliver on the promise may have diminished their popularity, but not that of the chicken."[5]

By the time Thornton Prince III opened his chicken joint on Charlotte, the people living in the neighborhood around him were ready for some nostalgic celebratory fare. Families like the Princes had been streaming into Nashville for a while now, leaving their farms behind them. Most of them were working class, juggling a couple of jobs to make ends meet, so they didn't have time to whip up old-fashioned feasts. Sure, the city had its good points—the excitement, the entertainment, the chance of a job that paid better wages than farm labor had—but many of them felt a little homesick. They missed downhome Black Southern cooking.

But while the BBQ Chicken Shack's fried chicken itself might have had the nostalgic edge of Sunday dinners on the grounds, the hot chicken's accoutrements—the spongy, factory-produced white bread and the crinkle-cut pickle chips—were a sign of just how modern and urbane Thornton Prince's new joint was. Yes, I'm talking about that bread that today seems so commercial and tasteless when compared to the hearty, fibrous, nutritious loaves we pick up from any grocery store bakery. In the 1950s, words like "industrial" were a selling point for American eaters. This was the era when Jell-O salads, frozen dinners, and creamed soup casseroles were the touted as cutting edge cookery, and every kid dreamed of eating dehydrated space-age food.[6]

Thornton Prince III also modeled his new venture on one of Nashville's archetypal restaurants, a style of restaurant that also traded on a longing for a certain mystical, pastoral past: the meat-and-three. This category of restaurant was known for letting diners order one meat and three sides (well, here in Nashville we say it's a meat and three vegetables, but those veggies feature mac and cheese, hushpuppies, and candied yams). These businesses gave diners a way to eat labor-intensive Southern comfort food favorites on the quick and cheap.

The meat-and-three is one of those things Nashville likes to claim as its own, to the irritation of our sibling southeastern cities. I'll compromise. Let's say the idea arose in the Mid-South. And when did it get started? Well, the earliest reference to this style of dining in the *Tennessean* was a 1922 advertisement for the Little Gem, a white-owned downtown lunch counter. For thirty cents, customers got "soup, one meat and three vegetables, cornbread and hot biscuits, with something to drink." A slice of pie cost an extra dime. Come summer, the restauranteur added sliced tomatoes, onions, and slaw, and he did it without raising the price.[7]

Other businesses adopted and adapted the concept for themselves. Hap Townes and his son, who were white, sold the same style of menu at their eponymous Nashville restaurant. And there was Walter and Susie Swett, a Black Nashville couple who already owned a gas station/grocery store. In 1952 they bought the Joyland Tavern. They never intended to serve food there, but they had ten children to feed, so every night, they sat their kids in a corner of the tavern for a family dinner. Soon, customers started joining them. In 1954, they launched Swett's Dinette a few blocks off Jefferson. Their business is still serving customers today.[8]

The food sold at Swett's and the BBQ Chicken Shack and other businesses like them would soon be called soul food. Where the meat-and-threes and even the chicken shacks could be found in both white and Black communities, soul food was Black. It was a way for African American parents to connect their children back to their rural roots, and it was a way for African American eaters to name the role Black cooks had in developing Southern cuisines.[9]

For centuries, Black chefs and home cooks alike had been critical agents in crafting the region's foodways, melding African, European, and Native traditions and ingredients and tastes. Their contributions, however, had sometimes been ignored, sometimes been claimed by white slaveowners and employers (think what the Sayers family had done with the food Ann Currine had cooked in their Wood Park kitchen), and sometimes been caricatured as being simplistic or primitive or base.

Soul food reclaimed African American food traditions as being something "constructed *by* African Americans *for* African Americans," scholar Sheila Bock wrote in *I Know You Got Soul*. And the soul in soul food disconnected the dishes from the history of slavery and oppression, replacing the loss with the love Black cooks had shown when they prepared food for their families and friends. It was about nurture and nutrition and resilience. Black foodways—soul food—were part of the bond that held Black communities together in racist America, and the cuisine helped the cooks heal the wounds caused by the prejudice around them.[10]

Soul food was also a way to preserve Black America's disappearing histories. As my attempt to reconstruct the Prince family's story demonstrates, most African American lives were systematically omitted from the records that made it into the archives and libraries and government collections. Black Americans stored their memories in other types of sources such as food. Those sources must stay alive for the memories to survive for future generations. "Whenever I go back to my sisters and brothers, we relive old times, remembering the past," chef and author Edna Lewis explained. "And when we share again in gathering wild strawberries, canning, rendering lard, finding walnuts, picking persimmons, making fruitcake, I realize how much the bond that held us had to do with food."[11]

Lewis's recognition of this was part of what made her the "brilliant, subversive, and political a writer she was," Francis Lam wrote in his profile of her, "an empowered woman who claimed the story of her people—Black, rural, a generation away from enslavement—as a story

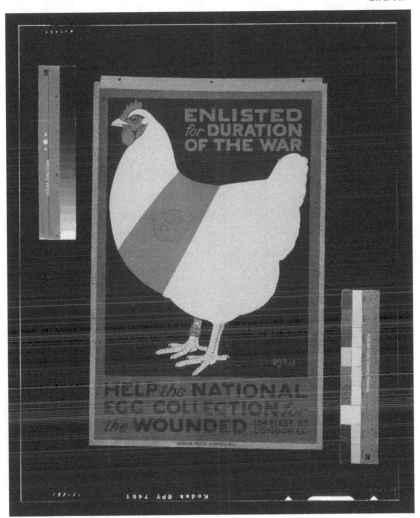

FIGURE 4.3. R. G. Praill, "Enlisted for duration of the war. Help the national egg collection for the wounded" (1915). Library of Congress, object no. LC-USZC4-11169

of beauty whose rightful place is squarely at the center of American culture. I marveled at her language, at its beauty and evenness, even as the ideas underneath it were fierce. It's a story of dignity and resistance."[12]

At least, that's how some folks talked about African American foodways. Not everyone agreed. Some, particularly among the Black Power movement, would argue that soul food was unhealthy physically—all that lard—and spiritually—that heritage of oppression. They urged the Black community to abandon the dishes. "Soul food came to be infused with many different meanings," Bock wrote, "including racial pride, cultural achievement, survival, comfort, oppression, filth, and danger." Or, as food writer and scholar Kyla Wazana Tompkins argued in *Racial Indigestion*, eating in America is a political act.[13]

The BBQ Chicken Shack was a family business, though only Thornton Prince III listed it as his primary job. He was the manager and the cook. His brothers, sons, and nephews pitched in as they could, but they all kept their day jobs as mailmen and mechanics and printers. They came to the BBQ Chicken Shack after hours and on weekends. For them the restaurant "was just a little substitute to try to get over," current owner André Prince Jeffries said. "Try to get some more bills paid." Her dad, Bruce Prince, was one of those part-time employees. The son of Thornton's brother Boyd and his wife Clara, Bruce had grown up with Thornton Prince III's kids, first on the farm out Gallatin Pike and then on Willow Street in South Nashville.[14]

Since most of the men had other jobs, the restaurant was closed for lunch, opened for dinner, and then stayed open later than any other restaurant in town: midnight during the week and 4 a.m. on the weekends. "That's one tradition that I try to keep, being open that late," Jeffries said. "It's grown on me. I'm a night owl now."[15]

The late-night hours meant the BBQ Chicken Shack wasn't a place for kids. Growing up, Jeffries only ate hot chicken as leftovers. "My father would bring it home and put it on the stove on Saturday night," she remembered. "When we'd get up on Sunday morning, getting ready to go to Sunday school and then to church, I'd always see that little greasy bag on the stove. Hey, we were tackling it because he wouldn't bring more than one or two pieces, and that would make us mad." She got used to the taste of it after it had sat overnight, and to this day she still prefers to leave her hot chicken to age a bit, a process that lets the hot penetrate even more deeply and evenly through the meat.[16]

The BBQ Chicken Shack was one of the safe spaces for African Americans in segregated Nashville, somewhere Black adults could eat and chat and unwind without worrying about what white folks might be thinking or planning. It was also someplace they knew they would receive service, and they would receive it on a first come, first served basis. No one would ask them to step out of line or out of the way simply because a white person showed up. When their food came out of the fryer, they could sit right down at a table and eat, no taking their food to go or hustling to the back.[17]

Eventually some white people did show up, complicating things a bit. The BBQ Chicken Shack's late-night hours made it a popular hangout for musicians after a gig. "When he drove to the Opry on Saturday nights, he could smell something really wonderful but couldn't figure out where it was coming from," wrote Lorrie Morgan, country singer and daughter of George Morgan, a Country Music Hall of Famer who was a regular on the Opry stage from the late 1940s through the early 1970s. One night, her father tracked the smell to the BBQ Chicken Shack. He fell for the restaurant's food and its hours, so he told his friends about it. Pretty soon, the Opry stars were headed there after every performance.[18]

The Prince family had a dilemma. In the Jim Crow South, Thornton Prince III couldn't serve white and Black customers in the same room, yet he didn't want to turn away his new star-studded white clientele. He needed a place to seat Morgan and his cronies that wouldn't unseat his Black regulars, something that obeyed the letter of de jure segregation while booting the spirit of the prejudicial ordinances right out the kitchen door. The Princes constructed an ingenious compromise. Black eaters stayed put. "We sat out front on these benches," Jeffries said as she rubbed one of the unpadded white booths. Then the family built a separate room for their white guests, but it was at the back of the building. White customers walked through the main dining room and the kitchen to reach it.

"Black people have never been segregated from the Caucasians," Jeffries continued. "Caucasians separated us. . . . As far as segregation is concerned, that is a Caucasian problem." She clapped her hands together and shook her head. "Have mercy!"

By the mid-1950s, however, change was coming to Nashville. In 1954, the United States Supreme Court ruled that public schools had to deseg-

FIGURE 4.4. Benjamin Jefferson Davis Jr., *Must Negro-Americans Wait Another Hundred Years for Freedom?: Against Tokenism and Gradualism* (1963). Collection of the Smithsonian National Museum of African American History and Culture, gift of the family of Dr. Maurice Jackson and Laura Ginsburg, object no. 2010.55.75

regate. They could have announced a timeframe for it; instead, the justices said desegregation had to happen with "all deliberate speed." Many communities used that wishy-washy language to push desegregation off for years or even decades. In Nashville, however, a young Black man named Robert Kelley had to walk past all-white East High School, over the Cumberland River, and through downtown to all-Black Pearl High School. His family filed a lawsuit in 1956, arguing the city should open East High to him. The Reverend Henry Maxwell filed a similar suit because his kids were bused from South Nashville to the other side of the city, a forty-five-minute ride. To settle these cases, the courts announced that beginning in the fall of 1957, Nashville public schools would desegregate one grade per year in what became known as the "Nashville Plan."

Compared to many other cities, desegregation was relatively peaceful in Nashville, but this may have been because residential segregation and urban renewal had already separated the races from each other.

De jure segregation may not have seemed as necessary; Gerald Gimre's projects and his zoning codes had ensured Black Nashvillians and white Nashvillians would not live, study, eat, or work together no matter what the law said.

The school board gerrymandered the school districts so that only about a hundred Black first-graders were eligible for desegregation in 1957. Nine enrolled. White "segregation academies" and white flight further undermined efforts to integrate the schools. Seven years later, fewer than eight hundred Black students were in formerly all-white schools. Black teachers and principals faced demotions or layoffs as the city consolidated the system.

Desegregation had turned out to be a two-edged sword for many African Americans. Racism severely limited their lives and opportunities. They had poorer school systems and fewer good job options. They were prohibited from moving into the best neighborhoods. They were denied loans and mortgages. They were expected to treat all white individuals with deference, even while they were mistreated. Any challenge to this system was punished with violence.

At the same time, segregation gave African Americans even more reason to develop separate businesses and community centers. Black schools, churches, and businesses became sites of resistance where the next generation learned about Black heroes and Black history. The BBQ Chicken Shack might not have lasted if it hadn't first been fostered within Nashville's Black neighborhoods.

––––––––––

Ever the romantic optimist, Thornton Prince III married one last time. On August 21, 1954, he wed twenty-two-year-old Katie E. Dobson, a girl at least thirty years his junior. Though Katie was considerably younger than Thornton, she already had her own failed marriage behind her. She had first married in 1953, a partnership that clearly hadn't thrived.[19]

Thornton Prince and Katie Dobson's wedding was no fancy church to-do. Their officiant was a Williamson County Justice of the Peace. The clerk scrawled "Do not Publish" in the top right corner of the marriage record, an intriguing invocation. The May-December couple may have been hiding their relationship from disapproving family members, or it could have been one or the other of them was embarrassed of their previous marriages, or it may have indicated a shotgun wedding after Katie suspected she'd be delivering a seven-month baby, or maybe they'd been living together unwed and did not want to shock their neighbors. Thornton signed the marriage license "James T. Prince," perhaps as a further obfuscation?[20]

Sherron Denise Prince was born to Katie and Thornton sometime in 1955, and the small family set up house together at 1920 Patterson Street in a house that was walking distance from the BBQ Chicken Shack. Theoretically they were living in the middle of Gerald Gimre's new Nashville. A few blocks to one side, Baptist Hospital was expanding, a bevy of doctors' offices exploding around it. Two blocks to the south of them, the city was developing, widening and paving Church Street. Charlotte Avenue itself was being transformed into a major east-west artery two blocks to the north. But the Princes were living in one of the segregated by-waters Gimre hadn't yet targeted. A 1962 picture from the street showed a double row of outhouses leaning higgledy-piggledy in the foreground. A woman in a white dress stood between two of them, walking toward one of the handful of outside ground spigots the tenants all shared because they had no running water inside their homes.[21]

Before Gimre could dismantle Patterson Street and all the other places like it, Nashville had to pass its first housing code, something he had proposed eleven years earlier. When Gimre brought the code back up in 1956, builders and real estate lobbyists resisted, arguing that the building codes were sufficient, but everyone knew those regulations gave landlords and property owners a giant loophole. Yes, if a contractor added plumbing to a dwelling, the plumbing had to meet codes, or if they put in electrical wiring, someone would inspect the electrical connections. But if a landlord erected a building that had no plumbing or electricity? No one would call them on it. Nor could the city enforce building codes on any pre-existing, unremodeled structures. Until Gerald Gimre had his housing code, Thornton Prince III's landlord could leave his tenants trapped in the nineteenth century.[22]

Gimre's proposed codes shouldn't have been controversial: every dwelling would have to have a sink and a bathroom facility and a water heater, and all of them would have to connect to the city's water and sewer systems. Each home would need central heating. Every bedroom would have at least one window facing the outside. Every occupant would require at least one hundred square feet of living space.[23]

The rudimentary nature of the codes is a reminder that urban renewal wasn't just about making the city prettier or richer or whiter. It was also about safety. One September day in 1958, for instance, a downtown rooming house went up in flames. Firemen arrived within minutes of the call, but they were already too late to save the building or the residents still trapped inside it. Two men died. One, a nineteen-year-old employed by the Mist-O-Matic Car Wash just down the street, burned to death within shouting distance of his older brother who heard him crying, "I can't make it" and "I'm smothering!" The fire inspector discovered that the building, which was riddled with frayed wiring, had a basement that had no outside access. The owner had divided that bottom floor into multiple apartments, which is where the deceased teenager had been living and where he had died.[24]

To Nashville's slumlords, though, Gerald Gimre's proposed regulations sounded ridiculous and onerous. They convinced the city council to strike the requirements for water and sewer access. They also got rid of mandatory rodent proofing, and they lowered the minimum space to seventy square feet for an adult, one hundred square feet for a couple and thirty-five square feet for a child. One member of the NI IA estimated that about half of Nashville's fifty-one thousand dwellings would fail to pass those standards, even in their reduced state. The homes on Patterson Street certainly didn't meet them.[25]

Patterson Street was just one of the many derelict corners of Nashville Gerald Gimre wanted to uproot and replace. In 1955, the Nashville Housing Authority already oversaw 4,503 low-rent dwelling units in ten housing projects—five white and five Black—and they expected to have an additional 808 units available before the year was out. In addition, the Capitol Hill Redevelopment Project was in full demolition mode, and Gimre's office was beginning to look for new projects. And it appeared Gimre and his team had a new ally in President Dwight D. Eisenhower, the first Republican president to have shown any interest in the move-

FIGURE 4.5. Carl Giers, "N.E. Nashville, showing Cumberland River and Edgefield, Tenn." (c. 1870). New York Public Library, object no. NYPG92-F35

ment that was now being called urban renewal. At noon on August 2, 1954, President Eisenhower had signed the first Republican-sponsored housing program into law.[26]

The new housing bill was a chance to expand these projects, taking the movement outside downtown and into the rest of Nashville. Gerald Gimre launched yet another survey of the city's blighted areas. This time he directed his staff to focus on the east side of the Cumberland River.

Like Willow Street and Hell's Half Acre, East Nashville's Black neighborhoods developed during and immediately after the Civil War, growing out the refugee camps that had sprung up there during the conflict. Also like Hell's Half Acre, East Nashville had considerable economic diversity. The neighborhood of Edgefield in particular was filled with professionals, businesspeople, and skilled laborers, and the Nashville Normal Theological Institute / Roger Williams University trained Black pastors. Edgefield had also been where Benjamin "Pap" Singleton lived when he launched the Exoduster movement. Disenchanted by Reconstruction's failure, Singleton believed that African Americans had no hope of finding equality within the former Confederacy. He proposed establishing new all-Black colonies in the western territories. Twenty-five thousand other freedpeople agreed with him and followed him to Kansas; 2,407 of these migrants left from Nashville.[27]

But by the 1950s, parts of East Nashville were as underdeveloped and impoverished as Willow Street, Hell's Half Acre, and Patterson Street. Gerald Gimre started talking about a new plan, one of even greater scale than the Capitol Hill Redevelopment Project. He called it the East Nashville Urban Renewal Project.

Unlike the Capitol Hill initiative, which had wiped away an entire community, the East Nashville project would focus on "reclaiming" or rehabilitating as many existing structures as possible; only the irredeemable would be razed, Gimre promised. Because he now had his building codes, the city would be able to sort what could be saved from what couldn't. On September 4, 1956, the City Council passed the East Nashville initiative eighteen to one.[28]

Councilman W. Y. Draper, the lone dissenter, wrote an editorial in the *Tennessean* explaining his unpopular stand.

> Under no stretch of the imagination and the American way of life, as I have known it, can one justify the seizure of private property, dislodge the owner or occupant and demand certain improvements to be made at the owner's expense. . . .
>
> And, to force such an issue that is beyond their control is unconstitutional, un-American and nothing short of communism-socialism in our own back yard. If we must have urban renewal, let's get to the bottom of the trouble. Let us increase their income, improve their minds and build a spirit of community pride through education. If this is what we mean by urban renewal, I AM FOR IT.[29]

Of course, that wasn't what anyone else in city government meant by urban renewal.

Then President Eisenhower discovered he didn't actually want to be in the business of rehabilitating and rebuilding American cities. In early 1957 he froze the funding for any housing initiative that wasn't a disaster recovery program. Nashville was one of dozens of cities that was suddenly trapped in the middle of a dramatic makeover, unable to proceed.

Nashville's mayor Ben West happened to be that year's president of the American Municipal Association. He joined a group of enraged mayors who stormed DC to protest this action. Urban renewal wasn't something that Nashville's leaders had wanted in the beginning, West argued. He couldn't even pin responsibility for it on over-zealous do-gooders like Gerald Gimre. The whole mess had been started by the feds. Now it was theirs to help clean up. Thanks to the money Eisenhower had promised to send, the NHA had already unhoused six thousand people in Davidson County,[30] and the final stages of the Capitol Hill Redevelopment Project would displace more. So the president only wanted to fund disaster recovery? Well, wasn't Nashville facing a federally created disaster![31]

Congress stepped in, approving the original amount the Eisenhower administration had requested and adding two hundred fifty million dollars to the pot, but from then on the federal government would be an ever-more unreliable partner, waffling and jiggling on urban renewal for the rest of the program's existence, leaving city planners, municipal leaders, and neighborhood residents continually unsure whether they'd be able to finish the projects they launched.[32]

Funding restored, the East Nashville Urban Renewal Program officially started on Monday, May 5, 1958, at the home of John D. Sharpe Sr. That morning, a city housing inspector sat down with him to explain what he needed to do to meet the city's new codes, a conversation that occurred under the watchful eyes of the mayor, the city council, Gerald Gimre, and local journalists, of course.[33]

A team of five housing inspectors fanned out across East Nashville. And they would only look at East Nashville, Gerald Gimre promised. "I was the token Black," Richard Gordon remembered. He inspected every building that was owned or inhabited by African Americans. His four white colleagues worked their way through the white portions of the district. The inspectors moved quickly, and the results were as bad as the NHA had predicted. At the beginning of October, the city's chief inspector announced that of the 588 homes inspected so far, only eighty-nine had met the new standards.[34]

Once the home inspections were underway, Gerald Gimre announced that the Nashville Housing Authority would begin buying up four hundred acres in East Nashville. They would raze every structure on those properties, subdivide the land, and resell it to private developers, hopefully at a profit to the city. They started with a ten-acre site the NHA had designated for the private development of apartment buildings for white families displaced by urban renewal. The demolition began at 2:05 p.m. on Tuesday, April 19, 1960. At the ceremony celebrating the first house to fall, Mayor Ben West bragged that the East Nashville project showed that as a city "we are burgeoning, we are blooming, we are blossoming.' "[35]

But city officials weren't the only ones working toward a vision of what new Nashville should be and who it should serve. Though West's office pretended all was well, the ceremony had started five minutes late because Ben West's schedule had been thrown into disarray that morning when three thousand members of the Black community marched on his office to protest the bombing of City Councilman Z. Alexander Looby's home at daybreak.[36]

This stage of Nashville's civil rights struggle had started in February 1960. A few weeks earlier, students in Greensboro, North Carolina, had sat at a segregated downtown lunch counter and demanded service. Inspired by their example, students from Fisk, the American Baptist Theological Seminary, and Tennessee A&I organized similar protests in Nashville, and they inspired middle class Black shoppers to boycott the downtown businesses.

When the police arrested the protesting students, Looby headed up the team of lawyers defending them, probably the reason someone had tossed dynamite at his house that morning. After ascertaining that no one was injured, the protesters had marched from Fisk to downtown where the mayor met them on the courthouse steps. Diane Nash, a Fisk University student who would help found the Student Nonviolent Coordinating Committee, demanded, "Mayor West, do you think it is wrong to discriminate against a person solely on the basis of their race or color?"

Mayor Ben West had worked for voting rights reform and Nashville's token school desegregation plan. He had fought efforts to gerrymander the voting districts, and he had stood against the poll tax. His actions had won over many Black Nashville voters, and he depended on them to win reelection. He also depended on the city's white businessmen, however.

"Yes," he replied. He added, "That's up to the store managers, of course."

As wishy-washy as the mayor's support was, it helped turn opinion for the protestors. "Whites Only" signs came down on May 10.[37]

Thornton Prince III was again living alone on Patterson. On February 8, 1956, a Davidson County judge granted Katie a divorce, ruling that Thornton Prince had abandoned Katie, "or turned her out of doors, and refused or neglected to provide for her."

His marriage to Katie Dobson Prince had been rocky almost from the beginning. She'd already left him at least once before, or maybe he had left her. Anyway, on February 10, 1955, a court had dismissed a divorce case she had brought, ruling that "the parties have become reconciled and have cohabited [sic] and lived as man and wife since the filing." Whatever reconciliation occurred did not last long.[38]

The divorce decree gave Katie Dobson Prince full custody of their daughter Sherron, and it ordered Thornton Prince to pay ten dollars a week in child support. He also was supposed to cover a hundred dollars' worth of Katie's legal fees.[39]

A month later, he appealed the amount of his child support payments. He claimed that he was "only employed part-time as a handyman" and earned "on an average of twelve dollars to fifteen dollars a week." And the child was so young, he argued, he didn't need to pay nearly that much money to Katie for Sherron's upkeep. It's curious that the restaurant is not mentioned in this appeal. Yes, the Chicken Shack was still open, and he still ran it. No, neither he nor Katie told the judge about whatever income he earned from the BBQ Chicken Shack. The court dismissed his payments altogether.[40]

If hot chicken hadn't already been invented by 1956, Katie Dobson Prince would have been a wonderful candidate as its progenitor.

After the divorce, Katie Dobson and her daughter moved back to her parents' house in South Nashville. She went to work for Christ the King Catholic Church, first as a member of their cafeteria staff and then as a maid.[41]

But she hadn't given up on love. In 1962, she married twenty-one-year-old Mason Baker. Where Thornton Prince was a couple decades too old for her, Baker was much too young. Katie Prince was a twice-married mother of about thirty. No matter how good Baker was to her, he never could have given her the support she needed. Their marriage lasted about as long as her marriage to Thornton Prince III.[42]

FIGURE 4.6. Unidentified, "Pinback Button from SNCC" (c. 1965). Collection of the Smithsonian National Museum of African American History and Culture, object no. 2012.159.6

Then she tried again, partnering up with a man named John Perkins. Though the couple was together by 1966, they did not marry until 1975. Perhaps Katie Dobson Prince Baker was a little scarred from her previous three failed marriages.[43]

What in the world had happened to this woman? Why had she chosen three ill-advised partners, one of whom hadn't lasted a year, one of whom was decades too old for a girl of twenty, and another of whom was much too young for a thirty-year-old woman with a child?

Katie Prince Perkins had grown up in a stable home with parents who stayed together for their entire lives and were clearly supportive of their children into adulthood, but her parents hadn't been able to protect their children entirely. On May 29, 1951, Katie Perkins' sixteen-year-old sister Lula was with her boyfriend, a nineteen-year-old private named James Whitt Oldham who was on leave from his post at Fort Pickett, Virginia. They'd gone to hang out with one of Oldham's friends. The conversation turned to the game of Russian roulette, and Oldham and his friend had pulled out a pistol to show Lula how it was done. Lula was out of her league, but like most sixteen-year-olds, she probably couldn't admit it. And then, disaster. As Oldham was spinning the pistol's cylinder, the gun "accidentally went off" in his hand.

FIGURE 4.7. The footstone to grave of Thornton Prince II. His wife Mary lies beside him. His son Thornton Prince III is buried in an unmarked grave somewhere close by. Photo: Rachel Louise Martin

The bullet struck Lula Dobson in the head just above her right temple, killing her instantly.[44]

The police arrested Oldham, but a grand jury refused to return a true bill against him. The press gave the entire tragic incident unfortunately predictable coverage. Her death warranted only two mentions: three paragraphs the day after the shooting and two paragraphs when the jury handed down its decision. In each account, one of the paragraphs is dedicated to explaining the game of Russian roulette and each one said that the chance of her actually being shot was only one in five.[45]

Eighteen-year-old Katie Perkins must have been devastated by all of this—her sister's death; the jury's failure to prosecute James Oldham; the *Tennessean*'s account, which left out any sense of who her sister was. It was, everyone outside the family seemed to agree, just too bad, an unfortunate accident. Katie must have been livid, robbed of her sister and betrayed by everyone who was supposed to seek justice on Lula's behalf. And what must the mood in her family home have been like after that? How did the Dobson family handle the trauma of Lula's sudden death? Was all of that part of what had sent Katie running into marriage after marriage?

Whatever had happened to her, Katie Perkins finally seemed to find peace and stability with John Perkins. They remained together and married until his death. She never remarried again.

Thornton Prince III was not so lucky. After the divorce, he'd gone back to his bachelor lifestyle, living alone and running the Chicken Shack into the wee hours. He died on February 15, 1960, of a cerebral thrombosis, or a clot that drained the blood from his brain. He could possibly have survived the event, but he had already been weakened by diabetes.[46]

One of his daughters filled out his death certificate, though she didn't sign her name so there is no way to tell which one she was. He was buried in a small country cemetery back in Williamson County, his body laid to rest somewhere near where his parents were interred. No one bought him a gravestone.[47]

His obituary, however, introduced an unexpected curveball. It listed his surviving children, including "four daughters, Mrs. Dorothy Prince Davis of Chicago, Ill.; Mrs. Ozella London, Mrs. Georgia Cunningham, and Sherron D. Prince, all of Nashville, Tenn." Wait, Georgia

Cunningham? Wouldn't you love to know who she was? Me, too. I searched the records, but I found no good answer, not even enough for speculation. Who was her mother? Was she the actual first person to cook hot chicken?[48]

CHAPTER 5

Fry in Spitting-Hot Oil

Jumping Jefferson Street Brought Low, 1961–1968

The wide-eyed chicken seemed to know something was up. Alarmed, it had pulled back its surprisingly mobile beak to bare its gritted teeth at the customers entering Helen's Hot Chicken. Of course, if the bird wasn't tipped off by the flick of flame painted where its wattles should have been, the smell of poultry spitting in hot oil and spice surely would've done it.

Launched in summer 2014, Helen's had quickly become one of the staple hot chicken shacks, both here in Nashville and across the region. Founders Jeremy Mallard and LaSonya Morrow had named the business after Jeremy's grandmother who had run a popular Nashville soul food joint in the '80s called Helen and John's. This new Helen's had started out small, just a mid-century trailer parked on an empty lot. They chose to place their food truck a few blocks up from the Cheatham Place projects on the boundary of Germantown, a gentrifying corner of the city. At first, they didn't even have seating, but after a few weeks, they added a pop-up tent and some picnic tables. They painted their trailer with that terrified chicken, framed the entire vehicle in dancing flames, and then emblazoned it with "Helen's Hot Chicken, It's Hella Hot!" The chicken wouldn't have been the only thing that was hot that first summer. The inside of the trailer must have been sweltering in the July heat with the fryers popping.[1]

Word about the new business spread quickly. Folks from the neighborhood started lining up alongside hot chicken aficionados from across Middle Tennessee. By October they had saved money up, enough to open their brick-and-mortar store. As of March 2020, they had expanded to seven locations in three states, but their shop on Jefferson Street was still their flagship location. The business was perched in one of the corner storefronts in Otey Plaza, right across from Fisk University. They shared the building with a shoe store, two tax prep options, a check-cashing store, a nail salon, a hair braider, an electronics repair shop, and the offices for a hospice service.[2]

At one time, 80 percent of the Black-owned businesses in Nashville were based on Jefferson Street, a place that belonged to all of Black Nashville, not just the neighborhood's residents. Since the Civil War, Jefferson Street has been where Black Nashvillians could shop, eat, learn, and worship safely, separated from racist white Nashvillians. It was a protected space, free of the prejudice, limitation, and violence that characterized Black life in the rest of Nashville, "the only street African Americans can claim in this whole city," as one lifelong resident told a reporter for the *Tennessee Ledger*.[3]

Like most of Nashville's other historic Black neighborhoods, this one began as a refugee camp built on the outskirts of a Federal fort. Jefferson Street itself was a wagon road that ran along one edge of the barricade. When the Army pulled out after the war, the Fisk Free Colored School took over their grounds and rechartered itself as Fisk University. The school was soon a leading institution of African American higher education.[4]

Meharry Medical College—the first African American medical school in the South—moved across the street from Fisk, and in 1912, the state established Tennessee Agricultural and Industrial State Normal School

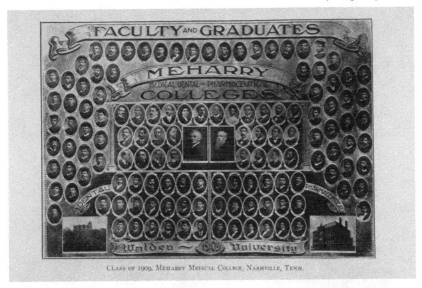

CLASS OF 1909, MEHARRY MEDICAL COLLEGE, NASHVILLE, TENN.

FIGURE 5.1. I. L. Thomas, "Class of 1909, Meharry Medical College, Nashville Tenn." (1910). New York Public Library, object no. NYPGR2786766-B

(today's Tennessee State University) on the far western end of Jefferson, creating an economic and residential corridor for Black Nashville. On July 4 of that same year, the city opened the thirty-acre Hadley Park, the first Black park in the city.[5]

Developers built subdivisions around the schools. Some of the homes were gracious Craftsman bungalows or Italianate villas, built for the professors, lawyers, and bankers who lived in the neighborhood, places like Samuel Bridges had bought for Caroline.[6] Most of the houses were more modest, just a handful of rooms wrapped in brick or lumber slat siding and erected on handkerchief lots.[7]

The students and professors became a guaranteed economic base and a cultural force in the growing community. Graduates were the heart of a new professional class. Businesses catered to their needs: Brown's Hotel, William Hawkins' North Side Ice Cream Company, Crowder's Barber Shop, K. Gardner's Funeral Home. The street soon had four different department stores where African Americans could try on clothes instead of having to buy them on sight alone and a movie theater where African Americans didn't have to climb into a segregated balcony.[8]

FIGURE 5.2. Kenneth F. Space, "Fisk University, Fraternity Easter Dawn Dance" (1936–1937). National Archives, photo no. 26174845

Jefferson Street was also a powerful cultural force in the Mid-South. By the mid-twentieth century, country music might have dominated white Nashville's music scene, but Jefferson Street drew the best jazz and blues musicians. The Del Morocco, Club Baron, and Stealaway Clubs hosted Aretha Franklin, Otis Redding, Ray Charles, James Brown, Joe Tex, Little Richard, and B. B. King. In 1963, Etta James took over the New Era Club to record *Rocks the House*, her first live album. One man told Tennessee State University professor Learotha Williams Jr. about the day he saw Tina Turner standing on the corner of Jefferson and 18th, right about where Helen's Hot Chicken is now.[9]

Jimi Hendrix—who came to Nashville before he was famous, back when he was still called James—said that his time playing at Jefferson

Street's Club Baron taught him the guitar. "You had to really play," he told an interviewer from the *Los Angeles Free Press* in 1967. "It was one of the hardest audiences in the South . . . they hear it all the time. Everybody knows how to play git-tar. You walk down the street and people are sitting on their porch playing more guitar . . . That's where I learned to play, really, in Nashville" (ellipses in original).[10]

Or as Learotha Williams put it, "Nashville is the Music City, but North Nashville gave it its rhythm."[11]

Yes, in the 1960s Jefferson Street was in its prime. Few of its residents and shoppers knew its death was already planned.

President Eisenhower hadn't wanted to spend money on urban renewal, but that was because he had another project in mind. Ike liked infrastructure. He was especially excited about superhighways, or what we today would call interstates. The superhighways would link city to city, easing commercial and personal travel. They would also connect city to suburb, allowing more and more Americans to go out and buy a little piece of land upon which to build their own personal castles. "A modern, efficient highway system," he said, "is essential to meet the needs of our growing population, our expanding economy, our national security."[12]

Ike's proposed interstates were not a new idea. Congress had created a Federal-Aid Highway Program in 1916, and it had spent the next thirteen years debating how to construct national expressways. In 1939, the US Bureau of Public Roads had finally issued an official proposal for what the highway system might look like. The roads networked like the arteries of a body, flowing across the country. In 1944, Congress officially launched the campaign but provided no funding for it. Eisenhower made the interstate system one of his pet projects. Perhaps this was a remnant of his time as a general when he'd worried about how he could move troops into battle. The president finally got to sign the *Federal-Aid Highway Act of 1956*.[13]

Nashville, a mid-sized city that should've merited a single interstate or maybe two, used its centralized location and powerful national politicians to land three of the new expressways: Interstate 65, connecting the Gulf of Mexico to the Great Lakes; Interstate 40, connecting the Atlantic to the Pacific; and Interstate 24, connecting Illinois to the Tennessee/Georgia line, the shortest of the three.

When the planning maps were published, no politician or planner or journalist alerted the Black residents that the proposed roadways plowed their way through the heart of most of Nashville's Black neighborhoods. No one noticed how they tore through South Nashville, separating Gertrude and Thornton's Willow Street home from its surrounding neighborhood. No one said they barreled around East Nashville, hacking away at three of its four borders. No one worried that the downtown interchanges planned for the interstates would destroy the handful of streets that had escaped the Capitol Hill Redevelopment Project. No one pointed out that the proposed route for I-40 would decimate Jefferson Street, ramming through its termini and following the midline of the neighborhood.

Local officials were supposed to hold public hearings where residents would have a chance to voice concerns about the coming projects. And so in May 1957, the State Highway Department held one public hearing, Nashvillians' only chance to discuss where the roads would go and who would be affected. Since most people hadn't heard about the project, they had no idea they needed to be concerned. Many people living around Jefferson Street didn't even know they would be affected by the roadways until early 1964 when real estate investors started approaching them, asking to buy their land. The speculators urged the locals to take whatever cheap price was offered for their homes. The government, the outsiders claimed, would condemn the land and seize it. In fact, however, the speculators expected to resell it to the feds at a steep markup.[14]

The influx of interested investors tipped the community off, and local Black leaders began investigating. As the shape of the plan became public knowledge, the neighborhood demanded answers. The community members knew the damage done by the construction project would reach beyond the I-40 corridor, that when the bulldozers razed the buildings, they would tear apart the fabric of the entire community. Congressman Harold M. Love tried to resist the devastation coming to Jefferson Street and the rest of his district. "We can't find a person in this community who remembers the so-called 'public hearing,' " Congressman Love said. "Well, when this is over, they're not going to be able to say they didn't know what effect I-40 would have on the people of North Nashville."[15]

Love challenged the Planning Commission and the NHA to talk about how they planned to rehouse not only the people displaced by the infrastructure program but also the businesses. Moving a business wasn't as easy as stacking up product in a new storefront and flipping a sign from CLOSED to OPEN. When a business moved, it had to build up a new customer base in its new location. And what about those businesses left behind on Jefferson Street, the ones who would not be displaced but who would struggle to survive because their customers were being forced out. "Where will businessmen find new customers?" he asked.[16]

But Gerald Gimre wasn't eager to listen to negative opinions of the work he had done in building the city's housing projects, clearing Hell's Half Acre off Capitol Hill, reconfiguring East Nashville, and bringing the federal interstate program to town. And he wasn't interested in facilitating some public discussion of his upcoming plans. By 1964, he had been at the Nashville Housing Authority for twenty-five years and running slum clearance/urban renewal in Nashville for over thirty years. Gerald had slogged through the apathy and the bureaucratic mire of both the municipal and the federal governments to improve Nashville's housing. Under his leadership—and many times despite the city's leaders—Nashville had built 4,503 public housing units, replacing miles of substandard urban lodgings. And Gimre had created the ordinances that let the city determine whether a structure was habitable. Thanks to him, tens of thousands of the city's residents now had electricity and running water, they used indoor toilets and central heat, and they fell asleep at night without worrying whether their child was coughing from tuberculosis. He had led the city when it revamped Capitol Hill, and under his guidance, Nashville was midway through the East Nashville Urban Renewal Project. And he had more rehabilitation and reconstruction plans almost ready to launch. What he didn't have was time for dissension. "I think the NHA has made tremendous strides during the first twenty-five years," he told a reporter for the *Nashville Tennessean*, "but I expect even greater strides in the next twenty-five years." Gimre put his considerable political muscle behind making sure that happened.[17]

The Princes' BBQ Chicken Shack was almost one of the interstates' casualties. It was safe over on Charlotte Avenue, but only barely, a mere four and a half blocks from the beltway that would loop about downtown, separating the business district from residential areas.[18]

Immediately after Thornton Prince III's death, his brother Alphonso took over the management of the BBQ Chicken Shack (which the 1960 city directory called the "Barbecue-Chicken Salad Restaurant," for God knows what reason). Alphonso Prince's reign did not last long. He died on December 30, 1960, suffering from a brain bleed, a condition worsened by the fifteen years he'd spent battling heart disease and high blood pressure. Next, William B. Prince Sr., another of Thornton's brothers, assumed management of the store, though he also kept his job as a dispatcher for the post office.[19]

William Prince Sr.'s biography sounded astonishingly like Thornton Prince III's. He'd married in March 1919 when he was still a teenager, wedding Eula Epps, another Williamson County kid. The couple had a child together in October 1919, a son they named William Brooks Prince Jr. Less than a year later, though, the couple had separated. Eula went back to live with her parents. William Prince Sr. relocated to Nashville, taking a job as a live-in houseman for a wealthy East Nashville family. Then just before Christmas 1920, Eula moved to Indianapolis, and she sent William Prince Jr. to live with his paternal grandparents, Mary and Thornton Prince II. William Prince Sr. filed for divorce on July 21, 1921. In his complaint, he told the court that he and Eula had "resided together for a short time" before she "willfully and maliciously deserted . . . without a reasonable cause." He swore he "did all in his power to make defendant a good husband" and she had "no cause or excuse for such desertion." He petitioned for "exclusive custody and control" of his son.[20]

The court granted his request, and the judge took it a step further. Not only was Eula Prince denied any custody rights to her son, she

FIGURE 5.3. Kenneth Space, "Fisk University, Library Circulation Desk" (1936–1937). National Archives, photo no. 26174838

was also "enjoined from tampering with said child or endeavoring to prejudice him against complainant [Will] or complainant's mother and family, where the child is now."[21]

William Prince Sr. wasn't put off by his first failed attempt at love, another way he was like Thornton Prince III. In mid-December 1922, he married Grace Darling Peden. Grace and William Prince Sr. settled into a house a few blocks off Jefferson Street that the 1930 census taker valued at three thousand dollars (that year, they were also one of only two families on their block to own a radio set). But though the census taker said the home belonged to William, it was actually Grace's possession.[22]

Grace Peden had grown up in the neighborhood, the daughter of two working class parents who wanted their children to have a better

life. The Pedens valued education and hard work. The parents' investment in their kids' lives paid off for Grace and her older sister Mattie,
both of whom became high school teachers, a highly respected position
within the Black community. Grace Peden Prince worked her way from
being a cadet teacher in 1924, a role very similar to being a teacher's
assistant, to being a probation teacher. Then she went back to school
at Fisk and completed some graduate work in education, finally earning the rank of being a full teacher.[23]

William and Grace Prince did not have any children together, but
they also did not bring William Prince Jr. to Nashville to live with them.
When Eula Epps Prince returned to Tennessee in 1924, she sued her
ex-husband for full custody of their son. She claimed no one had told
her about the divorce until six months after the court's decision, but
the judge didn't buy it. The court had a record of her being "regularly
served with a subpoena." Well, she said, now she was remarried—her
new name was Eula Collins—and she was ready and eager to raise her
son herself, especially since he wasn't getting a good raising with his
grandparents back in Tennessee. She charged that the Prince family
was leaving "him to drift where he will and to go in rags and squalor,"
and she alleged that her son was "in very improper and detrimental
surroundings."[24]

Eula Collins had tried to reclaim William Prince Jr. without the help
of the courts. One Sunday night, she had gone to visit her child, the
first time she'd seen him since he had been an infant. From the description, it sounds as though she did not warn the Prince family she was
coming. She simply showed up, "went in the house," and "told them
she had come to see the baby and started to kiss it." Unsurprisingly, her
son was not happy with this sudden attention from a stranger, and he
ran to his grandmother for protection.

"What is the matter with the baby?" Collins asked.

"He thinks you have come to steal him and carry him off," one of
William Prince Sr.'s sisters, replied. "He is afraid of you."

Eula moved to grab the boy, and the sister picked up a shovel and
shook it at William's ex-wife. One of William Sr.'s brothers ordered
Eula Collins to go home. As she retreated, Thornton Prince (the II not
the III) threw a piece of coal at her, hitting her in the head.

It must have been a terrible night for everyone involved. Collins clearly believed she had some sort of transcendent connection to her son that should have survived the past three years of silence. Discovering he had no memory of her must have been heartbreaking.

The Princes may have overreacted (though we only have Eula Collins' account of what happened that night, which doubtless omitted much of what she said and did to escalate the confrontation), but from William Prince Jr.'s behavior, they had given him love and support and connection and stability. The way he turned to Mary Prince for protection and comfort was how a child would turn to a mother in a time of distress, a move that psychologists today might well say showed he had a secure attachment relationship with her. And the charges of neglect? He was a country kid who was too young to be in school. What Eula Collins called rags and dirtiness might have been well-loved play clothes he'd worn romping about.[25]

On January 24, 1924, the court dismissed her petition and ordered her to pay all the costs of the suit. A few months later, Thornton Prince II died, but still William Prince Jr. stayed in Franklin with his grandmother and Aunt Maggic.* The two women raised him, got him through high school, and sent him off to become an undertaker. Mary purchased a house in Franklin, and William Prince Jr. opened Prince Brothers Funeral Home there. He married, and he and his wife appeared to have had a happy marriage. But still, William Prince Jr. had been abandoned by his mother and left behind by his father. He was an almost-orphan.[26]

Or at least that's how we understand it today. But Grace and William Prince Sr.'s decision to leave William Jr. with his grandparents may have been what they thought was best for the child. They were a working couple in an era when professional childcare was hard to come by and city living put children's health—especially Black children's health—at risk. Many parents of that era left their children with country relatives, especially when they were young. Restauranteur Sylvia Woods, the

---

* A decade later, some of Thornton Prince III's children would need somewhere to live. William B. Prince Jr. and his wife took them in, perhaps remembering how his extended family had stepped up to provide for his raising when he needed them; Censuses. Thelma Battle, *We Ran Until Who Lasted the Longest: A Local Collection of True Ghost Stories and Other Miscellaneous Testimonies* (Franklin, TN: Williams County Historical Society, 2007), 37.

"Queen of Soul Food," remembered that when she was three years old, her mother placed her with her South Carolina grandmother. It was 1929, and her mother was moving to Brooklyn to earn money, funds the family needed badly. She left her daughter behind because in South Carolina, Woods could run and play and eat food off the farm and breathe fresh air and drink uncontaminated water. A couple of decades later, Sylvia decided to do the same thing for her own children, sending them back to South Carolina for extended visits. And the South Carolina relatives also taught Woods and her children the foods they cooked in their Harlem restaurant.[27]

Grace and William Prince Sr. were still living in her house near Jefferson Street when the I-40 controversy started four decades later. Their road was one of the byways set to be truncated and hacked apart. Her home was slated to be torn down to make way for the embankment separating the neighborhood from the highway.

―――――――――

Determined to save Jefferson Street, local residents formed a group they called the Interstate 40 Steering Committee. Its chairman was Dr. Flournoy Coles, the associate director of Fisk University's race and poverty research program. The group didn't only protest the proposed routes; they came up with an alternate one they wanted the interstate's planners and engineers to consider. The new option swung north and followed the Cumberland River, avoiding Jefferson Street and most of the Black businesses in Nashville. To make their proposal irresistible, the Steering Committee hired an engineering firm to draw up recommendations for how to make the new route work.[28]

Planning officials on both the municipal and the federal levels couldn't seem to decide whether they wanted to engage in the public debate about the placement of the expressway or not. In October 1967, an official for the US Bureau of Public Roads promised to investigate whether "the proposed routing of Interstate Highway 40 will isolate North Nashville's university community." He challenged the I-40 Steering Committee to provide "'sufficient documentation' . . . to support the group's charges." If they did, he said, "work will be halted." Then other federal officials announced that it was too late to find a new route for

FIGURE 5.4. The dead-ended road where Grace Peden Prince's home once stood.
Photo: Rachel Louise Martin

the roadway. If the local people were unhappy, they should have come to the 1957 public meeting and voiced their opinions then.[29]

Undeterred, the I-40 Steering Committee kept lobbying. They asked that all work be halted for ninety days so that the city and the community could confer, and the Metro Council voted unanimously to grant that request. The federal government refused. Next the Steering Committee hired Z. Alexander Looby and Avon Williams to take their case to court. At the hearing, a city planner, who should have been expected to be on the side of the officials, told the judge to choose the Steering Committee's route because the planned roadway would decimate Nashville's Black business community. The judge refused to stop it. He reiterated what other earlier arbitrators had said: the people should have objected at the public meeting in 1957.[30]

The Steering Committee appealed the decision, and an official for the highway department promised to block all contracts so construction couldn't begin. When the federal court turned down the appeal, he released the funds. Finally, the Steering Committee asked the US Supreme Court for relief. The Federal Highway Administrator, however, was finished dallying. Work on I-40 began at the end of February 1968. Bulldozers tore through the community before the Supreme Court could hear the case. The I-40 Steering Committee continued fighting, reaching out to the president and the governor for relief, but the battle was lost.[31]

Mrs. Willie Duncan was one of the first people to lose her home. She lived with her two widowed sisters in the small house she'd purchased with her husband some fifty-two years earlier. The three women—none of whom could drive—were having to move to a neighborhood that had no shops within walking distance, but she was sure they would get by, somehow.[32]

And as Congressman Harold Love had predicted, the destruction affected all of Black Nashville, not just the people slated to lose their homes and businesses. It split the neighborhood in two. Journalist Reginald Stewart described what it was like to drive there after the roadwork began. Streets were bisected by the highway. Streetlights the construction crews had dismantled weren't re-erected. Potholes threatened his tires. "I just drive by luck now, hoping that when I get into some areas the streets aren't closed, and if they are open not so bumpy that they will rattle my little bug apart," he wrote. "Although we pay taxes, all sorts of taxes."[33]

Reavis Mitchell, a historian at Fisk, had family throughout the neighborhood. One of his grandfathers had owned a business at 10th and Jefferson, which was about a block from the building where Thornton Prince III had been living when his car was stolen. "The Interstate cut him off from half his market," Mitchell remembered.[34]

The interstate was also inaccessible from Jefferson Street, and it blocked residents from reaching the rest of the city. By the time the expressways and their interchanges and their bypasses were finished, many suburbanites could reach downtown faster than the folks living around Jefferson Street.

In the end, fifty percent of Jefferson Street's residents moved. One hundred twenty businesses closed. I-40 destroyed "620 Black homes, twenty-seven apartment houses and six Black churches," urban historian Raymond A. Mohl estimated. "It dead-ended fifty local streets, disrupted traffic flow and brought noise and air pollution to the community. It separated children from their playgrounds and schools, parishioners from their churches and businesses from their customers."[35]

Black leaders tried to mitigate the damage. In March 1968, Flem Otey III—the scion of a prominent Nashville family that had launched a number of Black-owned businesses around Fisk University including a grocery store on the plot where Helen's Hot Chicken now stands—led a group of forty Black businessmen to Atlanta to meet with representatives from the US Department of Labor and other federal agencies.[36] They asked the agencies to subsidize their businesses while they relocated and found a new customer base. The government offered them little tangible help.[37]

Black entrepreneurs needed this assistance because they could not rely on the financial systems available to their white peers. In late 1969 the Middle Tennessee Business Association released a study of Black-owned establishments in Nashville. At one time, the association's researchers found, there were 555 businesses catering to Black Nashvillians, and 83.2 percent of them had been owned by African Americans. Now four hundred of the businesses owned and operated by Black Nashvillians "have been and/or will be adversely affected by the construction of Interstate 40."[38]

Representatives from five Nashville banks teamed up to offer one million dollars in business loans to the displaced businesses. It was an admirable initiative, but it would turn out to be a pittance of what was needed. "Negro businesses, like a swimmer barely able to keep his head above water, have had a cement block tied to their necks and then are offered a life preserver," one community member said.[39]

Then the Tennessee Highway Department erected steel fences in front of the surviving businesses and homes along Jefferson Street. The construction workers even dismantled front porches to put them up. The department didn't try to hide the purpose of the fences. They weren't to protect the residents. "They were put up 'to discourage commercial development along that part of Jefferson Street,'" the department's chief engineer told a reporter for the *Tennessean*. "We felt that no one would be willing to buy any of these homes for commercial development if there was a fence there." Many worried that Jefferson Street could not recover and that its gutting would spell the end of independent Black Nashville.[40]

CHAPTER 6

Fry Again

Black Nashville Fights Back, 1968–1973

Morena is a modest street, mostly 1950s houses of red brick or tan siding, each set a couple dozen feet back from the road. It's the sort of place folks keep their lawns a uniform inch and a half high and their boxwoods trimmed. But this isn't a showy place. Most of the homes are just a hair too small to be proper ranch houses; they're more like ranchettes.

The small size of the homes had bothered André Prince Jeffries when she was a child. She wanted more space, a little room to breathe. She begged her parents to buy her a larger house somewhere else, but they always refused, perhaps because they were living right next door to her Grandmother Clara, Boyd Prince's widow. Or maybe they liked how centrally located they were, three blocks from Jefferson; four blocks from Fisk; across the street from Ford Green Elementary, where Wilhelmina taught first-grade and André attended school; one block down from Washington Junior High, another of André's alma maters; and only six blocks from Pearl High, her high school. What was once their front yard is now a parking lot, razed when Ford Green Elementary School was transformed into Pearl-Cohn Magnet. The neighborhood

FIGURE 6.1. Kenneth Space, "Fisk University, Students Studying in Library" (1936–1937). National Archives, photo no. 26174842

still has the feeling of a 1950s dreamscape, however; somewhere kids are safe riding their bikes to and from school even though I-40 is now the terminus of Morena's western end.[1]

Though André Jeffries grew up close to the Jefferson Street nightlife, she wasn't the type of kid to sneak into the clubs to hear Jimi or Etta play. She led a protected childhood. Her mother made sure of it. Her mother Wilhelmina believed in virtue and hard work and education. Not that she wasn't fun. She was the sort of mother who would do handstands with her daughters and join the board of the National Christian Missionary Convention. She was voted most outstanding teacher by her fellow faculty, and she was a Girl Scout troop leader for at least a dozen years. She served as the chairwoman of the Ford-Greene Social Service Committee, and she loved to travel.[2]

André Prince followed her mother's example, studying hard and becoming a leader in her church youth group. The summer before her senior year of high school, André Prince signed up to take a current events class at Pearl High School. The topics that summer were supposed to center on things like "Promoting Better Race Relations," but then the FBI released its annual crime data. Nashville, the Bureau said, was the most dangerous city in the state, and almost half of all crimes were committed by teenagers. Perhaps because the students at Pearl knew the racial assumptions underpinning that statistic in the minds of most of the *Tennessean*'s readers, they all sat down and wrote letters to the editors. The editors thought André Prince's was the best, and they printed it in a Sunday issue.[3]

"To the Editor:" she wrote, "Being a teenager, I consider this a very serious problem. . . . Parents who permit their children to be rushed into adulthood should be pitied. Allowing them, before maturity, to wear make-up, date, view degrading movies and to read obscene materials in many cases leads to degradation."[4]

Had the teenage André always been so in line with who her mother wanted her to be? Or was this a very public way of acknowledging her mother was always right? According to food writer Kevin Alexander, the women of the family may have been reacting against the attitude the Prince men had toward marriage and relationships and morality. Jeffries told him that her father Bruce Prince took after his Uncle Thornton in one important way: Bruce, too, had women on the side. But Wilhelmina and André may also have been playing out what Evelyn Brooks Higginbotham called "the politics of respectability," or the idea that African Americans could prove they deserved full citizenship by disproving white stereotypes about them, by staying above reproach.[5]

At this point in our narrative—but just for a moment—the tale of hot chicken and the story of Nashville's development diverge. So imagine William B. Prince Sr. over on Charlotte, continuing to fry up chicken and André Prince back on Morena, laughing, growing, and studying,

FIGURE 6.2. Fort Negley is in the foreground. War Department, "Tennessee – Nashville" (1936). National Archives, photo no. 68148972

while I tell you the story of how the Black neighborhoods learned to beat the Nashville Housing Authority.

In September 1960, the NHA had started discussing two new urban renewal projects. One of the projects was focused on the streets around Vanderbilt University. The other targeted the Edgehill community in South Nashville. Neither community wanted to be renewed, at least not by the clear-cutting methods the NHA tended to use, and both fought back. The residents affected by the University Center Urban Renewal Project should have had the better chance of winning their battle. They were educated, white, and socially connected. But they lost. Edgehill's residents, on the other hand, were Black and predominantly working class, but they forced Gerald Gimre's urban renewal juggernaut to make some concessions.[6]

The Edgehill community was another of Nashville's historic Black neighborhoods that had begun as a refugee camp. When the Union Army took control of Nashville in 1862, it chose to put its largest forti-fication, a star-shaped edifice named Fort Negley, on top of St. Cloud Hill. Though the hill is only the seventeenth highest hill in Davidson County, it is very steep, which made it an excellent defensive site. Over six thousand soldiers and more than 2,770 refugees and local free Black workers quarried limestone and hefted rocks up the slopes. When they finished their work, Fort Negley was the largest inland masonry forti-fication built during the war. The soldiers and the refugees settled in camps underneath the growing fortress. Some of the African Ameri-can men were given tents, but most were forced to camp in the open under armed guards. Those uncovered camp sites were the seeds of the community that would become Edgehill.[7]

When Gerald Gimre had begun his work in Nashville almost thirty years earlier, Edgehill had been a relatively good neighborhood, espe-cially compared to streets like Patterson and Willow. But each of the projects the city's planners undertook had unhoused thousands of Black Nashvillians, and the NHA had built a fraction of the number of units needed for the people they had displaced. People forced out by the housing projects and the Capitol Hill Redevelopment Project and the East Nashville Urban Renewal Project had pushed their way into the city's remaining Black neighborhoods—places like Edgehill and North Nashville. These communities that had once belonged to the Black middle class and intelligentsia were now becoming overcrowded and under resourced. Was this the actual purpose of urban renewal, Fisk economics professor Dr. Vivian Henderson and others like him started asking, "actually creating more potential slum areas?"[8]

Local and federal authorities blamed each other for the growing housing crisis. National administrators said that providing sufficient new housing was one of the responsibilities of the local housing authority. Gerald Gimre pointed at the "red tape and attitude" of the Federal Housing Administration. "The FHA has developed all types of squeaks and wheels that need greasing," he claimed.[9]

On August 15, 1961, the Nashville City Council approved the Edge-hill project, but the vote was not unanimous. The council members representing Edgehill and the downtown districts all raised concerns. "We don't want it rammed down our throats," one of them said. He'd heard about the East Nashvillians who had lost their homes without being given enough in compensation to go out and buy something new. And by that point, Z. Alexander Looby said "he opposes the principle of urban renewal."[10]

For a while, the conflict over the location of the interstates slowed down the work on the Edgehill Urban Renewal Project. Local leaders and residents used the time to organize their uprising, and they watched what worked and what didn't for the I-40 Steering Committee. The people of Edgehill decided they weren't just fighting for their neighborhood. They would take aim at the entire redevelopment program, and they asked civil rights organizations and nonprofits to join them in their fight.

They launched their first attack on June 13, 1966. That day, the Nashville Christian Leadership Council and the Nashville Chapter of the NAACP "charged that a 'general climate of racism'" undergirded urban planning in Nashville. They specifically cited the city's public housing complexes, which were theoretically desegregated but remained overwhelmingly sorted by race. City officials all claimed to be shocked at the accusations. They ran colorblind operations, the officials said. The applications for public housing didn't even include questions of race any longer. What the agency didn't say was that every applicant had to come into the office for a face-to-face meeting before they could be assigned a unit, so the agency didn't need to include a box regarding race on the application.[11]

The Edgehill Citizens Organization, the Tennessee Council on Human Relations, and the Tennessee Commission on Human Relations joined forces to send the Nashville Housing Authority a notice demanding that they "'cease and desist' from acquiring property within the [Edgehill] project" until they had proposed a way to rehouse the Edgehill residents in better housing than they had now. They sent copies to Mayor Beverly Briley, the NHA Board of Commissioners, the regional Housing and Home Finance Agency Office, the director of HUD, and members of the US Senate's Government Operations Subcommittee. Next, the South Street Community Center, the Edgehill Methodist Church, and the Nashville Community Relations Council joined the fight. Now eight local and state organizations were organized against the new urban renewal plan. Two hundred fifty people showed up to the next town hall meeting.[12]

Some of the allies of the Edgehill uprising started challenging white Nashville's view of itself as a racially tolerant, or even progressive, place. "No amount of commercial advancement, business progress, or cultural growth is going to make Nashville a first-class city if we forget the Negro minority," lawyer and civil rights leader Avon N. Williams told the readers of the *Tennessean*. White people—white Nashvillians—needed to take responsibility for fixing the inequality they had benefitted from. "We have the white liberal who is willing to let the Negro advance as far as he can. But this is no longer enough," Williams wrote. "Now, it is no longer enough."[13]

Part of the reason local Black residents were so fired up about the proposed renewal project was that they had invested their lives and their livelihoods in these properties. The people may have been poor—eighty percent of them could qualify for public housing—but fifty-five percent of them owned their own homes outright, no mortgages, no loans, no liens. No, they didn't want to leave their neighbors and their churches and their shops, but they also knew the NHA had the bad habit of paying the market value of their homes, not the replacement value.[14]

Lysanders Hadley, a sixty-five-year-old, had bought his house when he was twenty. The NHA had said his dwelling was worth four thousand dollars, but a similar home in another neighborhood would cost about ten thousand dollars. "They'll be leaving me outdoors and in debt," he said. "I don't like that."[15]

Or there were the Sanfords. He was seventy-two and she was sixty-seven. "Prior to the urban renewal project," their lawyers wrote on their behalf, they "had so arranged their affairs that they would have ample income to enjoy living their remaining years." They owned their home outright, but the city only offered them $5,500 for it, not enough for them to buy "decent, safe, and sanitary" housing elsewhere in Nashville. Their comfortable retirement would be over.[16]

Or there was Willa B. Clark. For fifty-five years she lived in the home she'd been born in. In 1961 the city took her home so it could expand the neighborhood's elementary school. They paid her five thousand dollars for her property, and she used the money for a down payment on a seven-thousand-dollar house nearby. Now the city was claiming that second house, paying her only $5,750 for it.[17]

"I would remind you that these dwellings represent for their owners a financial investment," Fisk University professor Dr. Edwin Mitchell told a group of white Nashvillians, "and that, as businessmen, they do expect and do obtain a return on their investment."[18]

The city representatives responded by publicizing a list of the subdivisions and housing projects they expected to build. "Paper homes on the drawing board do not afford shelter either from the elements or from discontent," Edwin Mitchell retorted.[19]

The leaders of Edgehill's resistance movement didn't stick to town halls and city council meetings and marches. Some of their younger members had a feel for showmanship. The action that must have offended Gerald Gimre the most was an event they called a "cultural-educational tour." The housing activists escorted Edgehill residents through Belle Meade, Nashville's swankiest neighborhood. The highlights of the tour included the governor's house, the houses of several bank presidents, and Gerald Gimre's home. This was the house that had belonged to Leslie and Nettie Boxwell. When Leslie Boxwell had died in 1960, he had left the house to Gimre as a life estate.[20]

The committee invited the house owners to come and talk with the tourists. When the owners refused, the tour leaders stood on the "public sidewalk in front of their homes" discussing the homeowners' "business connections, their positions in the community, and how they could help solve the slum problem." Then they invited the homeowners to take a tour of Edgehill. None of the Belle Meade clan took them up on it.[21]

Publicity stunts behind them, the housing activists refocused on the question of segregation in public housing because they had hard data to prove the city was in violation of federal statutes and had no plans to mitigate the situation. In fact, if their current plans for Edgehill were implemented, racial segregation in the city and in public housing would worsen.

The city already had two public housing complexes built along the same road in Edgehill. Now they planned to tear down the surrounding single-family homes, many of which were "in good condition, or close to it," to construct two more in the same vicinity. The new public housing units would add 880 apartments and create one of the city's largest housing complexes. "The experience in our nation on the psychological

TABLE 6.1. Percentage of Black and white families in Nashville public housing complexes

Name of Complex	Total Units Occupied	Percentage Black Families	Percentage White Families
Andrew Jackson Courts	398	100 percent (398 families)	0 percent (0 families)
Cheatham Place	313	0.32 percent (1 family)	99.68 percent (312 families)
I. W. Gernert Homes	181	99.45 percent (180 families)	0.55 percent (1 family)
James A. Cayce Homes	333	0.90 percent (3 families)	99.1 percent (330 families)
James A. Cayce Homes (Addition)	277	0.36 percent (1 family)	99.63 percent (276 families)
James A. Cayce Homes (Extension)	91	0 percent (0 families)	100 percent (91 families)
J.C. Napier Homes	479	100 percent (479 families)	0 percent (0 families)
John Henry Hale Homes	499	100 percent (499 families)	0 percent (0 families)
Preston Taylor Homes	550	100 percent (550 families)	0 percent (0 families)
Vine Hill	296	0.34 percent (1 family)	99.66 percent (295 families)

effect of large masses of public housing definitely indicates that this is a bad housing practice," the coalition averred, and since all 880 of those units would be for Black families, it would create "racially segregated housing" and a "vast South Nashville Negro ghetto."[22]

Officially, the NHA had embraced open housing, but according to a 1966 study by the Tennessee State Advisory Committee to the US Commission on Civil Rights, only two complexes—the Tony Sudekum and Sam Levy homes—could be considered integrated. The rest were anything but, as Table 6.1 makes obvious.[23]

An NHA representative agreed that the new projects in Edgehill would worsen the city's segregation, but he argued that integration was only "a small factor" in any urban renewal plan. The regional chief for the US Housing Assistance Administration's Occupancy Section backed him up, agreeing that federal housing regulations do not "say that a local housing authority has to promote integration."[24]

Not all the federal officials agreed. The US Commission on Civil Rights sent a representative to investigate what was happening in Nashville's urban renewal districts. Four federal housing officials also came to Nashville to discuss Edgehill in particular.[25]

After reviewing the data and interviewing Edgehill residents, the federal authorities ordered the NHA to revise its housing plans for the neighborhood, advising that the planned apartments "should be either reduced or dispersed, to avoid racial concentration." Gimre and the mayor both grumbled about how much money the city would lose by having to restart the planning process. Besides, what other neighborhood was going to want to gain these families? The federal authorities also told the city to start meeting with the Edgehill residents, asking what they wanted to have happen in their neighborhood.[26]

Gimre had once championed community advisory boards. In 1938, he had been part of a three-person team that had cobbled together guidance for best practices among planning administrators, and part of their report had included the need for community engagement. When he had envisioned the conversation happening, however, he saw it moving in a different direction. His dream advisory board didn't inform the city planners what the neighborhood wanted. They worked with the planner to win over the people. The advisory board's purpose, Gimre and the rest of the committee had said, was to "educate the general public" and "serve as a nucleus from which the idea will gradually spread throughout the entire membership." He had little patience for the instructions that told him to plan town halls and build in time for public comments.[27]

Gimre's feelings were probably also hurt. He may have even still been angry about that tour by his house. He was not interested in this overdue community input, not now when he was nearing what he doubtless thought should be his victory lap. He'd been working in Nashville for thirty-five years at this point, saving Nashville's impoverished residents from their leaders. Thanks to him, people across the city now had running water and functioning septic systems and safe heating units. He had brought them paved roads and community recreational centers and a burgeoning network of hospitals and universities. And now they said he didn't have their best interests at heart? Now they wanted in on the conversation? Now they accused him of being a racist?

Rather than reaching out to the locals, Gimre and his office tried to placate the federal authorities. In December 1967, the city's officials offered a compromise on their plans for the Edgehill projects. They would build one hundred eighty units on either side of the existing buildings and then scatter another one hundred forty units across the neighborhood. They planned to make the clump of apartments "two-story garden type apartments, and the 'scattered' units may be duplex or triplex buildings," the new plan explained. The federal housing authorities accepted this compromise, but the team that had coalesced to protest the Edgehill Urban Renewal Project thought it was a gloss that masked the city's refusal to take their concerns and objections seriously. They formed their own citizens advisory group, determined to oversee NHA's actions whether Gerald Gimre liked it or not.[28]

By 1968, much of the money promised for urban renewal and other city planning projects had dried up. "The problem so often lies in the fact that the federal government sets programs and objectives," said Herbert Bingham, executive secretary of the Tennessee Municipal League, "but does not appropriate the money authorized. The money falls out, but the objectives go right ahead."[29]

But the furious Edgehill residents didn't blame the national program. They charged that the NHA had abused its power, turning the neighborhood into "a ghost town," letting squatters move into emptied buildings, and prohibiting residents from making repairs to their homes. Now, after years of forced neglect, city code inspectors were condemning homes and offering only their current market value. According to one analysis, the NHA had displaced 1,174 Edgehill families, but it had only erected two hundred new dwelling units in the neighborhood. It only planned to build five hundred ninety more. Worse, the NHA had only supported thirty percent in their relocation efforts. Partially because of that lack of support, 78 percent of the dislocated families had been forced to move away from the Edgehill neighborhood, breaking apart the community ties, separating families, and overcrowding other low-wage districts in the city. And now the city said they couldn't even finish what they started![30]

The turmoil and turnover meant that many businesses in the district either closed or relocated. By 1970, 75 percent of them were gone from Edgehill, including both of the neighborhood's two grocery stores. The area had become what we today call a food desert. No public transportation serviced the community, and many of the residents could not afford cars. The city councilman representing the district donated one thousand dollars to establish a free three-day-a-week bus from Edgehill to the closest grocery. Seventy residents used it on its first day of operation, and three hundred fifty people used it in its first week. His money kept the bus going for five weeks. He hoped that by showing the need, he could convince the city to add a new bus line, but both the NHA and HUD said they couldn't afford to keep the bus in operation. The Council also voted against it, defeating the measure twenty to nineteen. After the first month, the bus only ran sporadically when private citizens donated funds toward the effort.[31]

The struggles of the Edgehill activists and the I-40 Steering Committee had taught local African American advocates that they could resist the city's plans for their neighborhoods, but only if they acted swiftly, mobilized widespread community support, managed the media, and refused to surrender. A winning neighborhood was one that understood the principles of attrition: all they had to do was outlast the city's will for the project. In 1968, residents of North Nashville started hearing rumors that soon it would be their turn. They began to organize.

The Model Cities Programs, which Congress voted into law in the fall of 1968 as a part of President Johnson's War on Poverty, was the latest version of what had been called slum clearance in the 1930s and urban renewal in the 1950s. Its authors claimed that unlike the earlier programs, this one would free communities from the oversight and rigid guidelines that the federal government had imposed on urban renewal, encouraging planners to instead talk to local residents and factor in their perspectives in ways earlier initiatives had not. "Probably the most promising domestic program in the 1960s, Model Cities proposed to effect a significant change in the quality of life of selected American cities within the short span of five years," a group of analysts wrote of the project. "In contrast to other then-existent Federal assistance programs, Model Cities has sought a comprehensive approach to urban problems; it has sought to deal with social, physical and economic issues at one and the same time."[32]

"Many citizens apparently feel they have no clout with the governing bodies," said Floyd H. Hyde, HUD's assistant secretary for community development. "We have hopes that new avenues of citizen involvement can be opened up."[33]

The people of North Nashville had known an announcement like this might be coming. Their urban renewal was supposed to be part of the interstate construction process, but facing resistance to the infrastructure project, Gerald Gimre, the highway department, and the mayor's office had put this part of the program on hold. When Nashville's authorities signed on to the Model Cities program, Nashville's leaders left themselves some loopholes so they could abandon the community participation part of the project and turn it back into a more traditional urban renewal initiative whenever they chose. They hoped the idea of citizens' participation would ease some of the tensions around the future phases of development planned for the area. If it didn't, they would accomplish their purposes otherwise.

Since the local leaders were supposed to take "maximum opportunity for employing residents of the area in all phases of the program," they authorized a seventy-five-member Citizens Coordinating Committee (CCC). The city may have hoped that the size of the CCC would make it too large for consensus, cutting down on the organization's power, but local Black leaders had made note of the outs the government had left for itself in the Model Cities charter.[34]

Dr. Edwin Mitchell, a community activist and a professor of radiology at Fisk, became the CCC's first chairman. He found the Model City plan more ominous than hopeful. He gave a Lenten sermon at Christ Church Episcopal, my home parish. "Government and business here in Nashville, planning for progress instead of for people, have combined—perhaps unwittingly because it is custom—to create oppression of minority citizens that is unbelievable for those who will but consider," he told the white congregation. "Driven in large numbers from East Nashville and South Nashville by urban renewal and interstate highway construction, the Black community has been impacted within the North Nashville area. And now uncoordinated urban renewal and highway construction—the latter at an accelerated rate—descend like a plague upon its people."[35]

From the beginning, the CCC was frustrated with their inability to get clear answers from Mayor Briley's office. They felt that every time they asked a question about what plans the administration was making for North Nashville, they were given either vague or shifting responses. But they had one powerful ally. William J. Reinhart, the first Model Cities director in Nashville, understood their anger and believed in citizen participation, so on August 6, 1969, Reinhart wrote the mayor a pointed letter. Briley's office rewrote the letter, "reducing it 'to vague generalities,'" and then released the revised version. Reinhart, furious, threatened to release his version. The mayor sent him a new letter by messenger. This one ordered him to take his vacation and submit his resignation.[36]

The CCC saw this as a rejection of any true engagement by the city, and they planned to protest the mayor's actions. Four hundred Nashvillians attended the planning meeting. "If your home isn't worth fighting for," Dr. Mitchell told them, "then you tell your kids what is worth fighting for. We've had it. We've been patsies long enough." The audience circulated petitions demanding that the city immediately halt the North Nashville Model Cities Program "until residents are granted 'meaningful participation' in planning the project."[37]

The folks at the meeting listed a number of concerns with the project as it was shaping up. First, it would leave Nashvillians homeless. The planning document said the city would raze 5,080 buildings, but the protestors doubted the units would be replaced because "in all the years Nashville has had an urban renewal program, it has been able to provide just over five thousand public housing units." The people had little reason to trust Gimre's NHA. Over the years, the NHA had done little to either support displaced renters or subsidize the losses born by homeowners and businesspeople in the "renewed" areas. Nor had it equalized its zoning laws. Then protestors pointed to the embattled urban renewal effort in the Edgehill neighborhood as evidence of the city's willingness to deal unfairly with the people it had supposedly helped.[38]

"Participation without redistribution of power is an empty and frustrating process for the powerless," HUD's former chief advisor on citizen participation had warned administrators and urban planners in 1969. "It allows the power holders to claim that all sides were considered, but it makes possible for only some of those sides to benefit. It maintains the status quo." Nashville's residents were savvy enough to see that and angry enough to fight it.[39]

The city enacted a handful of its projects around North Nashville, but the district as a whole escaped. This would be the last traditional urban renewal program attempted in the city.

Gerald Gimre was tired, and he also had to be feeling out of touch and out of date. He retired on June 30, 1970, thirty-eight years after he had arrived in Nashville to create the city's first zoning code.[40]

Looking around Nashville today, Gimre's urban renewal projects gleam like scars across the landscape—the amputated roads that once connected Black Nashville to its business districts, the shaved slopes below Capitol Hill where people used to live and work, the winding ribbons of interstates that flow past the residents of Jefferson Street.

After a lifetime living in the city Gerald Gimre created, I started this project prepared to dislike him and decry his work. This study has forced me to mitigate that assessment. Gerald Gimre, like so many other white leaders before and since, had meant well. He had used his education and his power to work toward what he thought was best for this town. But he never stopped to ask the people he was trying to help what it was they wanted. He never consulted with them to see whether they had other needs or dreams that he could have used his office to facilitate. He could not hear them when they said his good works had done them harm. He just didn't listen. He had a plan for the city, but he forgot its people.

Gerald Gimre's life is a parable for the rest of us. To borrow a moth-eaten truism, the road to hell is paved with good intentions.

The more I learned about Gerald Gimre's life, the more parallels I saw to my own work. As an educated, well-meaning white woman, it's easy for me to find answers. I like being right. I feel good when I've been helpful. But it's painful, humbling, even humiliating to sit down, shut up, and admit I may have been wrong, that I may not have even been asking the right questions.

And yet here I am, writing a book. No, I can't quite make that reconcile, either.

And what had been going on at the BBQ Chicken Shack? Grace and William Prince Sr. had taken over the business, but they had both continued working their primary jobs. He was at the main post office helping to maintain and repair the postal vehicles,[41] and she was a high school English teacher.[42]

Grace Prince retired from teaching at the end of the 1965–66 school year, having put in forty-two years in the Nashville public school system. Four months later, she sued for divorce from William. She kept the house, perhaps because it had belonged to her all along, and she soon remarried. For her second marriage, she chose Lon Tucker, a man who attended her church.[43]

William Prince Sr. also remarried quickly. On June 21, 1967, he wed Maude Satterfield. The two had known each other—and perhaps been in a relationship with each other—for at least a decade.[44]

Grace and William had already separated once before. In 1958, William had left Grace to move in with Maude. Maude Satterfield had lived in Nashville for about twelve years at that point, working as a maid and living in a house about a block and a half away from Thornton Prince III's Patterson Street house. That may have been how she and William Prince first met. But by 1959, William and Grace Prince appeared to have reconciled, and Maude Satterfield again lived alone.[45]

But had the Princes made up or struck a compromise? As a teacher, Grace may not have felt free to sue for divorce. There are those politics of respectability again. She was supposed to set an example for her students, their parents, and her neighborhood. Yes, the code of ethics governing teachers' behavior was loosening. At one time, teachers' handbooks had specified everything from teachers' bedtimes to their church attendance. But would she have retained her respectability, seniority, and authority if she left her husband? It's questionable. So perhaps the best indication of how she really felt came at her retirement when she kicked her husband out.

Maude and William Prince Sr. found an eight-room stone house some seven blocks from the BBQ Chicken Shack, but their marriage was a short one. William Brooks Prince Sr. died July 4, 1973. Maude Satterfield Prince mourned him until her own death in 2011.[46]

She found ways to honor him and keep his memory alive. For over a decade, she wrote annual odes to him on Memorial Day and published them in the *Tennessean*. The other way she honored her husband was by keeping his family's business going. And so the BBQ Chicken Shack continued to rock along, selling afterhours hot chicken from its spot on Charlotte Avenue.[47]

CHAPTER 7

Find Your Own Spice

Ms. André Prince Jeffries and the Hot Chicken Heirs, 1974–1998

A young guy on his way to the barber shop next door stuck his head in. "Y'all open?"

"Nope," Dollye Matthews said. "Soon."

"Ok," the kid said. Then, "I'm hungry." He shut the door.

This storefront, the newest outpost for Bolton's Hot Chicken and Fish, should have been up and going long before this. "Davidson County," Matthews said, "you can't get anything as fast as you like." She sighed. "Permits and stuff, we were delayed a minute."

The new Bolton's was going into a South Nashville strip mall just a few miles down Bell Road from where Prince's Hot Chicken Shack's now was. Like André Prince Jeffries, the Matthews have had a hard time expanding their business beyond their original East Nashville location. This spot was their fourth attempt. They first put a branch in a downtown food court known as the Arcade. It didn't take. Then they'd tried Hickory Hollow Mall, but "I moved in the day McDonald's moved out," Matthews said. After three years, they escaped that failing spot and tried to establish a business over on 8th Avenue South, a road that ran into the Edgehill Hill neighborhood. Like much of today's Edgehill, their area was increasingly gentrified and trendy, so their landlord sold the building out from under them. Now in the winter of 2020, the Matthews were trying again.

Dollye and her husband Bolton Matthews have been running Bolton's Spicy Chicken and Fish since 1999, but their roots in hot chicken history stretch much further back. Bolton Matthew's uncle was Bolton Polk, Maude Satterfield Prince's cousin and a cook/manager at the BBQ Chicken Shack. Polk went on to launch the Prince family's first competitor, Columbo's Hot Chicken. He had been part of a new generation of hot chicken folks who helped keep the dish alive.[1]

Bolton Polk was born on October 8, 1923, in Columbia, Tennessee, just one county south of where Thornton Prince III had grown up. But the Polk family didn't stay on their farm long. By the time Bolton Polk started school, they were living in Davidson County.

They may have left because Columbia was a deadly place for Black men and boys. One man had been lynched there on October 10, 1905, accused of raping a white woman. In May 1924, Robert Wilson was arrested for the same alleged crime, but the case against him was so weak that the jury of twelve white Southern men sentenced him to only two years in prison. The judge set the sentence aside, an almost unprecedented act of justice in the Jim Crow South. Wilson didn't walk free, however. While he was still standing in front of the judge, the alleged victim's brother stood up in the courtroom, pulled out a gun and shot twice, killing Wilson in front of a room full of witnesses. The shooter was found not guilty.[2]

Three years later, eighteen-year-old Henry Choate was accused of attacking a teenaged white girl one morning, catching her on her way to her school bus. When he was brought before the victim, she said she could not identify him. That night, a mob of white men stormed the county jail, dragged Choate out, and hung him off the courthouse's second-floor balcony. Several days later, the girl's actual attacker was captured. African Americans who lived in Columbia at the time remem-

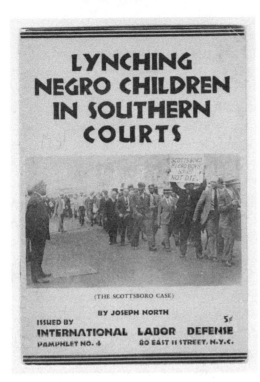

FIGURE 7.1. Joseph North, *Lynching Negro Children in Southern Courts* (1931). Collection of the Smithsonian National Museum of African American History and Culture, gift of the family of Dr. Maurice Jackson and Laura Ginsburg, object no. 2010.55.59

bered that the rope used to hang Choate was left dangling from the balcony, and it stayed there for months.[3]

Then in 1933, seventeen-year-old Cordie Cheek asked a white neighbor for the wages Cheek was owed. They fought, and Cheek won. A few days later, the white man paid his eleven-year-old sister a dollar to accuse Cheek of raping her. A mob of white men—at least one of whom was a county deputy—chased Cordie Cheek around the county before the sheriff arrested him. To protect Cheek, the sheriff took him to Nashville where a jury refused to indict him. The Nashville officials released him from custody, and he went to stay with his aunt and uncle who had a home near Fisk University's campus. While he was telling his aunt and uncle about his plans to escape to Indianapolis, two carloads of armed white men drove from Columbia to Nashville, invaded the house where Cheek had taken refuge, and abducted him. By the time the cars reached Columbia, Cordie Cheek was dead, his body slumped in one of the car's rumble seats.[4]

The Polk family never moved back to Columbia. They were still living in Nashville when World War II started. In January 1943, Bolton Polk enlisted in the Navy and went to work as a ship's cook, a job that was excellent training for the busy restaurants he would one day manage.[5]

After his discharge in December 1945, Bolton Polk came back to Nashville and worked a variety of jobs, first as a driver and then as a packer for a wholesale drug company; as a clerk for another drug company; as a janitor with Metro General Services; and then as a machine operator for the John Deal Company.[6]

By 1976, Maude Satterfield Prince had been running the BBQ Chicken Shack for three years. She'd been making do with the part-time help the Prince men provided, but she needed someone there fulltime. She may also have wanted to have some of her own family around. And she may not have loved working until 4 a.m. She asked Bolton Polk to join her.[7] Soon, he was the one running the business, working as its cook and manager. Maude Prince retained ownership of it.

Maude Satterfield Prince made one significant change to the Prince's family business during her time running it. In 1978 she relocated it, uprooting the BBQ Chicken Shack from its longstanding location on Charlotte Avenue and moving it north. Its new location was on the farthest edges of North Nashville. The only thing past it was a market, a McDonalds, and a bridge over the Cumberland River.[8]

Perhaps she had lost the lease to the original spot, though the old location sat vacant for about a year after the BBQ Chicken Shack left. Maybe this was part of the city's mid-seventies push to straighten out some of its zoning codes. Perhaps Bolton Polk preferred the new joint.

But if it was voluntary, Maude Prince's decision to change locations was a curious choice. The old spot was in her neighborhood, walking distance from her house. This new one was over three miles away, which meant it was also out of reach of any of its neighborhood regulars. It was also too far away to draw late night downtown revelers who wanted to eat their way out of a hangover, although by that point in Nashville's history, many less people were going downtown. After the Ryman had lost the Grand Ole Opry on March 15, 1974, fewer tourists found a reason to visit Broadway. Many of the residents had also left.[9]

Nashville's white business owners and municipal leaders loved to brag that they were one of the only cities in the nation successfully addressing their blight, but they had used urban renewal and the interstate projects to eliminate downtown's residences. They had gutted and bulldozed their way through the neighborhoods—primarily the Black neighborhoods—inside the city's borders. Most of the white leaders had left downtown over half a century ago. Now they were relocating their families, businesses, churches, and events again, moving even farther out of town—sometimes even out of Davidson County—to the new suburban developments spidering out from every interstate exit ramp. They used neighborhood covenants and "discerning" real estate agents and unequal banking practices to control who could buy the houses, which meant their new homeplaces were up to 98 percent white, and then they used the interstates to wall their new developments off from the places where Black Nashvillians lived. Under their care, Nashville grew increasingly segregated.[10]

And the city emptied. In 1950, almost 56 percent of the homes in Davidson County were within Nashville's borders. By 1958, that percentage was down to less than 48 percent. The city, one set of housing analysts found, had added only sixty-three hundred housing units in the past eight years while the county had gained twenty-eight thousand. And 44 percent of the city's gain, or 2,656 of the new units, had been additions to the town's housing projects. The 1960 census had confirmed those findings. For the first time in Nashville's history, the city's population had fallen. Nashville had 6,964 fewer residents than it had a decade before, but Davidson County had gained 72,580 people.[11]

One particularly astute census taker pointed out that urban renewal had caused part of Nashville's population loss. In 1950, the Capitol Hill area had two hundred homes housing 351 families, or somewhere around twelve hundred or even thirteen hundred people. That neighborhood was gone now.

And the Capitol Hill Redevelopment Project's effect had extended beyond the official slum clearance district. "In an area centered at the downtown district, the Census Bureau counted about twenty thousand people ten years ago," another census worker told a local reporter.

"This time, only about ten thousand were numbered in approximately the same area." Some of them had moved because they wanted to live elsewhere. Many more had been displaced as landlords changed their houses into doctors' offices or lawyers' offices or parking garages.[12]

One editorial cartoon from the era depicted a split screen picture of life in Nashville. One side was the city's downtown, the other was a suburban neighborhood of tract housing. A family—a businessman with a fedora, a housewife in heels, and their three kids, two boys and a little girl—were fleeing for the suburbs. The family was clearly white. Perhaps the newspaper understood the unspoken causes of flight to the suburbs, even if they didn't say it.[13]

"We thought that we were saving the city," former Mayor Bill Purcell explained to me. "But that wasn't going to save the city. There is no city that has been successful merely as a collection of suburban places."

These boosters of the 1970s insisted the downtown restaurants and groceries and department stores would survive, kept afloat by weekday businesspeople and weekend partiers. And they kept their tax base growing by endorsing the 1963 consolidation of Nashville and Davidson County into one giant metropolitan unit. Only a handful of people asked what downtown would look like when Nashville became a nine-to-five and a midnight-to-three sort of place.

Life had not gone according to plan for André Prince Jeffries. After she'd graduated from Pearl High in 1964, she'd gone less than a mile down Jefferson Street to enroll at Tennessee State where she planned to study biology and become a pediatrician. But she was also in love.

She'd started dating Kermitt Jeffries her sophomore year of high school, just about as soon as her mother said she was old enough to do so. He was a friend of her older brother, and he seemed so attentive and romantic. When she turned up pregnant, there really was nothing to do but marry the man. They wed on June 22, 1965. She was eighteen and he was twenty-two. She dropped out of school to have her baby, a little girl she named Yeae. A few years later, she had another daughter named Semone.

Kermitt, however, was no longer either romantic or attentive to his wife. He started gambling, disappearing every weekend to play cards and lose money. André Jeffries knew she couldn't raise her girls in that sort of tense, unhealthy environment, so she left him.

She lived with her parents briefly while she got back on her feet, then she found a job at the Jefferson Street YMCA and started to rebuild her life as a single mother.[14] A little work experience on her resume, she moved on to a position as an accounting clerk with the Metro Assessments Office. Her income there was higher than it had been at the Y, but money was still tight. Her parents helped her make ends meet, and they subbed in on childcare. A *Tennessean* photographer once published a picture of Wilhelmina Prince mid-babysitting duties. She rested on a stone planter wearing a stiff wool boater hat whose edge was brimmed in a striped ribbon. Her older granddaughter sat beside her, hands primly clasped. The younger one was napping on her lap. Wilhelmina gazed into the distance, smiling peacefully.[15]

In 1980, Great Aunt Maude Prince announced her retirement. She had decided Jeffries should take over the BBQ Chicken Shack. André Jeffries knew nothing about running a restaurant: she didn't like to cook and she had no idea how to fry a chicken. And then another complication, Bolton Polk announced that he was leaving to open his own place, Columbo's Chicken Shack. But Wilhelmina Prince, who was dying of breast cancer, told her daughter to accept the offer anyway. Plus, Jeffries told writer Kevin Alexander, she'd had a dream. In the dream, she'd been in charge of a restaurant that had more customers than it could handle. That had to be a sign, right?[16]

André Prince Jeffries' first few years were tough. Not only was she clueless as to how to run the business, but she was also—in longstanding Prince tradition—treating the BBQ Chicken Shack as her second job. Managing the business was what she did after her day in the assessor's office ended. After a couple of years, Maude Prince handed ownership of the restaurant over to André Jeffries, and Jeffries finally left her job with Metro, going to the Chicken Shack full time.[17]

About three years after she took over the business—perhaps once she had her own feet under her enough to start making the restaurant

FIGURE 7.2. Myspiritanimalisamanatee, "Nashville Hot Chicken Drumsticks" (2017). Wikimedia Commons

her own—Jeffries began making changes. First, she renamed the restaurant. "I took out the BBQ because this was never barbecue," she said. A family business should be named for the family, she decided. She called it Prince's Hot Chicken Shack.[18]

Next, she added heat levels. Before that, everyone who ate at the restaurant simply ordered hot chicken, no spice preferences available. And what came out of the kitchen had a little kick, but it wasn't what today's hot chicken fans would consider real heat. The chicken was somewhere around what today's eaters call mild. This decision set her apart from Bolton Polk's new restaurant and all the others that would follow him. For many years, she'd be the only chicken joint where patrons could choose how much pain they wanted in their meal. The categories of spice became an effective bit of marketing. Customers could talk about who was tougher, and many other journalists, those either braver or stupider than I am, love to write about what happens to the human body when it is exposed to extreme spice. But if you would like to read a graphic description of what happens when you decide you want your food to hurt you, well, I recommend grabbing a different book. Pain doesn't cause me pleasure when I eat. And I feel no guilt about that. The original chicken was mild, after all."[19]

Finally, André Prince Jeffries relocated the business. The store was too out of the way, and it was also a dangerous spot, perhaps because of its isolation. "When I took over, it seemed like every weekend we were getting robbed," she said.[20]

In 1989, André Jeffries loaded up her family's booths, the twenty-four-inch cast iron skillets they'd always fried the chicken up in, and two ancient gas stoves, even though the replacement parts were now obsolete, and trucked them over to 123 Ewing Drive in East Nashville.[21]

The Ewing Drive spot was on the edge of East Nashville, just past where the earlier twenty-two-hundred-acre East Nashville Renewal Project had reached. And by 1989, Jeffries and her team could feel certain that no future urban renewal project would be coming for them. That movement was dead when President Ronald Reagan won office.[22]

The Reagan administration wouldn't be underwriting up to 90 percent of the cost of rebuilding impoverished districts of a city. No way. It believed unrestricted capitalism would cure all urban woes. "Let the local entity, the city, declare this particular area, based on the standards of the percentage of people on welfare, unemployed, and so forth, in that area," Reagan said. "And then, through tax incentives, induce the creation of businesses providing jobs and so forth."[23]

Reagan's first year in office, his administration had cut fifty-seven housing grants down to nine block grants. Then he introduced a series of tax incentives that were supposed to draw businesses into urban areas. New businesses would mean jobs, the administration theorized. Jobs would mean more workers with more money to spend on rent and shopping. More money spent would mean fewer people on the government dole (which would be a good thing because the tax breaks would mean less money coming in). A new initiative needed a new name. Model Cities were out. The grants in this trickle-down approach to urban development were called Enterprise Zones.[24]

Nashville, a city with plenty of fiscally conservative voters who'd gotten used to spending the federal government's dime, would have to change its ways. Gerald Gimre must have rejoiced that he was already retired. Adapting to Reagan's new non-program would fall to a different set of administrators.[25]

The Metro Planning Commission had to shift its focus. Since Gerald Gimre had helped the city create a zoning code and then forced the city to adopt a housing code, the planning commission had worked with the NHA and other housing reformers to increase and enforce building regulations. Now they were to ease up. Under Reagan's plan, the Enterprise Zones were supposed to be the least restricted spaces in Nashville. The new president wanted "to put an end to 'annoying regulations' that now require contractors to take more time with projects."[26] Some area builders rejoiced, but the Planning Commission and housing advocates were less pleased, for obvious reasons. One coalition of twenty-seven inner-city neighborhood, tenant, and church organizations called the change "a misguided . . . effort which could leave local citizens of the special zones without protection." The lack of regulations didn't just include builders and contractors, a spokesperson for the organization explained. It included questions of environmental pollution and workers' rights. It meant grant money could be reallocated on a whim. Then the Metro Council voted to take two and a half million dollars in HUD funds away from inner city poverty relief and use it to widen a road.[27]

In June 1986 when the US House passed a new $16.3 billion housing bill, the new era had truly begun. The legislation halted all new public housing construction unless contracts had already been signed. The Enterprise Zone program was the only urban development initiative available moving forward.[28]

Residents and politicians in Nashville didn't know what to think about the new program. Who and what did they want their city to become in the future? And were the Enterprise Zones going to get them there?

Gerald Gimre wasn't in Nashville to see the dismantling of his work. On October 27, 1980, the vestry of Christ Church held their monthly meeting. Gimre had let one of the members know he was interested in reaching a settlement with the church. He wanted to leave Nashville, but Leslie Boxwell's bequest had kept him trapped in Nashville. Boxwell had given Gimre his Belle Meade home as a life estate, which meant it was Gimre's to use and enjoy as long as he lived, and as long as he lived in Nashville. After Gimre's death, however, the house would go to Boxwell's church, which was Christ Church. Gimre had approached the church about buying him out once before at the end of 1976. That time, either the church or Gimre backed away from the negotiation, but in 1980, Gimre and the vestry reached an agreement. Two months later, the house had sold for $185,000, or a net profit of $173,000 for the congregation. The vestry promised to invest the monies "at a favorable interest rate" and send Gimre an undisclosed cut of the annual dividend.[29]

The possible influx of funds was well-timed for Christ Church, which had just celebrated its sesquicentennial and had its campus named to the National Register of Historic Places. In the past year, the church had spent thirty-four thousand dollars repairing their stained glass windows and then turned around and installed a new roof and an industrial-grade kitchen. The vestry wanted those improvements to be just the beginning of the changes to the Christ Church campus. They dreamed of putting a sound system in the nave, and they wanted to refurbish and repaint the interior of the structure, which was several decades out of date. Plus, they had to undertake additional federally mandated maintenance to their historic façade. They were also continuing their usual charitable commitments, raising over two hundred thousand dollars to fund a world missions initiative and funding a project at the University of the South. And they were doing all of this while searching for a new rector, a search which had already failed twice.[30]

Gerald Gimre left Nashville and moved back home to Marshalltown, Iowa. Most of his siblings had moved to warmer climates like California and Arizona, but his unmarried sisters, Alta and Gladys, were still there. Gerald Gimre died on August 10, 1991, in Marshalltown's VA hospital. He was ninety-four years old. He named Christ Church of Nashville as the trustee of his estate, which he had willed to St. Luke's Community Center, an Episcopal community house, food bank, and outreach center in Nashville.[31]

In 1982 Bolton Polk opened Columbo's Hot Chicken Shack just off Broadway in the heart of Nashville's tourist district, right where Nashville's drinkers could stumble in both during and after their buzz. It was a small storefront wedged between a fire station and a plate manufacturing company that specialized in religious art and masonic ornamental plates. He served his own version of hot chicken made with a dry rub, which differentiated it from Prince's wet rub. He added his wife's chess pies and potato salad.[32]

Downtown Nashville was floundering. By the 1980s, lower Broadway, where today the bachelorettes reign, was at best scummy and at worse dangerous, a handful of honky-tonks catering to tourists who wandered about, dazed by rhinestones, whiskey, and country cover bands. Then came the lawyers' offices, banks, and insurance corporations, which emptied as soon as business hours ended. Ringing all of that were strip clubs, car lots, and interstates. One night in January 1987, *Tennessean* journalist Alan Bostick visited the district and reported what he saw: "splattered blood stains on the pavement," the homeless who "ooze out of the cracks in the sidewalk at nightfall," and the trash clogging in the gutters. This was the Nashville of my childhood.[33]

"I was still not sure about Nashville, and I'm not sure Nashville was sure about Nashville," Bill Purcell said to me. "It was not clear what we wanted to do. . . . There was a history and a practice of believing that if you did not have it here, we could go to Chicago or New York or Atlanta to buy it or see it or do it."[34]

"It's all well and good to want to be the Athens of the South and to be a center of learning, but it's the city's obligation to ensure that it's so," Purcell continued. "A city has to be safe, the whole city, not just parts of it or neighborhoods in it. By and large, this is the late '80s now, downtown Nashville was suffering from Nashville's own decision that the future of downtowns was not certain and certainly not required."

We were talking in the conference room of his law firm, which overlooks downtown. "We had made periodic efforts to salvage what we had and other competitive efforts to knock down and replace what we had," Purcell beckoned me to the window. He pointed out the places where there was once a garbage incinerator, derelict buildings, and empty lots, right in the heart of the city. "Only about nine hundred people lived downtown," he said. I haven't found an exact number, but from the evidence I've seen, I think his estimate is close to accurate.

Born in Philadelphia, Bill Purcell had come to Nashville for law school, worked briefly for a law firm an hour west of town and then returned to Nashville as a member of the Tennessee House of Representatives. After a few years, Purcell was promoted to the house majority leader. He and his wife moved to East Nashville, settling into one of the refurbished Edgefield homes.

At about the same time, Bolton Polk moved Columbo's down along the river. That was where Bill Purcell first encountered the dish. "As soon as I had this hot chicken, I knew it was unlike anything I'd ever had," he said to me. "It was one of the best things I ever had."[35]

It was also a dish unique to Nashville, something most white Nashvillians assumed did not exist. "Unlike some towns, such as Kansas City with its beef and Memphis with its barbecue, Nashville didn't have a signature cuisine—unless you count our deep-rooted love for garden-fresh vegetables and super-sweet desserts," Bernie Arnold wrote just about the time when Purcell became the house majority leader. But Bill Purcell knew differently. He'd eaten hot chicken.[36]

Columbo's, unfortunately, did not last in its new spot. It was trapped by the growth happening around Nashville. In the late 1990s, Nashville won an NFL football team. The Houston Oilers became the Tennessee Titans. Columbo's sat right where the new football stadium was supposed to go. Bolton Polk closed his restaurant rather than relocating it. Bill Purcell needed a new spot for his chicken fix.

Prince's Hot Chicken Shack wasn't half as convenient as Columbo's had been, but Bill was desperate. One day he made the six-mile trip to the northern reaches of East Nashville and wandered up to the Prince's window to order. That first brown baggie of hot chicken was a life-changing meal both for him and for André Prince Jeffries.

Soon Purcell was a regular. While he was in Tennessee's legislature, he started taking meetings with colleagues, constituents, and reporters at Prince's. "My legislation passed more easily," he said. "My vote totals went up." That may have happened because his guests loved the chicken, but he might also have used it as a threat.[37]

When he brought newbies to try hot chicken, he would always pull André Jeffries aside and tell her to ignore whatever heat level they ordered. "He'll tell us to give it to them hot," she said, "don't give it to them mild. You don't know if he's their worst enemy or what!"[38]

"After three bites I figured out he didn't ask reporters to lunch because he liked them," journalist Gail Kerr wrote of her first meal with Purcell. "He was trying to kill us off, one by one. It's a long, slow death over several days when the hot chicken just, well, stays with you."[39]

"He never has it mild," André Jeffries once told a reporter for the *Chicago Sun-Times*. "I don't know how he can eat it and go right back to work. Usually when people eat it hot, I see them in the small room the rest of the day. He has an iron stomach."[40]

"There is hotter food," Bill Purcell told the same writer, "but this is the hottest I have ever enjoyed." Then he threw some hot chicken shade. "I eat hot chicken because it is Prince's Hot Chicken Shack. If you want something different, you should go to a medium chicken shack, though they do not exist because nobody wants that."[41]

"My last act as majority leader was to declare Prince's Hot Chicken the finest restaurant in Tennessee," Bill Purcell said.[42]

In 1999, Bill Purcell became Metro's mayor, and he served two terms.[43] He decided it was time to make hot chicken famous. "Since he's been in office, the hot chicken places have increased five-fold," Bill's policy advisor bragged a couple years into the mayor's reign, that's "something the mayor considers one of the great accomplishments of his administration."[44]

In the late 1990s, neighborhoods across Nashville were in crisis. White flight and a couple of decades of urban neglect had taken their toll. The War on Drugs had destroyed young Black futures, though young people of all races and genders used drugs at roughly the same rate. Rampant disfranchisement, worsening educational inequality, sinking economic opportunities, and skyrocketing unemployment helped turn many poor minority neighborhoods into places of frustration, limitation, and violence.

The city—and the nation—needed a revolution in housing laws, a re-envisioning of its educational system, a reimagining of its judicial code, a reformation of its prison system, and an explosion of public health outlets. What it had to work with were the Enterprise Zones.

Nashville's city planners decided their new zone would be a monster that gobbled up most of South, North, and East Nashville. A few locals cheered the proposal, ready for anything that would help them fight for their city. Others warned that the project was unlikely to produce the miraculous results the city promised. A handful worried that it could actually worsen economic and racial segregation. And the residents of the Edgefield Historic District in East Nashville were livid. Their neighborhood was not "blighted," they said. They voted unanimously not to join the enterprise zone.[45]

Gentrification seems like a contemporary movement, a product of the early 2000s and the rise of the Millennial hipsters, but today's move into the cities actually began in the late 1970s when a small trickle of people returned to the neighborhoods their parents had abandoned to urban renewal. Most of these "urban pioneers" were young, white, and educated, middle-class professionals intrigued by the new historic preservation movement. They watched PBS's *This Old House* (which first aired in 1979), and they read Jane Jacobs's poetic obsession with sidewalks. In New York City, they made Hell's Kitchen into Clinton. In Charleston, they bought up single houses near the Battery. In Nashville, they snapped up the turn-of-the-century mansions in East and North Nashville that landlords had subdivided and neglected. They remodeled them back into single family homes, and then they banded together to spread their message of historically minded renovation.[46]

"A lot of folks simply wrote East Nashville off when the interstate came through here," East Nashville's councilman told the *Tennessean*. In 1978, Metro Council made Edgefield the city's first historic district. These preservationists were proving that actually the interstates had brought opportunity. With the new district in place, the councilman was working to "downzone" Edgefield and then put a historic zoning overlay on it, limiting demolition, new construction, and reconstruction. "We've stabilized property values and the future's mapped out," he said.[47]

Some of the older residents loved what historic preservation meant for their neighborhood. Edgefield resident Elizabeth Carter had lived near the James Cayce homes since the 1940s. When she moved in, she said, it "seemed ideal to her growing family." Now many of the older Victorian homes had been so abused that they were "beyond the point of saving and were razed during federal urban renewal." But with the help of the newcomers, her "neighborhood is rising again, like a phoenix."[48]

Not everyone appreciated their new neighbors, however. In 1991, disgruntled locals fought back with fire, literally. At least fifteen homes were burned while they were being remodeled, causing a minimum of a million dollars in property damage. The newcomers are "searching for a bargain and an opportunity to restore the past glories of the houses," the arson investigator explained. "Yet, many older residents resent the newcomers and residents say passions may run high enough to spark an arson."[49]

The new homeowners' paths were eased by the redlining and disinvestment that persisted for Nashville's Black residents. "Modern urban planning is formed by particular entanglements with power and race," Ted Rutland wrote in *Displacing Blackness*. "The power of modern planning is expressed . . . in the creation of material conditions that act upon individuals and populations."[50]

Mark Thompson, a community advocate, analyzed the 4,139 Davidson County home mortgages granted in 1987. He discovered that though Black low-income neighborhoods housed 12.1 percent of Davidson County's families, residents there received only 2.9 percent of the mortgages. In contrast, 19.7 percent of the families lived in white upper-income neighborhoods, and they had received 45.4 percent of the mortgages granted that year. Though the laws had changed, the racist patterns propagated in housing and banking had not.[51]

The Enterprise Zone again put the longtime residents into conflict with the new ones. The urban pioneers ran headlong into the fight. After voting against joining the zone, they tried to extend their historic overlay across the section of low-income housing that separated them from the James A. Cayce Homes. If they had succeeded, they would have instantaneously unhoused as many as five thousand people who were living in the overcrowded multi-family housing without providing any new housing for them.[52]

The housing authority and the council agreed to cut Edgefield out of the new Enterprise Zone, but that meant they also had to remove the Cayce Homes as well as Edgefield Manor, another housing development. The people in those projects were the ones in Nashville who most needed the economic development, job training, and other perks that were supposed to come with the Enterprise Zone. "It's unfortunate," a Metro Development and Housing Agency official agreed. The fight to bring the Enterprise Zones to Nashville floundered, never having the pull, splash, controversy, or funding earlier attempts had.[53]

The first time I visited Prince's Hot Chicken Shack—this was way back in 2015, some three and a half years before someone propped a brick on an SUV's gas pedal and ended an era—the restaurant was in a strip mall that gentrification hadn't touched yet. On one side of it was Entrepreneur Clothing; a deep bass rhythm pumped through its open door onto the street. Next to that was a customer-less Chinese restaurant and a nail salon. The parking lot was potholed, and when Prince's was busy, guests bumped their way to an unpaved lot next door. The area was best known for prostitution and drug deals.

Though André Prince Jeffries had moved the restaurant to Ewing Drive because of the crime on Clarksville Pike, she still had trouble with theft. Now, though, it was tourists picking off her memorabilia. As we talked, she pointed to the places where something used to hang in the restaurant. Many pieces had been stolen: photographs of her family, plaques and awards given to the restaurant, and a set of autographed plates from the celebrities who frequent Prince's.

Jeffries had hoped to move the restaurant again, somewhere nicer and newer. "We were supposed to move to 10th and Jefferson, but a lot of politics got involved," she said a little sadly. A year later, that corner would be part of a giant new baseball complex for the Nashville Sounds. I asked her what her dream restaurant would look like. "If I had it my way, we'd have a shack-type building but upscale on the interior with a big old potbellied stove in the center of it," she told me.

"My mother always said, if you have what people want, they will make their way to your door," Jeffries said, patting the table in front of her. "You can tell, this is certainly not an upscale bird place. This is my little hole in the wall, but people have made their way here from all over the world. All over the world."[54]

CHAPTER 8

Plate on White Bread

Hot Chicken Goes Global, 1998–2020

Steve Younes was tall and lanky and bearded with hair that probably lightened to ginger in the summer. He looked remarkably like who he was: a college-educated white guy who worked with computers during the day and obsessed about perfecting hot chicken at night. And he had learned to nail hot chicken; he was the 2018 Hot Chicken Festival amateur cooking champion.

"I'm a little more over the top than the prior winners," he admitted. "When I won, I brought the hot chicken trophy to restaurants; I brought it to day care; I brought it to work. Now it's displayed at home so you see it as soon as you walk into the room." He'd even brought it to the 2019 Hot Chicken Festival and paraded it through the streets of East Nashville.[1]

Younes was not the most logical champion hot chicken cook. Born in upstate New York, he'd come here as a teen. After four years of college at Middle Tennessee State University, he'd moved to East Nashville in

2008, just as hot chicken was catching on beyond the Black community. "It was cool, all the diversity that we had back then," he remembered.

His first taste of hot chicken was at a joint where patrons chose between pizza, barbecue, hot chicken, and salads. He hadn't expected that meal to change his life. He and his friends hadn't gone there for the food; they were celebrating after a flag football game. "It wasn't like the original places," he admitted, but something about the dish caught him anyway. "I had that experience," he said. "Everyone knows it who's had hot chicken: you're miserable, unhappy, but you have this euphoria."

Shortly after that, he moved just down the road from Prince's East Nashville spot and became one of Jeffries' regulars. He preferred Prince's style to Bolton's style. "It's the dry rub," he said. "I like having the sludge to eat."

Steve Younes had always loved to cook, and he looked for recipes that would be a challenge to do correctly. Hot chicken became one of his experiments. He started out by testing different recipes, finding his level of heat and what methods he thought gave him the best results. Then he launched a campaign of endless tweaking. "It's the data thing," he admitted. Slowly he homed in on his ideal chicken.

The 2018 championship wasn't his first time at the competition. He had entered in the amateur cooking challenge in 2016, but he'd miscalculated what the judges would want. "The flavor was there but the heat wasn't there," he said. "I didn't want them to suffer." When he came back to try again two years later, he wasn't as merciful, and the judges rewarded him for it.

But Younes worried that he was becoming part of the problem. That diversity that had once drawn him to East Nashville? Every year, his neighborhood became whiter and more middle class. He'd watched as both the families who had lived in the area for generations and the artists who had once made East Nashville hip were priced out of the district.

He had tried to find ways to fight against these trends. A few Black Fridays ago he'd found a website that promoted Black-owned businesses, so he made a point to begin shopping at as many of them as he could. When it came time for him to decide how to plate his hot chicken for the judges, he decided not to use the red-and-white checkered papers that have become ubiquitous among Nashville's white hot chicken entre-

FIGURE 8.1. The Krystal Burgers where Thornton Prince III's BBQ Chicken Shack was located. The cranes in the background are part of a large construction project on Patterson Street. Photo: Rachel Louise Martin

preneurs. Instead, he tried to find something a little more homegrown, something that felt like his family. He went to a thrift store, bought some plates and wrote "Hot damn!" on them. And above all, he would not be opening a hot chicken joint. "It kinda feels like the Elvis effect, if you will," he said. "We [white male cooks] come in and go, 'Oh, well, how can we make this in a way that everyone feels comfortable?'"*

But would those actions be enough to save the East Nashville he'd loved? "My friends describe me as a pessimist," he admitted.

East Nashville's gentrification was partially Mother Nature's fault. Tornadoes struck Nashville on April 16, 1998. It was a rare double-tornado event, and those two were just two of thirteen different funnel clouds to cross Middle Tennessee that day. The first of the Nashville tornadoes

* In the summer of 2020, Younes won a second Hot Chicken Festival championship. A few months later, he opened Surfin' Bird, a to-go hot chicken place in an incubator space in East Nashville.

touched ground at 3:30 in West Nashville and followed Charlotte Avenue to downtown, passing right overtop the Krystal that stood where the BBQ Chicken Shack used to be. It swept through the city's business center, crossed the Cumberland River and aimed itself at the heart of Edgefield. The track of its damage was almost three-quarters of a mile wide and fifteen miles in length. Thankfully, there was only one fatality, a Vanderbilt student who was pinned by a tree in Centennial Park and eventually died of his injuries. The second tornado touched down at 5:15 p.m., and it also rammed through East Nashville, a funnel powerful enough to wrap a sheet of metal the size of a barn roof around a utility pole.[2]

Because the two tornados happened so closely together, it was hard to know which part of the East Nashville damage could be attributed to which funnel cloud, but by the time night fell, fifteen hundred homes had damage and hundreds of homes in the district were destroyed. St. Ann's Episcopal Church lost its entire nave. Tulip Street Methodist's main wall, made of brick, had crumbled under the force of the winds. Nearly the entire quadrant of the city was without electricity.[3]

A Tornado Recovery Board formed to coordinate the relief efforts in East Nashville, and several of the members of the board were neighborhood advocates who had long dreamed of remaking and revitalizing their district. The tornado meant they would have the funds, attention, and opportunity to reimagine what their community could be in the future. They realized this was their chance to control what happened next in their quadrant of the city.

The Tornado Recovery Board morphed into a Regional/Urban Design Assistance Team (R/UDAT). Its sole purpose was to make suggestions for the redevelopment and rehabilitation of East Nashville. The board members guided the creation of new public/private partnerships, helped plan new infrastructure that would tie the neighborhood to downtown, created design guidelines to ensure all new construction fit their vision for the area, and encouraged outsiders—both those from New York and those from West Nashville—to see East Nashville as an investment opportunity. They used pictures of the destruction to show wealthier folks the wonderful, damaged, under-maintained East Nashville homes they could rehab into showpieces. "For all its fury in tearing things apart, the tornado—for the first time in many decades—built a bridge across the Cumberland and brought our entire city together," one man wrote in the *East Nashvillian*.[4]

The committee meant well. "The two greatest treasures East Nashville offers are its diversity and authenticity," the members of the R/UDAT wrote in their final report. "Throughout the nation, new 'neo-traditional' communities are being planned and developed in the hope of replicating the feeling that this community offers."[5]

The R/UDAT supported people like March Egerton—a white local real-estate developer who focused on helping businesses move into the district, transforming a TV repair shop into a coffee spot, a gas station into a trendy café, and an old metal-working garage into a hair salon— and white local gallery owners Meg and Bret MacFayden who launched the Tomato Art Festival, which swelled to thousands and then tens of thousands of visitors a year.

Many of the R/UDAT's biggest fans were the white professionals who'd moved to East Nashville in the 1970s and 1980s. "The neighborhood moment that had started and flourished here was a result of no assault or threat and did not arise from disaster," Bill Purcell reflected fifteen years after the storm. "It came from a shared desire nearly a generation before to protect what was and is so good and so special about the place and the people East Nashville nurtured through two centuries. . . . We discovered all over again what our neighborhood meant to us. And the city understood, many for the first time, how special the people and the place were."[6]

Unfortunately, the families and communities that had settled East Nashville and lived there for generations began to be bought out, unable to compete with the rising cost of property. This was the neighborhood-in-flux that Bolton and Dollye Matthews chose for the rebirth of Columbo's restaurant.

Shortly after the tornado, Bolton Polk came to his nephew and said he wanted the younger man to learn how to make hot chicken. Polk was finally ready to share his secret recipe.[7]

Owning a chicken shack wasn't a logical career move for either Bolton or Dollye Matthews. Dollye at least knew the basics of how to quarter and fry a chicken, but Bolton, the one his uncle wanted to be the cook, had to learn which part of the chicken had white meat and

FIGURE 8.2. Amy C. Evans, "Customers in line" (2008). Southern Foodways Alliance

which had dark. "The whole nine yards," Dollye said. "He had to start from scratch."

The couple had met because they both owned janitorial services. Well, more accurately, they met because Dollye had hired Bolton. She ran a business called Quality Maintenance, and one day she subcontracted a job to his firm, Matthews Janitorial, which specialized in floor work. "He was a floor specialist," she told me.

Now they would be running a restaurant together, just as soon as Bolton Matthews learned to fry. The two Boltons got to work. They spent weeks frying chicken together before Bolton Matthews mastered his uncle's techniques. Then Bolton Polk gave the younger man his blessing to re-create his restaurant. Bolton Polk even gave the Matthews his original cast iron skillets, some of which they still have to this day. Dollye suggested they add a hot fish sandwich to the menu to give a little variety to their offerings and to differentiate themselves from Prince's and the other chicken joints that were just beginning to pop up.

Dollye and Bolton Matthews opened Bolton's Spicy Chicken and Fish in a small, low concrete block building on Main Street just a block from East Park where the annual Hot Chicken Festival now takes place. When

Plate on White Bread

they found it, however, it didn't look like much. They didn't even have running water in the building. After they had paid to have it piped in, the Health Department inspector showed up and told them the building was condemned. They begged him for mercy. "The man said, 'Well, if you can seal the ceiling to the wall and the wall to the floor, we'll give you a permit to use the building,'" Dollye remembered. "He and I spent days caulking" (but she pronounced it *corkin'*, just like my grandfather used to).

When Bolton's first opened, Matthews fried his chicken to a single level of heat just like Bolton Polk had always done. Then Matthews started experimenting with his uncle's classic spice blend, adding levels of heat. Today, Nashvillians debate which is the hottest, Prince's or Bolton's. Dollye assured me they win that contest, though like André Prince Jeffries, she seldom eats anything hotter than mild or maybe medium, about the heat level Bolton Polk's chicken used to be. She also doesn't know everything that goes into the current spice mixture. That secret belongs to Bolton Matthews alone.

"I know some ingredients," Dollye said. "I don't care to know it all." Then she teased me with a couple of details: one of their ingredients had to be registered with the state before they could start using it. "A tablespoon of that in a seventeen-story building and everybody gotta go," she said. And they have worked with franken-pepper scientists who are experimenting with newer, hotter, more concentrated peppers. That's why Dollye never hires anyone under the age of twenty-one. Kids can't be trusted around materials like that.

The Matthews ran their business alone for about the first six months. On the day they had their first five–hundred-dollar day, Dollye told her husband that it was time for them to find some help. "That might not sound like much money," Dollye said, but remember, "back in the day a fish sandwich was three dollars; the chicken sandwich, that was $4.50. Takes a lot of sandwiches to make five hundred dollars."[8]

After Bolton's opened, Nashville saw what may have been the oddest venture in the hot-chicken story, HOTchickens.com. It opened in 2001 when the Internet felt new. No, it wasn't a hot chicken delivery service; it was a physical restaurant. And yes, the .com was part of the name and even on the building's sign.

147

The restaurant was founded by country music stars Lorrie Morgan and Sammy Kershaw. Morgan learned to love hot chicken by eating it with her father, the same George Morgan who had once frequented the BBQ Chicken Shack, forcing the Princes to add a separate back room for white guests. According to the rumors swirling around Nashville, Lorrie was using her father's recipe, which he stole from Polk. Or maybe Polk had leaked it to him. Or perhaps he sent a piece of Polk's chicken off for chemical analysis and then used the forensic scientists' report to re-create the Columbo experience in his fry-daddy at home (seriously; that version even made it into a newspaper account).[9]

Dollye Matthews tried not to laugh when she heard that last one. He didn't get Polk's recipe, she insisted. "They all came out of the kitchen together, the elders of the Prince family and Uncle Bolton and Lorrie Morgan's dad," Dollye said. "Then they split." Oh, and one other problem with that theory: Bolton Polk had used a dry rub. He was the only hot chicken maker to do so. Some Nashville diners insisted the problem was even greater than the question of a dry rub versus a wet sauce. If George Morgan had actually been the only person outside the Prince/Bolton duo to see how hot chicken was properly made, he hadn't passed the secret onto his daughter, they said. Her chicken was good, but folks suspected she added her spicy sauce after the chicken was fried, not before as was proper.[10]

But the thing everyone remembered from HOTchickens.com was its dining room, and it sounds overwhelming. Food writer John T. Edge described HOTchickens.com as "a gingham-trimmed fast-food outlet that . . . reflects the peculiar Nashville geek-in-a-cowboy-hat zeitgeist."[11]

It was "ferns and shiny chrome by country kitsch decor in a bland brick ranger, and a giant-screen video playing (what else?) Lorrie Morgan videos," folklorists Eric and Paige La Grone Babcock wrote.[12]

The venture didn't last long. Debts from the restaurant drove Kershaw into Chapter 13 bankruptcy. "Perhaps if the couple had invested in the actual URL instead of a bricks-and-mortar restaurant, it might still be kicking out some income for them," was one local food writer's snarky yet accurate assessment.[13]

Their marriage ended in mutual restraining orders. Morgan tried again, underwriting Lorrie Morgan's Hot Chicken Cafe inside a gambling resort in Alabama. That effort attracted a governor's office investigation.[14]

In 2007 Mayor Bill Purcell was wrapping up his second term in office, and he knew that this was probably the end of his political career, that it was time for him to return to private life. After so many years of visiting Prince's, after dragging almost two decades of eaters along with him to the restaurant he called his second office, he decided it was time to make Prince's Hot Chicken Shack famous. "Why?" André Jeffries asked rhetorically. "Because he knows I have to pay my bills."[15]

Bill Purcell was also looking for a way to celebrate the city, which was approaching its bicentennial. "Hot chicken is truly our indigenous food," he explained. "It seemed a way to convene the city around something special to us, worth celebrating but also allowed everybody to participate."[16]

He decided to turn his love for hot chicken into an annual festival. He founded a festival committee, and they decided to put the festivities in East Park in the heart of Edgefield. This would put the gathering close enough to downtown that people could come and go from the official city celebrations, but it wouldn't be swallowed up by other events happening. "And I was the mayor," Purcell added, with a little smirk. "East Park was close to where I live."

The festival quickly grew in popularity, introducing people to the dish. Hot-chicken cooking and eating contests became part of events around the city.

Hot chicken's new-found popularity was helped along by national and international forces. East Nashville's gentrification was well under-way by the time the event began, and many of the transplants were looking for a way to feel like they, too, were authentic Nashvillians. Hot chicken provided that. Those transplants were soon to gain thousands of fellow hot chicken travelers. Nashville was on the cusp of exploding.

In December 2007, the housing market collapsed. After several years of record prices driven by shaky mortgage lending habits and speculative investment practices, the housing economy of both the nation and the globe began to correct itself. And the rest of the economy followed closely behind it. Nashville—the city whose mayors claimed was recession-proof—shed fifty-three thousand jobs in construction, business services, and retail. Manufacturing, which had already been declining, lost another twenty percent of its workers over the next two years. By the time the workforce in Nashville finished contracting, about 197,100 Nashvillians had lost their jobs.[17]

Foreclosures followed. In 2008, 4,203 Nashville homeowners lost their homes, a 178 percent increase over two years earlier. Minority families were affected more often than white families were, which accelerated the gentrification happening in places like East Nashville and Edgehill. Houses changed hands, going from the Black families who had owned them to newer white residents who had the funds to buy into Nashville's housing market.[18]

And then in 2010, the flood struck, decimating large swaths of the city. In the aftermath, even more of the original residents were displaced, unable to afford the cost of renovating their properties and unable to resist the money developers were offering for their homes.

Some of the changes that have come to places like East Nashville are beneficial to everyone. Crime rates are falling. Education is improving. Some historic homes are being carefully restored. Restaurants and coffee shops and boutique clothing stores form the heart of new, trendy business districts catering to a hipster crowd.

But the people who have lived there for generations are getting priced out of their homes. Some of the Black residents whose ancestors first settled East Nashville are being forced into the suburbs where white Nashvillians used to live. Others are ending up in overcrowded, low-income pockets of the city.

In this era of change and loss, residents and visitors alike are anxious to celebrate what is historic about the town. Hot chicken has become shorthand for the area's various traditions, a de rigueur part of being from here.

By 2010, hot chicken had left the Black neighborhoods. New restaurants specializing in the dish were popping up across town. "They're like pizza places, all over," André Jeffries said. "Everywhere you look, there's a new one opening."[19]

Isaac Beard was the first of the new generation of white hot chicken restaurateurs. He started Pepperfire Chicken in 2010 after a decade of taste testing other restaurants' chickens and three years perfecting his own. "I believe I was born to do something with hot chicken," he told food columnists Jane and Michael Stern. "I am a hot-chicken evangelist."[20]

On August 9, 2012, the most successful of these new ventures opened its doors. Hattie B's, owned by Nick Bishop Jr and his dad Nick Sr.—a white family from the Prince's hometown of Franklin—launched their first store in Midtown, right in the heart of a new, hip area. "Hattie B's is almost in both Music Row (the area where country recording studios are located) and the campuses of both Vanderbilt and Belmont Universities, making it a much nicer area than Prince's seedy strip mall," food blogger Dan Angell wrote of his visit there. "The idea of being in a more protected area was appealing to us, and since you can't go through Nashville without having experienced hot chicken, Hattie B's was the choice." Soon the Midtown location had a loyal following. The Bishops opened a new spot on the edge of a rapidly gentrifying neighborhood once known as the Nations. By 2020, they had seven locations, including spots in Las Vegas, Atlanta, Memphis, and Birmingham.[21]

Did André Prince Jeffries worry about losing her customers?

"My customers, they try all these different places that are popping up," she said. "They come right back here. Might take 'em a little while, but they come back to the real thing. They tell me all the time, 'You still got it.' 'Course that makes me feel good. Have mercy." Her only question, she insists, is which family member will take the restaurant next.[22]

"The newbies come in a little bit cocky, a little snobbish," Dollye Matthews said. "If you came seven years ago, no, you're not the one that put hot chicken on a map. If you came three years ago, your hot chicken *might* be good." She thought there was room enough in the hot chicken market for all the good cooks to find a place as long as they "stay humble. Stay grinding. Do what you do and to try to perfect what you have." She paused. "That's my motto."[23]

André Prince Jeffries' response was moderated and politic, but Dollye Matthew's answer hinted at another conversation many white Nashvillians have refused to have about their new love of spicy poultry.

For generations this dish was cooked in Black kitchens by Black cooks. These chefs were trapped in underdeveloped communities that lacked access to even the most basic of modern amenities like running water. And then they were driven out of their homes when the city decided to make their neighborhoods better, but the improvements weren't made so that the displaced Black families could return and rebuild better lives. The renovations benefitted white Nashville.

Even when Thornton Prince III rallied his family to help him turn a favorite dish into a restaurant venture, his business was limited by the systemic racism around him. Real estate practices kept him from being able to place his business in a wealthy corner of Nashville. Banking regulations barred him from accessing business loans. Segregated seating arrangements forced him to put his famous regulars in a tiny, walled-off back room. And the BBQ Chicken Shack's location in the Black community—as necessary and protective as it was during the pre-Civil Rights Era—kept Prince from reaching the level of economic success that might have been possible if he could have put his restaurant elsewhere in the city. Systemic racism meant that hot chicken stayed in a corner of Nashville for almost seventy years before it exploded into the rest of the city.

Can Nashville—can America—ever overcome this heritage of hate and inequality? One day in graduate school, I went to a meeting at the Center for the Study of the American South. The speaker had spent the past year photographing the US/Mexico border, recording the terror and danger faced by undocumented workers who fled their homelands for the opportunities the United States represented.

It was the spring of 2008, and North Carolina was in the throes of an immigration debate and newly awakened by the pending nomination of Barack Obama. Issues of race and equality were on our minds, but we were also historians. We could all riff on the discouraging realities of modern America, like the fact that public schools were more segregated than they had been at any time since 1965 and income inequality was growing. Our conversation grew increasingly cynical.

Then William Ferris chimed in. Ferris is a noted folklorist whose wife is a prominent foodways scholar. He is one of those public intellectuals whose lists of achievements should make him terrifying, but he has a deeply kind streak that makes him a student favorite. Ferris said that the popularity of Mexican culture encouraged him. He pointed out that Mexican restaurants are growing ubiquitous, and in each establishment, customers met people affected by the immigration debate. Maybe restaurant-goers would get to know their servers, fall in love with their food, dance to the music they heard playing over the sound systems, and thus learn to empathize with immigrants.

At the time, I vehemently disagreed with him. It was the only time I dared to do so. I used the African American experience as my example. "Whites have eaten fried chicken for centuries now," I remember saying. "Segregation still exists."

But these days, I find myself hoping he was right. Is the hot chicken craze helping Nashville create a new history? Or is hot chicken being stripped of its cultural meaning? Can a simple chicken dish be trusted with healing the divisions that have taken generations to form? Or will it become nothing more than Nashville's newest hipster trend?

The erasure of Black cooks—and specifically Black female cooks—is nothing new. Today we call it cultural appropriation, but it is, to use a phrase favored by many a college undergraduate, as old as America itself. Beginning in Jamestown, Virginia, in 1619, these Black women experimented and labored, mixing the foods smuggled from Africa with imports from England and endemic plants and animals. Sometimes they did this independently, working over their own hearths. Other times they crafted this new cuisine in conversation with indigenous cooks or white slaveowners or employers. "From frontier cabins to plantation houses to the White House, from steamboat galleys and Pullman kitchens to public barbecues and fish fries and private homes without numbers," John Egerton wrote in *Southern Food*, "Black chefs and cooks and servants have elevated the art of American cookery and distinguished themselves in the process, and they and all other Americans need to see the story fully told."[24]

At the same time, the "frequent conflation of African American women and food has functioned as a central structuring dynamic of twentieth-century US psychic, cultural, sociopolitical, and economic life," Doris Witt wrote in *Black Hunger*. But this merging of Black women and food wasn't about casting them as America's culinary heroes or recognizing the contributions they had made to the creation of the South's cuisines. The very best the conflation could do was to produce Aunt Jemima, originally an enslaved Black Louisiana chef that post-bellum blackface vaudeville transformed into a racist caricature that marketers then morphed into a ploy to entice white buyers into purchasing pancake flour. More often, the conflation was used to tell a story of laziness and obesity and malnutrition and food stamps and poverty.[25]

When hot chicken left the neighborhood, it did so without taking its progenitors along with it. White tourists and white locals alike have coded ways of explaining why they don't go to Prince's or Bolton's but choose the white-owned hot chicken restaurants instead. A few years ago, folks would say the neighborhoods felt dangerous to them, which was a barely veiled way of saying white customers were uncomfortable going into Black spaces. These days, Yelp reviewers will say that some other business felt cleaner or the customer service in the white restaurants is always better or when they go to Prince's or Bolton's it feels like the cashier puts other people's orders ahead of theirs.

In February 2018 a local news station released a new promo they called "This Is Home." And of course, it included hot chicken, but the camera crew didn't head to visit André Jeffries at Prince's. They set up outside Hattie B's, panning past Nick Bishop Jr. who was flashing a peace symbol and holding a sign that said, "THIS IS NASHVILLE."

Yes, I'm afraid that vignette was very Nashville.

Conclusion

Dig In

There are people who order their chicken so hot that Jeffries sends them home to eat it in private. There are people who go with chicken one notch down. They sometimes ask for wet paper towels to lay over their eyes. Food reviewers warn hot-chicken newbies to wash their hands before using the restroom or touching any other sensitive body parts. But as we've established, I'm a wimp. I grew up in a household where adding garlic made a dish spicy. I ate my first leg of hot chicken on the day I interviewed André Prince Jeffries. I ordered my chicken mild. I added a side of coleslaw, figuring I could use it to cut the heat.

It was getting late, so I took my food to go like most of the other customers. By the time I placed my order, someone else was sitting in my booth. I stood along the wall, waiting for my food and balancing my recorder bag on my feet. A B-grade horror flick played on a flat-screen TV suspended on the wall across from me. I watched a plastic dinosaur chase stranded castaways down a beach.

André Jeffries saw me standing there. I heard an argument start up in the back. She told them to rush my order. "But she just got here!" a woman said. "No, she's been here for over an hour," Jeffries replied. A young man came out with my sack of food a few minutes later.

It was very good fried chicken, moist and crispy at the same time, but it was warmer than I like my food. While I'd love to talk more with André Jeffries, I'm not sure I'll ever be the hot-chicken devotee so many Nashvillians have become.

When I came back home in 2013, Nashville was more than ten percent larger than it had been when I left it less than a decade earlier, and it was surrounded by communities that had grown by as much as 44 percent.

The tourist strip along lower Broadway was busier and glitzier than ever. High rise condominiums had popped up among the business buildings. A new symphony center hosted concerts, speakers, and community events. The Nashville Convention Center and the Music City Center drew thousands of people to town every weekend. The Bridgestone Arena sat close to twenty thousand people and was home to the Nashville Predators hockey team, which had shocked their hometown and become a competitive club. Then Nashville had shocked everyone by becoming a hockey town, though we'd added our own spin on the sport by introducing some odd traditions involving catfish. And for some reason, bachelorettes from around the nation had started descending upon us, gaggles of girls in tutus and Stetsons.

Over that same short ten years, the neighborhoods Gerald Gimre had fought for forty years to remake had also changed. Edgehill had a coffee shop and an upscale taco joint and a Warby Parker. Downtown Nashville bristled with cranes as developers erected new mixed-use high-rises that had shops on the ground floors, hotels tacked to their sides, and condominiums rising up their central towers.

And East Nashville, a region of the city I remember as having a few antiquated businesses, many abandoned houses, and large public housing complexes, had become the most desirable spot if you were at all artsy, though by 2013, many of my friends could no longer afford to live there. Residents who tried to hold out when gentrification started faced not only higher property taxes but also a higher cost of living. And as always, the money they were offered for their homes usually did not equal the replacement value.

The 9th Annual Music City Hot Chicken Festival happened on July 4, 2015. It was an unusual Independence Day for Tennessee, with a high of only 82° and an almost guaranteed chance of rain. Diehard hot-chicken lovers still braved the weather, ducking under golf umbrellas or into the beer tents when rain started falling.

I showed up for the mid-morning parade that kicks off the day's official events. I was supposed to be meeting a guy for a first date. I was counting on André Prince Jeffries' theory, that this chicken would give us something to talk about. But as I got out of my car, I got a text from him saying he would be late. Then I realized I had forgotten my umbrella. It seemed an inauspicious beginning to both the relationship and the day.

I found a seat on a low concrete wall along the parade route and started making notes about the folks around me. Though the crowd's racial demographics didn't match East Nashville's neighborhoods or even the numbers in Nashville generally, it was the closest thing to a mixed gathering I've seen in Nashville outside of a sporting event.

But very few individuals mingled with anyone other than the people they came with. I wondered if that was partly because the weather kept numbers low. Groups could sit comfortably distanced from everyone else.

The parade was what Momma would call "homegrown." Two police on motorcycles led it followed by a small brass band. The rest of the parade was made up of four antique firetrucks that judiciously chirped their sirens, trying to show off for the crowd without scaring the babies; a series of municipal candidates and their supporters who hurled candy at bystanders; a couple of local businesses with people tossing beads out the doors of their company vehicles; one home-converted top-less wood-paneled station wagon labelled #TheDoose that carried a handful of very cool looking twenty-somethings; and three tatted-up members of the Nashville Rollergirls, who whipped in and out of the other groups.

After the parade, I walked back through East Park to the main stage, where the Shelby Bottom String Band was entertaining the crowd, filling time until Bill Purcell stepped on stage to say a few words.

"We're going to play Bill's favorite," the lead singer told the crowd. They started in on a Merle Haggard classic "Rainbow Stew." Purcell wasn't ready when they finished the song, so they soldiered on through another couple of numbers.

My guy showed up about the same time Purcell did. We wandered around, looking into our various options. Lines had started forming in front of each of the hot chicken tents. He told me he lived down the road from the new Hattie B's in the Nations and ate there all the time. I told him the story of Prince's founding.

The line for Prince's stretched the length of the green, past the lines for Hattie B's and Pepperfire and Bolton's. At the end of the green, the queue took a sharp turn, wrapping around Prince's competitors.

A curious thing was happening. Folks at the back of the Prince's line stayed in their groups, chatting with the people they came with. But by the time they reached the bend in the queue, they were running out of things to say to their friends. They stood, arms crossed and hips cocked, staring into space. Then after a few more minutes of waiting, they started talking to the others in line around them, telling strangers the story of when they first tried hot chicken and trading insider knowledge of what to order from the other hot chicken joints.

I wanted to be able to take this moment of peace and unity and turn it into a rosy assessment of Nashville's—and the nation's—future.

Some things in Nashville today do look different. Multiple waves of immigration and refugee resettlement have remade our demographics. "Nashville entered the last decade of the twentieth century a black-and-white city whose place on the map of Country music was established but whose place on the map of international migration was questionable at best," wrote immigration scholar Jamie Winders. By 2010, 10 percent of the city's population were immigrants, and they accounted for almost 60 percent of the people who moved to the city. And it isn't just about the influx of Latinx immigrants. Nashville has more Kurdish immigrants than any other city in the nation, about sixty thousand Bhutanese, and seventeen thousand Egyptians.[1]

Many of the immigrant communities settled around the working class white South Nashville neighborhood where my grandparents lived before their deaths, transforming the community and bringing in new grocery stores, shopping centers, restaurants, worship spaces, and customs. But as has happened over the past one hundred fifty years, as the new residents moved in, the original residents fled. If my grandparents were still alive, I doubt they would have stayed.

Nashville is in now the middle of its fifth fit of urban planning. This time we call it Nashville Next, and we say it's a way to handle gentrification. The city is growing almost faster than developers can manage. Historic neighborhoods are being razed and renewed. The suburbs are expanding. Fields are being replaced by paved shopping paradises identical to those spreading across the nation. My friends have moved to the neighborhoods we grew up avoiding. They ask me to meet them for drinks or haute Southern cuisine in places I remember as industrial wastelands.

And as they—as we—move into the Gulch and East Nashville and Germantown and North Nashville and Edgehill, other people move out, families are displaced, and communities that have weathered the previous waves of urban planning break apart.

Midway through the research for this project, I found a speech given by Dr. Edwin Mims, professor emeritus of English at Vanderbilt, to a group of local Rotarians in 1949. He was harsh in the way only a post-tenure professor can be. He had little patience for his audience of well-meaning do-gooders. It was time, he said, "for more realistic idealists with patience, courage and faith who see Nashville as it is and what it may become . . ."

> Nashville's problems demand community statesmen who think about, care about, and plan for the city. . . . We need to ask ourselves uncomfortable questions that cannot be brushed aside in our complacency. . . . For certain historical reasons we have been slow to develop community consciousness that causes men to make sacrifices for the public good. . . . The only thing left is for us to love Nashville, and if enough love her, think of her, plan for her, she will rise.[2]

What would it mean for Nashville to finally rise, for it to move past being the capital of country music or the bastion of the bachelorettes? Is there a way for us to finally build a city where every resident has an equal chance to thrive?

A surprisingly connected question: Whose chicken is this anyway? What do we mean when we say we're making it spicy, "Nashville style"?

The cultural appropriation of this Black dish created by a Black woman and cooked in Black kitchens is symbolized by the very label we applied to it. Calling it Nashville hot chicken implies that this is the city's food. It ignores the reality: in the 1980s and 1990s, someone like me with deep roots in this city, could be born here and reach adulthood here without having ever encountered hot chicken. What claim do I have to the dish?

But if it isn't Nashville hot chicken, what is it?

"I would call it soul-food hot chicken," Dollye Matthews said, "because it developed in the Black community. When you say Nashville hot chicken, it's like taking it away from where it came from once again. Stealing that identity."

I get why she liked that option. Soul-food hot chicken leaves room for folks like Bolton Polk who helped popularize the dish. But the term skips over the time when hot chicken belonged to the Prince family alone, an era that spanned either a couple or a few decades.

Calling hot chicken "soul food" also plays off of (or plays into?) the politics of the term. When food is called soul food, that means it can, as Doris Witt wrote, be "uncritically embraced as the essence of blackness or else dismissed as an inauthentic, blackface product of white radical chic or black bourgeois 'slumming,'" depending on the speaker and the audience.[3]

Is it more accurate to call it Prince's hot chicken? That choice also isn't perfect. It takes a dish invented by a woman and gives credit to the man who figured out how to market it. The hot chicken getting fried up in all these various kitchens didn't belong to Thornton Prince III. It was a product of that unnamed Black woman who had wanted to teach him—or at least his taste buds—a lesson.

I've always been bothered by the namelessness of the woman who invented hot chicken. When I started this project, I knew I couldn't uncover who she was, so I searched for the names and stories of some of the women who may have been her: Jennie May Patton, Gertrude Claybrook, Mattie Crutcher, Mattie Hicks, Caroline Bridges, Dorothy Prince, Ozella Prince, Katie Dobson.

In the process, I have found an unexpected moment of redemption. Thornton Prince III, William Prince Sr., and their brothers and sons made a few dollars off of this woman's chicken for a few years. But no matter when the first BBQ Chicken Shack opened—whether it was 1936 or 1956—André Prince Jeffries has been running the business longer than Thornton Prince III possibly could have. Before her, the restaurant supported her Aunt Maude. After André, the business will be passed along to her daughters.

For most of the time that the Chicken Shack has been in business, the angry woman's chicken hasn't belonged to the Prince men. It's been what kept the women of the family independent. It let them prosper. It won them awards and international attention. It brought celebrities from Jerry Seinfeld to the British royal family through their front doors.

I bet the woman who first made hot chicken would be pleased, whoever she is. That man, he's finally had his comeuppance.

Epilogue

Wash Up

At 12:36 a.m. on March 3, 2020, a tornado touched down at John C. Tune Airport, a regional airport whose lights I can see from my apartment. From my neighborhood in West Nashville, the funnel cloud pummeled Tennessee State University, destroying the agricultural research center and doing thirty million to fifty million dollars in damage. It then barreled through North Nashville, running parallel to Jefferson Street. After it crossed the interstate and reached the Cheatham Place Housing Project, it turned slightly south, following Jefferson Street into Germantown and over the bridge into East Nashville. It passed over Bolton's, causing "extensive damage," according to early reports. The tornado ran due east through East Nashville, obliterating a popular business district called Five Points. A friend and former coworker who worked as a bartender at a trendy cocktail joint on the edge of that neighborhood was leaving work with his girlfriend when the storm arrived. They both died.[1]

From East Nashville, the storm followed I-40 east through Mt. Juliet where a woman found the green "TERMINAL" sign that used to hang on the John C. Tune runway some twenty miles away. It crossed Wilson and Smith Counties before hitting Putnam County. It ran along the northern edge of Cookeville, the county seat, then it finally dissipated. It had stayed on the ground for fifty-seven minutes and traveled over fifty miles, killing twenty-four people. Fifty thousand Nashvillians had no power, and almost fifty buildings in the city had been destroyed.[2]

After the storm, coverage of the destruction focused on what had happened in gentrified Germantown and East Nashville. The damage done in North Nashville, however, was at least as devastating. I waited a couple of days and then drove through after having worked a volunteer shift at one of the North Nashville community centers, following the path of the storm as it cut across the path of my story.

The ticky-tacky tall skinnies going up in the North Nashville neighborhoods did not weather the storm well. The houses being erected in this neighborhood were selling for a third of a million dollars, not the half a million or more that new houses were pulling on the other side of Charlotte Avenue. As a result, the construction of the North Nashville houses was considerably cheaper. An acquaintance posted a picture of a twin-set of houses in the Elizabeth Park section of North Nashville. Both of the stick-constructed houses had collapsed in exactly the same way. The top stories now rested on the homes' foundations, the first floor splintered and smashed absolutely flat. Neither home was occupied, which is the only reason no one had died in them.

Caroline Bridge's home—the Ann's Hacienda Hotel—escaped with some roof damage, though homes less than a block away were destroyed and an ancient oak had crashed through a neighboring house. The Cheatham Place Housing Projects were without power and had sustained minor damage, but they were recoverable. Many other Black-owned houses and businesses were not. The official tally of who will and will not be able to reopen has not yet been released, but it will include places like Joshua Mundy's three businesses: Music City Cleaners, an event venue, and a minority entrepreneurial space. He'd put them in a stunning century-old building that was reduced to rubble. If Mundy is able to reopen, it will not be in the same space.

And North Nashville residents and neighborhood advocates expected what will come next: the developers. They were out canvassing the neighborhood within forty-eight hours. "We know there are people already knocking on doors," a local nonprofit head said. "If they say they're going to put you up in the Omni for a week and give you one hundred thousand dollars cash, and you're staying in a house with no walls, you might accept that."[3]

If you or your parents bought a house for twenty-five thousand and someone offers you a hundred thousand, "you really think you're gaining," Dollye Matthews explained. But too many people around here, "they don't know how the other people live," she continued. "They don't know what it's like to buy at Whole Foods or Turnip Truck. Don't have a clue." As a result, people have taken the money offered to them because it looked impossible to resist and then discovered they could not afford to buy back into the community where their friends and families lived.[4]

Other families have tried to use their land to finally create some transgenerational wealth, TSU Professor Learotha Williams said. One day, he was visiting his barber, complaining about how the developers had started cold-calling him when he didn't even live inside the Nashville city limits. Another man said he'd had a guy waiting by his mailbox, trying to convince him to take a quarter of a million dollars for a quarter acre lot. And he could understand why that would seem irresistible, but he worried that this wave of development would finish what slum clearance and urban renewal and interstate construction and model cities couldn't: the erasure of the historic Black communities and the spaces they had built for themselves.

"You can go to a state or a town or a city that has a Native American name and not find a Native American person in there," Williams said. "As they [the names] become markers, they become tombstones of folks that were there and aren't anymore. That's the end of the story." He worried that would soon happen to Nashville's few remaining historic Black neighborhoods.[5]

The Friday after the storm, the *East Nashvillian* released their weekly newsletter. In this issue, they listed "a compilation of the status of East Side businesses affected by the tornado." They sorted the restaurants by category: Severely damaged or destroyed—closed indefinitely; damaged—closed until further notice; mild to no damage—will reopen within a few weeks or sooner; or mild to no damage—open for business.

Bolton's was not included in any of the four options. But Dollye had already updated hot chicken fans through Facebook. The South Nashville location was finally up and running, and they'd have the Main Street spot going just as soon as electricity was restored.[6]

March 11, 2020
Nashville, Tennessee

Notes

INTRODUCTION

1. Natalie Neysa Alund, "Prince's Hot Chicken Closed after Crash, Fire," *Tennessean*, December 29, 2018.
2. "Iconic Nashville Hot Chicken Restaurant Closed after SUV Crash Causes Fire," *NBC*, December 28, 2018, https://www.wpsdlocal6.com/news/iconic-nashville-hot-chicken-restaurant-closed-after-suv-crash-causes/article_5c3e885a-f197-5615-843a-ce170a291a13.html.
3. Natalie Neysa Alund and Lizzy Alfs, "Prince's Hot Chicken Location Will Not Reopen," *Tennessean*, July 29, 2019; Steve Cavendish, "Prince's Hot Chicken on Ewing Drive Will Not Reopen," *Nashville Scene*, July 26, 2019; D. Patrick Rodgers, "Prince's Original Location to Close 'Indefinitely' in Wake of Fire," *Nashville Scene*, December 28, 2018.
4. André Prince Jeffries, interview by the author, Prince's Hot Chicken Shack, Nashville, TN, March 18, 2015.
5. Interview with André Prince Jeffries.
6. *1983 Nashville (Davidson County, Tenn.) City Directory* (Taylor, MI: R.L. Polk and Company, 1983) 153; *1984 Nashville (Davidson County, Tenn.) City Directory* (Taylor, MI: R.L. Polk and Company, 1984) 172, 477.
7. Interview with André Prince Jeffries.
8. Interview with André Prince Jeffries.

9. Thayer Wine, "Hot Chicken!" *Tennessean*, October 28, 2002.

10. John T. Edge, *Fried Chicken: An American Story* (New York: G.P. Putnam's Sons, 2004), 132.

11. Jeffries interview; Thayer Wine, "Hot Chicken!"

12. Dollye Matthews, interview by Amy C. Evans, Southern Foodways Alliance, May 31, 2008, https://www.southernfoodways.org/interview/boltons-spicy-chicken-and-fish.

CHAPTER 1

1. "An Ideal Williamson County Stock and Grain Farm at Public AUCTION," *Nashville Tennessean*, July 20, 1919; Renee Chevalier, Randy Lee, Todd Petrowski, Amy Thomas and Mike Womack, "Wood Park (Sayers-Oman House)," Leadership Brentwood Class of 2008, http://www.brentwoodtn.gov/Home/ShowDocument?id=367.

2. "An Ideal Williamson County Stock," *Nashville Tennessean*.

3. For more on the history and significance of separate, external kitchens, see Deetz, *Bound to the Fire*, 20–23.

4. 1860 US Census, Williamson County, Tennessee, slave schedule, p.19–20 (written), James J. Sayers, digital image, Ancestry.com, accessed May 31, 2020, http://ancestry.com; 1850 US Census, Williamson County, Tennessee, slave schedule, p. 965 (written), J. J. Sayers, digital image, Ancestry.com, accessed May 31, 2020, http://ancestry.com.

5. Deetz, *Bound to the Fire*, 2, 16.

6. Kelley Fanto Deetz, *Bound to the Fire: How Virginia's Enslaved Cooks Helped Invent American Cuisine* (Lexington: University Press of Kentucky, 2017), 2, 16.

7. Deetz, *Bound to the Fire*, 62–63.

8. Deetz, *Bound to the Fire*, 23–27.

9. Michael W. Twitty, *The Cooking Gene: A Journey through African American Culinary History in the Old South* (New York: Amistad, 2017), 1–23.

10. Deetz, *Bound to the Fire*, 2.

11. Alice Randall and Caroline Randall Williams, *Soul Food Love: Healthy Recipes Inspired by One Hundred Years of Cooking in a Black Family* (New York: Clarkson Potter, 2015), 11.

12. Chandra Manning, "Working for Citizenship in Civil War Contraband Camps," *Journal of the Civil War* 4, no. 2 (June 2014): 171–73; David R. Roediger, *Seizing Freedom: Slave Emancipation and Liberty for All* (New York: Verso Books, 2014), Introduction; Amy Murrell Taylor, *Embattled Freedom: Journeys through the Civil War's Refugee Camps* (Chapel Hill: University of North Carolina Pres, 2018),

3–4; Eric Wills, "The Forgotten: The Contraband of America and the Road to Freedom," *Saving Places*, June 19, 2017, https://savingplaces.org/stories/the-forgotten-the-contraband-of-america-and-the-road-to-freedom.

13. Roediger, *Seizing Freedom*; Taylor, *Embattled Freedom*, 2, 9, 39–40, 44–45; Wills, "The Forgotten."

14. Abigail Cooper, "Interactive Map of Contraband Camps," *History Digital Projects*, 2014, https://repository.upenn.edu/hist_digital/1; Jim Downs, *Sick from Freedom: African American Illness and Suffering during the Civil War and Reconstruction*, (New York: Oxford University Press, 2012), 3–5.

15. Jonathan Mattise, "Nashville Caught in Battle between Growth and Preservation," Fox 17, November 7, 2017, https://fox17.com/news/local/slave-burial-sites-investigated-on-land-eyed-for-development.

16. John Cimprich, *Slavery's End in Tennessee: 1861–1865* (Tuscaloosa: University of Alabama Press, 2002), 52; Downs, *Sick from Freedom*, 164–66; Taylor, *Embattled Freedom*, 62–64.

17. Ira Berlin and Leslie S. Rowland, eds., *Families and Freedom: A Documentary History of African American Kinship in the Civil War*, (New York: New Press, 1997), 78; Tennessee Valley Archaeological Research, "Historic Background Research and Ground Penetrating Radar Survey Associated with the Greer Stadium Redevelopment Project in Nashville, Davidson County, Tennessee" (Nashville: Metro Parks and Recreation, 2018), 38.

18. Edward John Harcourt, "'That Mystic Cloud:' Civil War Memory in the Tennessee Heartland, 1865–1920" (PhD diss., Vanderbilt University, 2008), 21–22.

19. 1880 US Census, Williamson County, Tennessee, population schedule, p. 231 (stamped), dwelling 161, family 161, Billy Murrey, digital image, Ancestry.com, accessed November 12, 2019, http://ancestry.com; Williamson County, Tennessee, Marriage certificate p. 522 (1889), Prince-Maury, Tennessee Division of Vital Statistics, Nashville; 1900 US census, p. 0344.

20. 1891 Enumeration of Male Voters, Williamson County, Tennessee, p. unknown, number 57, Thornton Prince, digital image, Ancestry.com, accessed October 4, 2019, http://ancestry.com; 1900 US Census, Williamson, p. 0344; 1910 US Census, Williamson County, Tennessee, population schedule, p. 0557 (written), dwelling 128, family 131, Thornton Prince, digital image, Ancestry.com, accessed November 12, 2019, http://ancestry.com.

21. 1920 US Census, Williamson County, Tennessee, population schedule. P. 0351 (written), dwelling 160, family 172, Thornton Prince, digital image, Ancestry.com, accessed November 12, 2019, http://ancestry.com.

22. 1900 United States Census, Williamson County, Tennessee, population schedule, p. 238 (stamped), dwelling 101, family 101, Albert Patton, digital image,

Ancestry.com, Accessed May 31, 2020, http://ancestry.com; Williamson County, Tennessee, Marriage certificate no. 1387 (1910), Prince-Patton, Tennessee Division of Vital Statistics, Nashville; 1910 US Census, Williamson County, p. 0557; 1910 US Census, Williamson County, Tennessee, population schedule p. 0601 (written), dwelling 137, family 140, Albert Flemming, digital image, ancestry.com, accessed May 31, 2020, http://ancestry.com.

23. Williamson County, Tennessee, Marriage certificate no. 1387.

24. Williamson County, Tennessee, Marriage certificate no. 1818 (1912), Prince-Claybrook, Tennessee Division of Vital Statistics, Nashville.

25. 1900 US Census, Williamson County, p. 1560 (written), dwelling 210, family 20, Harden Claybrook, digital image, Ancestry.com, accessed November 12, 2019, http://ancestry.com; 1910 US Census, Williamson County, p. 7001 (written), dwelling 310, family 315, Rena Dennenham, digital image, Ancestry.com, accessed November 12, 2019, http://ancestry.com.

26. In 1900, 43.2 percent of them were in the labor force, compared with only 17.8 percent of white women; Claudia Goldin, "Female Labor Force Participation: The Origin of Black and White Differences, 1870 and 1880," *Journal of Economic History* 37, no. 1 (1977): 87–108.

27. Evelyn Nakano Glenn, *Unequal Freedom: How Race and Gender Shaped American Citizenship and Labor* (Cambridge, MA: Harvard University Press, 2002) 107–8.

28. US Social Security Applications and Claims Index, no. 410248137, Dorothy Lee Prince [Dorothy Lee Wright] [Dorothy Davis], digital image, Ancestry.com, accessed December 3, 2019, http://ancestry.com.

29. Davidson County, Tennessee, death certificate no. 20878 (1946), Jasper Lee Prince, Tennessee Department of Public Health, Nashville.

30. Davidson County, Tennessee, Registration card no. 305 (1917), Thornton Prince, United States World War I Draft Registration Cards, 1917–1918, Ancestry.com, accessed November 12, 2019, http://ancestry.com; "Stock," *Nashville Banner*, May 22, 1919.

31. Williamson County, Tennessee, Marriage certificate no. 2215 (1917), Prince-Dempsey, Tennessee Division of Vital Statistics, Nashville; 1920 US Census, Davidson County, p. 243 (stamped), dwelling 17, family 17, Thornton Prince, digital image, Ancestry.com, accessed November 12, 2019, http://ancestry.com.

32. Lois Meguiar Hadley, *Garnered Memories: Journals by Elizabeth Lois Meguiar Hadley*, Nashville Metro Archives, http://www.nashvillearchives.org/documents/garnered-memories.pdf.

33. Interview with André Prince Jeffries.

34. John T. Edge, ed., *Foodways*, vol. 7 (Chapel Hill: University of North Carolina Press, 2007) 2–4, 88–95; John Egerton, *Southern Food: At Home, on the Road, in History* (New York: Alfred A. Knopf, 1987) 21–22, 32–33, 36.

35. William D. McBride and S. Darrell Mundy, "Farrow-to-Finish Swine Production in Ten Counties of West Tennessee," Research Report, University of Tennessee Agricultural Experiment Station, 1987, 1, http://trace.tennessee.edu/utk_agresreport/90; "The Hog," *Breeder's Gazette*, August 10, 1922, 149.

36. 1920 US Census, Davidson County, p. 243; Hadley, *Garnered Memories*, 20, 120–21; *Marshall-Bruce-Polk Co.'s Nashville City Directory, 1920*, (Nashville, TN: Marshall-Bruce-Polk Company, 1920), 167, 547; "Rank and File," *Nashville Tennessean*, January 21, 1917; "Newman Cheek Buys Dillon Subdivision Tracts," *Nashville Tennessean*, January 4, 1925, "To Open Subdivision," *Nashville Tennessean*, July 16, 1929; "Statistical Record," *Nashville Tennessean*, September 18, 1929; "Statistical Record," *Nashville Tennessean*, April 13, 1930; "School Site Purchased," *Nashville Tennessean*, September 15, 1935.

37. *Marshall-Bruce-Polk Co.'s Nashville City Directory, 1922*, (Nashville, TN: Marshall-Bruce-Polk Company, 1922), 685.

38. Gary W. Dolzall, "The Tennessee Central Story, Part 1," *Trains*, September 1987; Carroll Van West, "Tennessee Central Railroad," *Tennessee Encyclopedia*, http://tennesseeencyclopedia.net/entries/tennessee-central-railroad; "Tennessee Central Railway Company: The Scenic Railway of the South," *The Official Guide of the Railways and Steam Navigation Lines of the United States, Porto Rico, Canada, Mexico and Cuba* (New York: National Railway Publication Company, 1923) 576–77; "Tennessee Central Railway," *American Rails*, https://www.american-rails.com/tc.html.

39. 1880 US Census, Williamson County, Tennessee, population schedule, p. 240–41; 1920 United States Census, Davidson County, Tennessee, population schedule, p. 42, (stamped), dwelling 211, family 212, Austin Prince, digital image, Ancestry.com, accessed November 12, 2019, http://ancestry.com; Holbrook & McClellan, "Bad Weather Hurts Lay," *Egg Reporter*, volume 17 (Mount Morris, IL: Watt Publishing Company, 1911), 16; *Marshall-Bruce-Polk Co.'s Nashville City Directory, 1920–21* (Nashville, TN: Marshall-Bruce-Polk Company, 1921), 471; *Polk's Nashville City Directory (1922)*, 471, 685; *Salmagundi 1910: Bascobel College* (Nashville, TN: Bascobel College, 1910) 71, http://digital.library.nashville.org/cdm/ref/collection/nr/id/7996; Williamson County, Tennessee, Marriage certificate no. 472 (1894), Prince-Foster, Tennessee Division of Vital Statistics, Nashville.

40. Louis M. Kyriakoudes, "Southern Black Rural-Urban Migration in the Era of the Great Migration: Nashville and Middle Tennessee, 1890–1930," *Agricultural History* 72, no. 2 (Spring 1998): 341–51.

41. Luther Adams, "'Headed for Louisville': Rethinking Rural to Urban Migration in the South, 1930–1950," *Journal of Social History* (Winter 2006): 408; Kyriakoudes, "Southern Black Rural-Urban Migration," 341–51.

42. Nashville Public library Foundation, "Nashville Rising: Our Story of the 2010 Flood," http://maps.nashville.gov/npl_2010FloodStory; Kent Travis, "Cumberland Rising," *Tennessean*, https://i.pinimg.com/originals/28/3f/37/283f372456a89db75ab8540e51be0946.gif.

43. A note about sources: most of these examples come from reports written about twenty years before the Prince's moved onto Willow Street. The *Nashville American* combined with the *Tennessean* at that point, and they only sporadically published lists of everyone who had died in the city; the new paper preferred to do obituaries, which only included the individual's whose families had the ability and the connections to submit a death report to the paper. The accounts from Willow Street and the surrounding neighborhood disappeared from the paper at that point, but it wasn't because of any improvements in public health; "Death's Reported," *Nashville American*, February 25, 1896; "Deaths Reported," *Nashville American*, March 18, 1896; "Deaths Reported," *Nashville American*, May 1, 1896; "Deaths Reported," *Nashville American*, September 20, 1896; "Death Record," *Nashville American*, May 3, 1899; "Death Record," *Nashville American*, June 17, 1899; "Death Record," *Nashville American*, October 12, 1899; "Death Record," *Nashville American*, December 15, 1899; "Death Record," *Nashville American*, June 26, 1900; "The Death Record," *Nashville American*, September 6, 1900; "Death Record," *Nashville American*, November 1, 1900; "Record of Deaths," *Nashville American*, March 19, 1901; "Death Record," *Nashville American*, August 10, 1901; "Death Record," *Nashville American*, August 22, 1902; "Death Record," *Nashville American*, August 29, 1903; "Death Record," *Nashville American*, March 22, 1904; "One Death and Others Are Ill," *Nashville American*, April 29, 1906; "Deaths," *Nashville Tennessean and Nashville American*, October 21, 1915; "Death Notices," *Nashville Tennessean and Nashville American*, February 28, 1918.

44. Kenneth Barnhart, "Negro Homicides in the United States," *Opportunity: Journal of Negro Life* 10-11 (July 1932): 212–14; Harrington Cooper Brearley, *Homicide in the United States* (Chapel Hill: University of North Carolina Press, 1932); "Deaths Reported," *Nashville American*, February 4, 1896; "Death Record," *Nashville American*, August 12, 1897; "Death Record," *Nashville American*, August 15, 1897; "Death Record," *Nashville American*, December 5, 1897; "Death Record," *Nashville American*, April 28, 1899; "Death Record," *Nashville American*, October 29, 1899; "Death Record," *Nashville American*, October 4, 1901; "Death Record," *Nashville American*, November 6, 1901; "Death Record," *Nashville American*, March 1, 1898; "Death from Smallpox," *Nashville American*, September 11, 1904; "Death Notices," *Nashville Tennessean and Nashville American*, December 14, 1914; "Negro Woman Killed, Murderer Arrested," *Nashville Tennessean and Nashville American*, February 21, 1916; "Deaths in the City," *Nashville Tennessean and Nashville American*, February 24, 1917.

45. John Linn Hopkins and Marsha R. Oates, "Shotgun Houses," in *Tennessee Encyclopedia*, 2017, https://tennesseeencyclopedia.net/entries/shotgun-houses.
46. Nat Caldwell, "Vet 'John Jones' Cites Need for Housing Aid," *Nashville Tennessean*, January 9, 1949; Caldwell, "1 Outdoor Spigot Supplies Water for 13 Families," *Nashville Tennessean*, January 11, 1949.
47. Hopkins and Oates, "Shotgun Houses."
48. Williamson County, Tennessee, Registration card no. 12027 (1942), James Thomas Prince, United States World War II Draft Registration Cards, 1940–1947, Ancestry.com, accessed November 12, 2019, http://ancestry.com.

CHAPTER 2

1. Mrs. William W. Geraldton, *Nashville Social Directory* (Nashville: Cumberland Press, 1911), 66; "For Rent-Residences," *Nashville Tennessean*, September 5, 1909; Dixie Rose, "YWCA Blue Triangle Branch Collection," Nashville Public Library, February 9, 2019, https://library.nashville.org/blog/2019/02/ywca-blue-triangle-branch-collection.
2. Gloria Ballard, "Blue Triangle Was the Y for Black Women," *Nashville Tennessean*, February 26, 1989; William Henry Harrison, *Colored Girls' and Boys' Inspiring United States History and a Heart to Heart Talk about White Folks* (self-published, 1921), https://www.gutenberg.org/files/57181/57181-h/57181-h.htm; Rose, "YWCA Blue Triangle Branch."
3. Ballard, "Blue Triangle Was the Y"; Marchelle Cannon, "Blue Triangle Part of Nashville History," *Nashville Tennessean*, October 19, 1986; Carrie R. Hill and Linda T. Wynn, "Blue Triangle YWCA (1919–1974)," *A Profile of African Americans in Tennessee History*, http://ww2.tnstate.edu/library/digital/Blue.htm; Bobby L. Lovett, *The African-American History of Nashville Tennessee, 1780–1930: Elites and Dilemmas* (Fayetteville: University of Arkansas Press, 1999), 123; *Marshall-Bruce-Polk Co.'s Nashville City Directory, 1926* (Nashville, TN: Marshall-Bruce-Polk Company, 1926), 613; Williamson County, Tennessee, Death certificate no. 468 (1918), Buela Claybrook, Tennessee Department of Public Health, Nashville.
4. Charles Edwin Robert, *Nashville and Her Trade for 1870* (Nashville: Roberts and Purvis, Republican Banner Office, 1870), 47.
5. Nellie Kenyon, "Yesteryear's Swanky Homes Bow in March of Progress," *Nashville Tennessean*, June 21, 1949.
6. H. B. Teeter, "Capitol Gaslit Era Gives Way to a New," *Nashville Tennessean*, June 26, 1949.
7. Mason K. Christenson, "'The Saloon in Nashville and the Coming of Prohibition in Tennessee" (MA thesis, Middle Tennessee State University, Murfreesboro,

2013), 11–15, https://jewlscholar.mtsu.edu/bitstream/handle/mtsu/3578/Christensen_mtsu_0170N_10152.pdf.

8. "TERA Housing Survey of State Finds $72,000,000 Fund Need," *Nashville Tennessean*, February 7, 1935.

9. "Slum Clearance," *Nashville Tennessean*, August 13, 1932.

10. "Editorial of the day: Housing and the Depression," *Nashville Tennessean*, September 16, 1932.

11. "Committee to Consider Slum Clearance Named," *Nashville Tennessean*, November 2, 1933.

12. "Gerald Snyder Gimre," *Pebbles Annual*, Marshalltown, IA, 1916: 20; "Pupils in Recital," *Times-Republican*, June 3, 1914; "May Festival Held," *Times-Republican*, May 15, 1915; "Concert at Elim Church," *Times-Republican*, May 18, 1915; "Thomas Post Plans for Memorial Day," *Times-Republican*, May 19, 1915; "School Children in Memorial Service," *Times-Republican*, May 31, 1915; "Senior High School Debates Completed," *Times-Republican*, December 18, 1915; "Work on Senior Class Play," *Times-Republican*, April 27, 1916; "'Between the Acts,' Given by Seniors," *Times-Republican*, June 9, 1916.

13. "Gimre," *Pebbles Annual*, 20; Marshalltown, Iowa, Registration card no. 14-237B (1918), Gerald Snyder Gimre, United States World War I Draft Registration Cards, 1917–1918, Ancestry.com, accessed May 31, 2020, http://ancestry.com.

14. "Boys Guest at Supper," *Times-Republican*, January 29, 1914.

15. "Gimre," *Pebbles Annual*, 20; "More Senior Boys than Girls in 1916," *Times-Republican*, May 17, 1916; "M.H.S. Class of 1916 Is Graduated," *Times-Republican*, June 10, 1916.

16. "High Percentage Physically Fit," *Times-Republican*, July 16, 1918; "Summon Men for Next Quota," *Times-Republican*, September 3, 1918; "Three After Commissions," *Times-Republican*, September 7, 1918; Joseph A. Whitacre and W. J. Moore, *Marshall County in the World War, 1917–1918* (Marshalltown, IA: Marshall Printing Company, 1919), 142, https://hdl.handle.net/2027/wu.89072939655; "Gerald Gimre," *Des Moines Register*, August 15, 1991.

17. "Art and Design 14 Students Exhibit Original Designs," *Daily Illini*, March 18, 1919; "Award Two Students Membership in ULAS," *Daily Illini*, April 23, 1919; "Appoint Ingram '20 as Editor of "Reptonian," *Daily Illini*, January 13, 1920; "Seniors with High Standings Receive Scholastic Honors," *Daily Illini*, June 16, 1920; *Ilio*, 1921, 69, 422, 520; University of Illinois, *Report—University of Illinois Board of Trustees* (1918–1920), 830, 840, https://hdl.handle.net/2027/uiug.30112020300908; "Exhibit Garden Models in Agriculture Building," *Daily Illini*, April 2, 1921.

18. City Planning Commission, "Zoning Ordinance," Warren, OH, 1925, https://babel.hathitrust.org/cgi/pt?id=uiug.30112113447152&view=1up&seq=5; "Zoning

Ordinance Acted on by Council," *Chronicle-Telegram*, October 9, 1928; "Take No Action on Zoning Ordinance," *Chronicle-Telegram*, December 28, 1928; Theodora Kimball Hubbard and Katherine McNamara, *Planning Information Up-To-Date: A Supplement, 1923–1928* (London: Oxford University Press, 1928) 5, https://doi.org/10.1002/ncr.4110180511; "City Planner Named," *Nashville Tennessean*, July 1, 1932

19. "Kiwanis Club Plans Local Zoning System," *Nashville Tennessean*, July 14, 1923; "Mayor to Hear Plea for Street Marking," *Nashville Tennessean*, August 17, 1923; "City Planning Commission of Seven for Nashville Proposed in Measure," *Nashville Tennessean*, February 6, 1925; "2 Bills Propose City Zoning and Planning Bodies," *Nashville Tennessean*, July 8, 1925; "City Council Passes Anti-Rabies Bill on First Reading," *Nashville Tennessean*, August 19, 1925; T. H. Alexander, "Taxable Values to Be Enhanced If Bonds Voted," *Nashville Tennessean*, December 13, 1925; "The Reasons for the Faith That Is in Us," *Nashville Tennessean*, December 15, 1925; "Legislature in Session," *Nashville Tennessean*, April 6, 1927; "City Planning," *Nashville Tennessean*, September 29, 1929; "City Planning Bill Put in Session Call," *Nashville Tennessean*, December 1, 1929; "City Planning Commission Bill to Be Introduced," *Nashville Tennessean*, December 2, 1929; "For a Better Nashville," *Nashville Tennessean*, December 2, 1929; "Council O.K.'s $2,600,000 Budget: Opposes City Planning Proposal," *Nashville Tennessean*, December 4, 1929; "Appointments to Zoning, Planning Bodies Approved," *Nashville Tennessean*, September 16, 1931.

20. "City Planner Named."

21. "The Gainsboro to Be Nashville's Most Up-to-Date Apartment House," *Nashville Tennessean*, July 3, 1927; "The Gainsboro, Nashville's Newest Apartment Ready by October 1st," *Nashville Tennessean*, July 3, 1927; "Exterior View of the Gainesboro Apartments," *Nashville Tennessean*, April 1, 1928; "Safety Board for Nashville Will Meet Here Today," *Nashville Tennessean*, June 9, 1932; "C. of C. Safety Board Adopts Principles Here," *Nashville Tennessean*, June 10, 1932.

22. "Plan Machine Shop," *Nashville Tennessean*, November 20, 1928; "Residents Resisting Placing of Business Houses on Harding," *Nashville Tennessean*, September 16, 1932; "Commission to Meet," *Nashville Tennessean*, October 27, 1932; "Commercial Building Permit is Denied Here," *Nashville Tennessean*, November 18, 1932.

23. "Effects of City Zoning Ordinance Is Explained," *Nashville Tennessean*, May 22, 1932.

24. "Effects of City Zoning Ordinance"; "Zoning Plans Are Outlined at Meeting," *Nashville Tennessean*, February 16, 1933; "Public to Discuss Proposed Zoning Law Here Tonight," *Nashville Tennessean*, July 11, 1933.

25. "To Study Zoning Maps," *Nashville Tennessean*, January 27, 1933; "Council Approves City Zoning Bill on Third Reading," *Nashville Tennessean*, July 20, 1933.

26. "Man Recovers Own Car, Arrests Negroes," *Nashville Tennessean*, July 10, 1933.

27. "Man Recovers Own Car."

28. *Marshall-Bruce-Polk Co.'s Nashville City Directory, 1924*, (Nashville, TN: Marshall-Bruce-Polk Company, 1924), 655.

29. *Caron's Directory of the City of Louisville for 1925* (Louisville, KY: Caron Directory Company, 1925), 1587; *Caron's Directory of the City of Louisville for 1926* (Louisville, KY: Caron Directory Company, 1926), 1577; *Caron's Directory of the City of Louisville for 1927* (Louisville, KY: Caron Directory Company, 1927), 1669; *Caron's Directory of the City of Louisville for 1928* (Louisville, KY: Caron Directory Company, 1929), 1739.

30. *Caron's Directory of the City of Louisville for 1928* (Louisville, KY: Caron Directory Company, 1928), 1589; *Marshall-Bruce-Polk Co.'s Nashville City Directory, 1933*, (Nashville, TN: Marshall-Bruce-Polk Company, 1933), 706.

31. *Marshall-Bruce-Polk Co.'s 1922*, 443; *Marshall-Bruce-Polk Co.'s 1924*, 430; *Marshall-Bruce-Polk Co.'s Nashville City Directory, 1931*, (Nashville, TN: Marshall-Bruce-Polk Company, 1931), 550; *Marshall-Bruce-Polk Co.'s 1933*, 706.

32. "J. B. [*sic*] Taylor, Negro Pastor and School Leader, Dies," *Nashville Tennessean*, February 26, 1946.

33. John Erwin, "Slum Clearance Project Wins Approval of US Which May Defray Entire Cost," *Nashville Tennessean*, December 13, 1933; "Zoning Action Deferred," *Nashville Tennessean*, October 28, 1932; "Dr. Crouch Named NHA Chairman," *Nashville Tennessean*, December 11, 1969; Doug Hall, "NHA Says Goodby [*sic*] to Retiring Gimre," *Nashville Tennessean*, July 1, 1970.

34. Nat Caldwell, "Need of Slum Clearance to Eradicate Crime and Disease Cited in Trades Council Report," *Nashville Tennessean*, October 26, 1938.

35. "Rats Costing City $1,000,000 Year, Says Overton; Plans War," *Nashville Tennessean*, December 11, 1938.

36. Robert Guy Spinney, *World War II in Nashville: Transformation of the Homefront* (Knoxville: University of Tennessee Press, 1998), 11.

37. "$10,000,000 More for Housing to Be Asked, Murrey Announces," *Nashville Tennessean*, March 12, 1935.

38. "Liaison Officers of 5 Southern States Map Housing Plans," *Nashville Tennessean*, August 23, 1934; "$10,000,000 More for Housing; "Government to Start Buying Land at Once for White Housing Project," *Nashville Tennessean*, May 15, 1935; "Big Cases Pend as US Justices Meet in New Quarters," *Nashville Tennessean*, October 7, 1935. City officials' willingness to negotiate with landowners meant that Nashville was not embroiled in the lawsuits pending against other city governments; these claimants argued that this was an example of eminent domain by the federal government, which was surely unconstitutional. The public housing planners in other places eventually get around this by agreeing

that the federal government will never condemn any property. That responsibility will fall to local governments; "Shift in Federal Policy Cuts Cases in Supreme Court," *Nashville Tennessean*, March 6, 1936.

39. The single-story structures would be for the 51 two-room apartments and 257 three-room apartments. The two-story townhomes would be for 85 four-room dwellings and 49 five-room houses; "Government to Start Buying Land at Once for White Housing Project," *Nashville Tennessean*, May 15, 1935; "Work to Begin Soon on Nashville's $3,200,000 White Housing Project," *Nashville Tennessean*, February 23, 1936; Charles W. Smith, "Uncle Sam Supplies Heat, Power, Water for Cheatham Square Dwellers, But Their Monthly Income Must Not Exceed $70," *Nashville Tennessean*, September 19, 1937.

40. "Reported $3,500,000 Housing Grant May Be Answer to Petition in 1933," *Nashville Tennessean*, May 29, 1935; "Slum Clearance Should Be Lasting Drive, Says Ickes," *Nashville Tennessean*, October 30, 1935; "Housing Plans Here Altered to Meet Costs," *Nashville Tennessean*, January 24, 1936; "Work to Begin Soon on Nashville's $3,200,000 White Housing Project," *Nashville Tennessean*, February 23, 1936.

41. "Slum Clearance Building Begins," *Nashville Tennessean*, February 18, 1936; "Bids Rejected on Low-Cost Housing Work," *Nashville Tennessean*, July 22, 1936.

42. "Nashville Leader in Building Boom Sweeping Over South," *Nashville Tennessean*, September 11, 1936.

43. "Bids Rejected on Low Cost Housing Work," *Nashville Tennessean*, July 22, 1936; "Dallas Firm Low Bidder for Local Housing Project," *Nashville Tennessean*, March 17, 1937.

44. The federal government passed the nation's first minimum wage act in October 1938. They set it at $0.25 per hour. That meant a minimum wage worker who worked forty hours a week, five days a week—no sick time, no vacation days—earned ten dollars a week or $43 a month or $520 a year. None of them could afford to live in Cheatham Place either. Another way of calculating this: in January 1938, the city of Nashville employed 2,622 people, and it paid out $284,940 in wages. That is an average of $108.67 per employee. Now, yes, some employees earned considerably more than that, but that means that many employees earned much less than that. Cheatham Place would have been out of their reach as well; "History of Federal Minimum Wage Rates Under the Fair Labor Standards Act, 1938–2009," Wage and Hour Division, https://www.dol.gov/agencies/whd/minimum-wage/history/chart; Jonathan Grossman, "Fair Labor Standards Act of 1938: Maximum Struggle for a Minimum Wage," US Department of Labor, https://www.dol.gov/general/aboutdol/history/flsa1938; United States Department of Labor Bureau of Labor Statistics, "Employment and Pay Rolls of the City of Nashville and

Davidson County, Tennessee, 1929 through 1938," *State, County and Municipal Survey Employment Pay Rolls 1929 through 1938* (Washington, DC: Labor Statistics Bureau, 1939) 7; Charles W. Smith, "Uncle Sam Supplies Heat, Power, Water for Cheatham Square Dwellers, But Their Monthly Income Must Not Exceed $70," *Nashville Tennessean*, September 19, 1937.

45. Editorial, "Going, Going– ," *Nashville Tennessean*, October 11, 1938; "City Will Ask for $12,000,000 Housing Fund," *Nashville Tennessean*, November 10, 1938.

46. "Cheatham Place Housing Project Dedicated," *Nashville Tennessean*, March 7, 1938.

47. "US Did Not Begin Low Cost Housing Until World War," *Nashville Tennessean*, March 6, 1938; "Housing Plan up to Council," *Nashville Tennessean*, May 23, 1938; Editorial, "Around the Mulberry Bush," *Nashville Tennessean*, October 18, 1938; "Nashville House Authority Urged," *Nashville Tennessean*, September 2, 1938; Editorial, "Why the Stupor?" *Nashville Tennessean*, September 4, 1938.

48. "Gerald Gimre Given Leave," *Nashville Tennessean*, October 28, 1938.

49. "City Will Ask for $12,000,000 Housing Fund," *Nashville Tennessean*, November 10, 1938.

50. "Housing Body Applies Today for Charter," *Nashville Tennessean*, November 7, 1938. Mayor Thomas Cummings angered many people around Nashville by naming his friends and cronies to the first Nashville Housing Authority board. At least one of the new board members had recently spoken against public housing. Three of them were known to support Roosevelt's political opponents. Several members of the board were bankers, others worked for the mortgage industry. J. C. Napier, a highly respected member of the Black community and the only Black member of the board, was over eighty years old and too ill to attend most meetings. Labor representatives, local politicians, public housing advocates, and Senator Kenneth D. McKellar all came out against the board. McKellar even told Cummings that Nashville would not receive any public funds until the entire board resigned and new members were named. Caving to the pressure, the entire board resigned on January 12. When he heard the NHA had resigned, Senator McKellar predicted that Nashville would soon receive money for slum clearance and housing projects. He met with US Housing Administrator Nathan Straus that afternoon. Cummings named a new housing authority the afternoon of January 18. Though none of them were recipients of public assistance, they were a better cross-section of Nashville life and less likely to profit from the construction or maintenance of public housing; "Housing Body Applies Today for Charter," *Nashville Tennessean*, November 7, 1938; "City Will Ask for $12,000,000 Housing Fund," *Nashville Tennessean*, November 10, 1938; "Mayor, Foley Said Planning Housing Trip," *Nashville Tennessean*, December 16, 1938; "Mayor, Foley Go

to Capital Over Housing," *Nashville Tennessean*, December 19, 1938; Mayor Silent on M'Kellar, Housing Meet," *Nashville Tennessean*, December 21, 1938; Editorial, "The Housing Impasse," *Nashville Tennessean*, January 8, 1939; "Politics Is Responsible for Resignation of 5 Authority Members, Mayor Charges," *Nashville Tennessean*, January 13, 1939; B. N. Timmons, "Housing Funds Seen Available for New Board," *Nashville Tennessean*, January 13, 1939; "Meet for New Housing Group Slated Today," *Nashville Tennessean*, January 19, 1939.

51. "City Will Ask for $12,000,000; B. N. Timmons, "'Belt' to Stop Slums Spread Here Planned," *Nashville Tennessean*, November 15, 1938, Bascom N. Timmons, "Housing Funds Lost to City; Bid 'Too Late,' *Nashville Tennessean*, December 9, 1938; "M'Kellar Says Housing Fund Hope Not Gone," *Nashville Tennessean*, December 10, 1938; "The Old Cow's Tail," *Nashville Tennessean*, December 10, 1938.

52. "Single Unit Dwelling Unit Abandoned by Board," *Nashville Tennessean*, April 8, 1939.

53. "Meet for New Housing Group Slated Today," *Nashville Tennessean*, January 19, 1939; "Mayor to Fly to Washington," *Nashville Tennessean*, March 27, 1939; "Single Unit Dwelling Unit Abandoned by Board," *Nashville Tennessean*, April 8, 1939; "More Housing Money Is Asked," *Nashville Tennessean*, June 3, 1939; Editorial, "Shoulder to the Wheel," *Nashville Tennessean*, June 30, 1939; "Housing Bids Planned Jan. 1," *Nashville Tennessean*, October 4, 1939; "Comfort on Low Incomes," *Nashville Tennessean*, March 18, 1940.

54. Ernest Lindley, "If World War Doesn't Come," *Nashville Tennessean*, April 26, 1939; B. N. Timmons, "City's Housing Fund Increase Chances Hurt," *Nashville Tennessean*, July 25, 1939.

55. "$98,000 Check Received Here for Slum Clearance Projects," *Nashville Tennessean*, September 1, 1939; "Housing Bids Planned Jan. 1," *Nashville Tennessean*, October 4, 1939; "Straus to Help Get More Cash," *Nashville Tennessean*, December 8, 1939.

56. Harry McEwen, "Housing Project Urged to Replace Slums Near Capitol," *Nashville Tennessean*, April 30, 1940.

57. E. Pluribus Unum, "Visitor Finds Capitol 'Slovenly,' Needing 'Face Lifting,'" *Nashville Tennessean*, January 13, 1939.

58. Reuel Hemdahl, *Urban Renewal* (New York: Scarecrow Press, 1959) 272.

59. *Marshall-Bruce-Polk Co.'s Nashville City Directory, 1924* (Nashville, TN: Marshall-Bruce-Polk Company, 1924), 814.

60. Davidson County, Tennessee, Death certificate no. 22701 (1933), Gertrude Prince Claybrooks, Tennessee Department of Public Health, Nashville.

61. Death certificate no. 22701 (1933).

62. Death certificate no. 22701 (1933).

CHAPTER 3

1. Betsy Rowlett, "Blighted Area Called 'Outrageous' Slum," *Nashville Tennessean*, April 24, 1949.
2. Rowlett, "Blighted Area."
3. "US to Speed Housing Here," *Nashville Tennessean*, February 8, 1941; "Housing Funds 'About Gone,'" *Nashville Tennessean*, April 22, 1941; Editorial, "Quiet Creation," *Nashville Tennessean*, April 22, 1941.
4. "Flag Brings $100,000 at War Bond Auction," *Nashville Tennessean*, September 24, 1942.
5. Marshalltown, Iowa, Birth certificate, Delayed Birth Records, no. 070013 (1942), Gerald Gimre, Iowa State Department of Health, Nashville; *Register of Commissioned and Warrant Officers of the United States Naval Reserve* (Washington: United States Government Printing Office, 1943), 527; *Register of Commissioned and Warrant Officers of the United States Naval Reserve* (Washington: United States Government Printing Office, 1944), 463; *Register of Commissioned and Warrant Officers of the United States Naval Reserve* (Washington: United States Government Printing Office, 1951), 371; "Gerald Gimre," *Des Moines Register*, August 15, 1991.
6. "Nashville Scouts' Own Page," *Nashville Tennessean*, December 10, 1933; "The Nashville Scouts' Own Page," *Nashville Tennessean*, November 3, 1934; The Tennessee Industrial School had been founded in the 1880s after a cholera epidemic orphaned a number of Nashville's children, more than there were prospective adoptive parents. Though it began as a private enterprise, the state took it over in 1885. The residents could live on the campus until they turned twenty-one. By the 1930s, there were six boys' dorms and three girls' dorms; Tennessee State Planning Commission, *Tennessee State Industrial School* (Nashville: Tennessee State Planning Commission, 1937) 1–23, 50–59, https://hdl.handle.net/2027/mdp.39015068445108; The Nashville Rotary Club organized the first Boy Scout troop at the Tennessee Industrial School in 1923. By the time Gimre moved to Nashville and started working with the boys at the school, there were seven troops there serving two hundred Scouts; "T.I.S. Owes Its Scouting to the Rotary Club," *Nashville Tennessean*, October 2, 1938.
7. "Nashville Scouts' Own Page," *Nashville Tennessean*, August 19, 1934.
8. "With the Nashville Scout Troops," *Nashville Tennessean Magazine*, October 17 1937; "The Nashville Scouts," *Nashville Tennessean Magazine*, December 26, 1937; With the Nashville Scouts," *Nashville Tennessean*, January 23, 1938; "Boxwell Renamed Scout Group Head," *Nashville Tennessean*, January 27, 1938; "With the Nashville Scouts," *Nashville Tennessean*, March 27, 1938; "With the Boy Scouts," *Nashville Tennessean*, April 17, 1938; "With the Boy Scouts," *Nashville*

Tennessean, May 22, 1938; "Officials of Boy Scout Council," *Nashville Tennessean*, January 23, 1941.

9. "Youths' Future Lies in Training, Courtenay Says," *Nashville Tennessean*, January 24, 1947.

10. "US Scout President Praises Nashville Council, Leaders," *Nashville Tennessean*, January 18, 1945; "Youths' Future Lies in Training, Courtenay Says," *Nashville Tennessean*, January 24, 1947; "L. B. Stevens Heads Boy Scout Council," *Nashville Tennessean*, January 9, 1948; "6790 Boy Scouts Active in Midstate," *Nashville Tennessean*, September 26, 1951; "Active Scouts Praise Program," *Nashville Tennessean*, January 23, 1952; "Boy Scouts of America, Forty-Fifth Annual Report" (Washington: United States Government Printing Office, 1954) 246.

11. Leslie G. Boxwell, "Necessity of a State Highway Department," *Tennessee Agriculture* 3, no. 1 (January 1914), 54; "Boxwell Primer, People and Positions, Leslie G. Boxwell," VirtualBoxwell.org, copyright 2020, http://www.virtualboxwell.org/primer/pp_boxwell.php; "Leslie G. Boxwell, Nashville, Tenn," *Men of the South* (New Orleans: Southern Biographical Association, 1922) 634; "Funeral Tuesday for L. G. Boxwell," *Nashville Tennessean*, September 25, 1960.

12. Boxwell, "Necessity of a State Highway Department," 54; "Leslie G. Boxwell," *Tennessee. The Volunteer State, 1769–1923*, volume 4 (Nashville: S.J. Clarke Publishing Company, 1923), 647–48; "Boxwell," *Men of the South*, 634; "Boxwell Primer, People and Positions, Leslie G. Boxwell"; "Funeral Tuesday for L. G. Boxwell," *Nashville Tennessean*, September 25, 1960.

13. "Boxwell Primer, People and Positions, Leslie G. Boxwell."

14. "Canker at the Heart," *Nashville Tennessean*, November 27, 1945.

15. Dollye Matthews, interview by the author, Bolton's Spicy Chicken and Fish, Nashville, TN, February 20, 2020.

16. "Negro Shot by Two Men Believed to Be Dying," *Nashville Tennessean*, September 13, 1936; "Negro Shot by Operators of Lunch Wagon," *Nashville Tennessean*, September 14, 1936; "Negro Shot by Operators of Lunch Wagon Improves," *Nashville Tennessean*, September 14, 1936.

17. "Nashville's Classified Business Director," *Nashville Globe*, May 3, 1940; "Officers Probing Hold-Up, Break-Ins," *Nashville Tennessean*, November 8, 1940.

18. *Marshall-Bruce-Polk Co.'s Nashville City Directory, 1940*, (Nashville, TN: Marshall-Bruce-Polk Company, 1940), 1427–30.

19. "Negro Argument Leads to Killing," *Nashville Tennessean*, January 18, 1941; "Springer," *Nashville Tennessean*, January 20, 1941; "Negro Indicted," *Nashville Tennessean*, January 29, 1941; Davidson County, Tennessee, Death certificate no. 370 (1941), Roscoe Springer, Tennessee Department of Public Health, Nashville.

20. Nelson, Winling, Marciano, Connolly, et al., "Mapping Inequality."

21. "Personals," *Nashville Globe*, August 4, 1944.

22. *Marshall-Bruce-Polk 1931*, 346; Davidson County, Tennessee, Marriage certificate no. 52946 (1934), Prince-Tillman, Tennessee Division of Vital Statistics, Nashville; "Real Estate Transfers," *Nashville Tennessean*, July 18, 1939.

23. Davidson County, Tennessee, death certificate no. 20878.

24. Davidson County, Tennessee, death certificate no. 20878; "Three Local Draft Boards List Names, Classifications," *Nashville Tennessean*, August 19, 1943; "How TB Kills," Médecins Sans Frontières (September 28, 2000), accessed November 18, 2020, www.msf.org/how-tb-kills.

25. *Minutes, Davidson County Tuberculosis Hospital* (December 1, 1939–April 1, 1949), 1142, Metropolitan Government Archives, Nashville Public Library, Nashville, Tennessee.

26. 9 *Minutes, Davidson County Tuberculosis Hospital*, 1148, 1151, 1155.

27. P. C. Hopewell, "Tuberculosis in the United States before, during and after World War II," *Tuberculosis and War: Lessons Learned from World War II*, 43 (2018): 179–87; "Fewer Deaths from 'TB' Reported for Tennessee in 1945," *Nashville Globe*, December 6, 1946.

28. "Health Department History, 1926–1960," *TN Department of Health*, https://www.tn.gov/health/history-of-public-health-in-tennessee/1926-1960.html.

29. T. V. Woodring, "The Problem of Tuberculosis," *Nashville Glove*, October 12, 1945; "Negroes Do Not Have More 'TB' than White, Report," *Nashville Globe*, April 5, 1946.

30. "1,500,000 City, Rural Homes a Year Urged to Beat Disease, Crime," *Nashville Tennessean*, August 2, 1945; "Truman Appeal Fails on Housing Measure," *Nashville Tennessean*, July 26, 1946; "Truman Signs 'Teeny Weeny' Measure for Housing Aid, Repeats Earlier Charges," *Nashville Tennessean*, July 2, 1948.

31. Frank Eleazer, "Smelly, Rat-Ridden Slums near Capitol Gag 'Sensitive' Senators on Housing Tour," *Nashville Tennessean*, April 20, 1949.

32. "Housing Survey in City Slated to Start Monday," *Nashville Tennessean*, January 6, 1949.

33. Charles L. Fontenay, "Capitol Area Still in Running for Auditorium," *Nashville Tennessean*, January 24, 1950.

34. "Confab Today on Slum Issue," *Nashville Tennessean*, April 29, 1949; "State Speeding Slum Appraisals," *Nashville Tennessean*, June 14, 1949.

35. Williamson County, Tennessee, Marriage certificate no. 512 (1944), Prince-Bridges, Tennessee Division of Vital Statistics, Nashville.

36. Davidson County, Tennessee, Death certificate no. 22361 (1934), Sam L. Bridges, Tennessee Department of Public Health, Nashville; *Marshall-Bruce-Polk 1940*, 114, 133; *Marshall-Bruce-Polk Co.'s Nashville City Directory, 1942*, (Nashville, TN: Marshall-Bruce-Polk Company, 1942), 104, 120; *Marshall-Bruce-Polk Co.'s Nashville City Directory, 1943*, (Nashville, TN: Marshall-Bruce-Polk Company, 1943), 103; "Legal Notices," *Nashville Globe*, August 4, 1944.

37. *Marshall-Bruce-Polk Co.'s Nashville City Directory, 1946*, (Nashville, TN: Marshall-Bruce-Polk Company, 1946), 428, 711; *Marshall-Bruce-Polk Co.'s Nashville City Directory, 1947*, (Nashville, TN: Marshall-Bruce-Polk Company, 1947), 438.

38. "Fourth and Cedar Business Area May Not Be Resettled," *Nashville Globe*, March 15, 1946.

39. "City Council Faced with Hard Decision," *Nashville Globe*, March 22, 1946.

40. Charles L. Fontenay, "Auditorium Foes Branded 'Selfish and Short-sighted,'" *Nashville Tennessean*, April 29, 1949.

41. Charles L. Fontenay, "All Bond Issues Approved," *Nashville Tennessean*, May 6, 1949.

42. "House Approves Slum Clearance," *Nashville Tennessean*, June 29, 1949; "Beautification Nearing for Capitol District," *Nashville Tennessean*, July 3, 1949.

43. "Federal Aid Denied Race-Barring Projects," *Nashville Tennessean*, December 3, 1949; Charles L. Fontenay, "Race Rule Won't Hit City Housing," *Nashville Tennessean*, December 3, 1949; "City Gets Funds for Capitol Hill from US Today," *Nashville Tennessean*, January 19, 1950.

44. "Historical Census of Housing Tables Home Values," *Census of Housing*, https://www.census.gov/hhes/www/housing/census/historic/values.html; Nellie Kenyon, "State Acquires All Properties in Capital Area," *Nashville Tennessean*, March 28, 1950.

45. "What Theater Men are Doing: News From Live Exhibitors All over the Country," *Motography* vol. 18 (November 3, 1917): 934; "Bijou Theater, Nashville, Tenn., the Equal of Any Colored Theater in the Country; Shows Vaudeville and Moving Pictures and Books through the Mutual Amusement Circuit," *Nashville Globe*, December 6, 1918; Eric Ledell Smith, "Bijou Theater," *African American Theater Buildings: an Illustrated Historical Directory, 1900–1955* (New York: McFarland, 2011), 202; "Bijou Theater," *Trials, Triumphs, and Transformations*, http://digital.mtsu.edu/cdm/singleitem/collection/p15838coll7/id/124/rec/1; Gabriel A. Briggs, *The New Negro in the Old South* (New Brunswick, NJ: Rutgers University Press, 2015) 46–47; Lovett, *The African-American History of Nashville Tennessee*, 108, 160.

46. Gene Graham, "Capitol Hill Project Gets Council Nod," *Nashville Tennessean*, April 30, 1952; Daniel R. Mandelker, "The Comprehensive Planning Requirement in Urban Renewal," *University of Pennsylvania Law Review* 116, no. 1 (November 1967): 44–54.

47. Bill Purcell, interview by the author, Belcher, Sykes, Harrington LLC, Nashville, TN, March 2015.

48. Gene Graham, "Group of Owners Threatens Action on 'Hill' Project," *Nashville Tennessean*, May 13, 1952; "Decision Delayed on Hill Property," *Nashville Tennessean*, May 22, 1952; Nat Caldwell, "Restoring Slums an Unequal Deal," *Nashville Tennessean*, June 20, 1952.

49. "Bijou Theater, Construction in Front of Theater, 1957 July 17," Metropolitan Nashville/Davidson County Archives, Nashville Public Library, http://digital.library.nashville.org/cdm/ref/collection/nr/id/5114.

50. At his death, Thomas was divorced with a young son, Thomas Edward Prince Jr. The boy went to live with Dorothy Wright, Thomas's only full sister. A few years later, Dorothy divorced her husband and moved to Chicago where she remarried. Presumably Thomas Prince Jr. went with her.

51. "Woman Bound Over on Murder Charge," *Nashville Tennessean*, June 28, 1949.

52. "Woman Bound Over"; Davidson County, Tennessee, Death certificate no. 49-11984 (1949), Thomas Edward Prince, Tennessee Department of Public Health, Nashville; "Woman Seeks Pardon in Manslaughter Case," *Nashville Tennessean*, April 3, 1952; In September 1952, just a few months after the housemate finished her sentence for Thomas Prince's death, the housemate was charged as an accessory to murder in another altercation, though this one happened in a tavern rather than her kitchen. She had a pistol in her purse, and a man tried to wrestle it away from her. Another man, presumably her friend, shot her attacker; "2 Are Charged in Pistol Death," *Nashville Tennessean*, September 8, 1952.

53. Like Mattie Hicks, Caroline Bridges had some powerful connections among Black Nashville's elite. Her lawyer was Z. Alexander Looby, the civil rights attorney who would be a critical part of the coming struggles for equality in Nashville.

54. *Marshall-Bruce-Polk Co.'s Nashville City Directory, 1951,* (Nashville, TN: Marshall-Bruce-Polk Company, 1951), 123, 578, 758; Davidson County, Tennessee, Circuit Court Minutes, p. 276 (1953), Circuit Court Clerk, Nashville.

CHAPTER 4

1. *Marshall-Bruce-Polk Co.'s Nashville City Directory, 1953,* (Nashville, TN: Marshall-Bruce-Polk Company, 1953), 1106.

2. *Marshall-Bruce-Polk 1953,* 1106.

3. "Hattie Moseley Austin, Founder of Hattie's Chicken Shack," Saratoga.com, undated, https://www.saratoga.com/aboutsaratoga/history/hattie-moseley-austin, accessed Nov. 20, 2020; "Clinton Negroes Bombed," *Nashville Tennessean*, February 15, 1957; Mike Epstein, "Chicken Shacks," *Forgotten New York*, December 21, 2004, https://forgotten-ny.com/2004/12/chicken-shacks-ken-clucky-fried-imitators-around-town-by-mike-epstein-of-satanslaundromat; Mike Sula, "The First Family of Fried Chicken: How Harold's Chicken Shack Grew from a Mom-and-Pop Stand to a Chain 62 Strong and Still Expanding," *Chicago Reader*, April 13, 2006, https://www.chicagoreader.

com/chicago/the-first-family-of-fried-chicken/Content?oid=921815; Kevin Starr, *Golden Dreams: California in an Age of Abundance, 1950–1963* (New York: Oxford University Press, 2009) 386; Victoria Joshua, "Chicago's Harold's Chicken Shack: History Behind the Taste," *Black Chicago Eats*, August 24, 2016, http://blackchicagoeats.com/haroldschickenshack; "Jimmy's Chicken Shack Harlem, NY, 1930–1980s," *Harlem World*, March 24, 2018, https://www.harlemworldmagazine.com/jimmys-chicken-shack-harlem-ny-1930-1980s; Justin McNelley, "Chicken Shack in Luverne Named One of Alabama's Best," *WSFA12 News*, July 5, 2018, https://www.wsfa.com/story/38582804/chicken-shack-in-luverne-named-one-of-alabamas-best; Naomi Tomky, "The Maker of Baton Rouge's Best Chicken Also Fought for Civil Rights," *Food and Wine*, December 17, 2018, https://www.foodandwine.com/travel/restaurants/chicken-shack-baton-rouge-civil-rights.

4. Edge, *Foodways*, 2–4, 88–95; Egerton, *Southern Food*, 21–22, 32–33, 36; Edna Lewis, *The Taste of Country Cooking*, 30th Anniversary Edition (New York: Alfred A. Knopf, 2006), 76; Francis Lam, "Edna Lewis and the Black Roots of American Cooking," in *Edna Lewis at the Table with an American Original*, Sara B. Franklin, ed. (Chapel Hill: University of North Carolina Press, 2018), 60.

5. Egerton, *Southern Food*, 242.

6. For more on this, see Aaron Bobrow-Strain, *White Bread: A Social History of the Store-Bought Loaf* (Boston: Beacon Press, 2012).

7. "Eat Lunch at Little Gem," *Nashville Tennessean*, January 6, 1922; "Eat Fried Chicken," *Nashville Tennessean*, August 2, 1922, *Marshall-Bruce-Polk* 1922, 777.

8. Hap Townes, interview with John Egerton, Southern Foodways Alliance, Nashville, TN, July 17, 2006; "History," *Swett's: Fine Food Since 1954*, https://www.swettsrestaurant.com/history; David Swett Jr., interview with John Egerton, Nashville, TN, July 17, 2006, www.southernfoodways.org/interview/swetts.

9. Doris Witt, "Soul Food: Where the Chitterling Hits the (Primal) Pan," in *Eating Culture*, edited by Ron Scapp and Brien Seitz (New York: State University of New York Press, 1998) 258–76.

10. Sheila Bock, "'I Know You Got Soul': Traditionalizing a Contested Cuisine," in *Comfort Food: Meanings and Memories*, edited by Michael Owen Jones and Lucy M. Long (Oxford: University Press of Mississippi, 2017), 165.

11. Lewis, *The Taste of Country Cooking*, xxi.

12. Lam, "Edna Lewis and the Black Roots," 59.

13. Bock, "'I Know You Got Soul,'" 164–69; Kyla Wazana Tompkins, *Racial Indigestion: Eating Bodies in the 19th Century* (New York: New York University Press, 2012) 3–4; Witt, "Soul Food," 258–76.

14. Davidson County, TN, Registration card no. 1054 (1940), Bruce Prince, ancestry.com, May 31, 2020, http://ancestry.com; *Marshall-Bruce-Polk Co.'s Nashville City*

Directory, 1958, (Nashville, TN: Marshall-Bruce-Polk Company, 1958), 187, 758; *Marshall-Bruce-Polk Co.'s Nashville City Directory, 1959*, (Nashville, TN: Marshall-Bruce-Polk Company, 1959), 187, 745; interview with André Prince Jeffries.

15. Interview with André Prince Jeffries.
16. Interview with André Prince Jeffries.
17. Frederick Douglass Opie, *Hog and Hominy: Soul Food from Africa to America* (New York: Columbia University Press, 2008) 100–102.
18. Interview with André Prince Jeffries; Kay West, *Around the Opry Table: A Feast of Recipes and Stories from the Grand Ole Opry* (New York: Center Street, 2007), "Lorrie Morgan."
19. Williamson County, Tennessee, Marriage certificate p. 408 (1953), Burrell-Dobson, Tennessee Division of Vital Statistics, Nashville; Williamson County, Tennessee, Marriage license no. 17 (1954), Prince-Dobson, Tennessee Division of Vital Statistics, Nashville.
20. Williamson County, Tennessee, Marriage license no. 17.
21. Davidson County, Tennessee, Affidavit of death, (2015), Sherron D. Prince, Davidson County, Nashville; Bill Kovach, "Prison Alley's Smell 'Awful,' " *Nashville Tennessean*, June 14, 1962.
22. Nellie Kenyon, "Slum Eradication Will Hold Major Part in City Planning," *Nashville Tennessean*, January 29, 1944; Eugene Dietz, "Survey for Giant City Face Lifting Due in 30 Days," *Nashville Tennessean*, November 13, 1955.
23. Eugene Dietz, "Council to Get Bill Compelling Slum Cleanup," *Nashville Tennessean*, July 3, 1956.
24. Charles Coates, "$35,000 Blaze Hits Hotel Here," *Nashville Tennessean*, September 3, 1958; William Keel, "Rooming House Probes Delayed," *Nashville Tennessean*, September 7, 1958.
25. Eugene Dietz, "Council to Get Bill Compelling Slum Cleanup," *Nashville Tennessean*, July 3, 1956; "City Council Passes 'Soft' Housing Code," *Nashville Tennessean*, December 19, 1956; Eugene Dietz, "Opposition Slight to Housing Code," *Nashville Tennessean*, January 17, 1957; "Housing Agency Gets City Code," *Nashville Tennessean*, January 25, 1957.
26. Advisory Committee on Government Housing Policy and Programs, "Report of the President's Advisory Committee on Government Housing Policies and Programs," HUD User, Office of Policy Development and Research, US Dept. of Housing and Urban Development, December 14, 1953, https://www.huduser.gov/portal/sites/default/files/pdf/President-Advisory-Committee-Dec14.pdf; "Longer Loan Key to Housing Plan," *Nashville Tennessean*, December 16, 1953, 6; "Public Housing Gets New Look," *Nashville Tennessean*, January 26, 1954; "Housing Bill Signing Slated," *Nashville Tennessean*, August 2, 1954.

27. Albert Cason, "Housing Authority Operates 4503 Units," *Nashville Tennessean*, April 23, 1955; Eugene Dietz, "Survey for Giant City Face Lifting Due in 30 Days," *Nashville Tennessean*, November 13, 1955; Bruce Gourley, "Baptists and the American Civil War: April 11, 1864," *Baptist and the American Civil War*, April 11, 2014, http://civilwarbaptists.com/thisdayinhistory/1864-april-11; Lovett, *The African-American History*, 76, 79–84, 174–75; Robert, *Nashville and Her Trade*, 47; Neil Websdale, *Policing the Poor: From Slave Plantation to Public Housing* (Boston: Northeastern University Press, 2001), 51–52.

28. Eugene Dietz, "Council Acts Tuesday on 2200-Acre Project," *Nashville Tennessean*, June 28, 1956; Eugene Dietz, "What Other Areas Will Be Renewed?" *Nashville Tennessean*, July 1, 1956; Eugene Dietz, "Council Grants Urban Survey," *Nashville Tennessean*, September 5, 1956.

29. W. Y. Draper, Letter to the Editor, *Nashville Tennessean*, September 20, 1956.

30. Eugene Dietz, "US Approves Urban Renewal Plan in County," *Nashville Tennessean*, October 18, 1957.

31. Lois Laycook, "West Asks Talk with President," *Nashville Tennessean*, March 26, 1957; Lois Laycook, "West Says Cuts Would Cripple War on Slums," *Nashville Tennessean*, March 27, 1957; "Mayor Sees Full Urban Renewal," *Nashville Tennessean*, March 28, 1957; "Eisenhower, West to Discuss Renewal," *Nashville Tennessean*, April 6, 1957; "Blight Fund Talk Cheers Mayors," *Nashville Tennessean*, April 9, 1957; "County Plans Family Shift," *Nashville Tennessean*, April 20, 1957.

32. "House Ups Cash for Reclamation," *Nashville Tennessean*, May 10, 1957; "Pact Reached on Housing Bill," *Nashville Tennessean*, June 28, 1957; "AMA Says Fund Curb to Kill Urban Renewal," *Nashville Tennessean*, July 26, 1957; "FHA Reaffirms Renewal Aims," *Nashville Tennessean*, August 10, 1957; "President Boosts Federal Housing," *Nashville Tennessean*, December 25, 1957; "Senate Upholds Housing Veto," *Nashville Tennessean*, August 13, 1959; "The President Is Challenged," *Nashville Tennessean*, August 21, 1959; J. W. Davis, "Housing Bill Veto Dared," *Nashville Tennessean*, August 28, 1959; Editorial, "Arrogant Housing Bill Veto Is Contempt of Congress," *Nashville Tennessean*, September 5, 1959; "Third Housing Bill Signed by President," *Nashville Tennessean*, September 24, 1959.

33. "Cities Urban Renewal Will Begin Monday," *Nashville Tennessean*, May 2, 1958.

34. Rose French, "Longtime Inspector Saw Housing Change," *Nashville Tennessean*, June 24, 2003; William Keel, "Urban Renewal in Nashville Leads Nation," *Nashville Tennessean*, October 5, 1958.

35. "Urban Renewal Share by City: $500,000," *Nashville Tennessean*, July 7, 1959; "East Nashville Clearance Set," *Nashville Tennessean*, October 17, 1959; "Revamp Start Set for E. Nashville," *Nashville Tennessean*, April 13, 1960; "Renewal Called Boon to City," *Nashville Tennessean*, April 20, 1960.

36. David Halberstam, "Integrate Counters—Mayor," *Nashville Tennessean*, April 20, 1960; "Renewal Called Boon to City," *Nashville Tennessean*, April 20, 1960.

37. Halberstam, "Integrate Counters—Mayor."

38. *Marshall-Bruce-Polk Co.'s Nashville City Directory, 1956*, (Nashville, TN: Marshall-Bruce-Polk Company, 1956), 709; Davidson County, Tennessee, Circuit Court Minutes, p. 439–41 (1956), Circuit Court Clerk, Nashville.

39. Circuit Court Minutes, p. 439–41.

40. Circuit Court Minutes, p. 439–41.

41. *Marshall-Bruce-Polk 1959*, 250; *Marshall-Bruce-Polk Co.'s Nashville City Directory, 1961*, (Nashville, TN: Marshall-Bruce-Polk Company, 1961), 787.

42. Williamson County, Tennessee, Marriage record, p. 109 (1962), Baker-Prince, Tennessee Division of Vital Statistics, Nashville.

43. "Dobson," *Nashville Tennessean*, September 1, 1966; Robertson County, Tennessee, Marriage record, p. 167 (1975), Tennessee Division of Vital Statistics, Nashville.

44. "Girl, 16, Killed Taking Lesson in Gun Roulette," *Nashville Tennessean*, May 30, 1951; "Motorist Indicted in Traffic Fatality," *Nashville Tennessean*, June 13, 1951; Davidson County, Tennessee, Death certificate no. 51-10175 (1951), Lula Mays Dobson, Tennessee Department of Public Health, Nashville.

45. "Girl, 16, Killed"; "Motorist Indicted in Traffic Fatality"; Davidson County, Tennessee, Death certificate no. 51-10175.

46. Davidson County, Tennessee, Death certificate no. 60-03141.

47. Davidson County, Tennessee, Death certificate no. 60-03141.

48. "Prince," *Nashville Tennessean*, February 19, 1960.

CHAPTER 5

1. Beth McKibbon, "Nashville's Helen's Hot Chicken Finally Arrives Downtown on Edgewood Ave," *Eater Atlanta*, February 24, 2020, https://atlanta.eater.com/2020/2/24/21150534/helens-hot-chicken-opens-edgewood-avenue-downtown-atlanta; "Tiny Restaurants Pack a Punch," *Tennessean*, September 18, 2014, https://www.tennessean.com/story/life/food/2014/09/19/riverside-grillshack-helens-hot-chicken-pack-punch/15787049; Jen Todd, "Helen's Hot Chicken to Open Saturday," *Tennessean*, July 1, 2014, https://www.tennessean.com/story/life/food/2014/07/01/helens-hot-chicken-open-saturday-germantown/11893387.

2. Chris Chamberlain, "Helen's Hot Chicken Opening Location on Jefferson Street," *Nashville Scene*, October 23, 2014, https://www.nashvillescene.com/food-drink/article/13056555/helens-hot-chicken-opening-location-on-jefferson-street.

3. Frank Ritter, "Negro Firms' Aid Need Cited," *Nashville Tennessean*, March 8,

1968; Tim Ghianni, "Rekindling the Flame that Was Jefferson Street," *Tennessee Ledger*, 39, no. 30, https://www.tnledger.com/editorial/ArticleEmail.aspx?id=82791.

4. Popular lore has long held that the area was named for the white slaveholder John Hadley, and in 2018, some activists pushed to have the park there renamed for Malcolm X. Local historian Betsy Phillips dug into the old city directories and census records to debunk that myth; Betsy Phillips, "Hadley Park's Name Is Already Subversive," *Nashville Scene*, May 31, 2018, https://www.nashvillescene.com/news/pith-in-the-wind/article/21007317/hadley-parks-name-is-already-subversive; Reavis L. Mitchell, Jr., "Jefferson Street," *Leaders of Afro-American Nashville*, 1999, http://www.tnstate.edu/library/documents/jeffst.pdf; James A. Hoobler, *A Guide to Historic Nashville, Tennessee* (Charleston: History Press, 2008), 103, 133; Tennessee State Library and Archives, "Nashville—Jefferson Street," *Mapping the Destruction of Tennessee's African American Neighborhoods*, accessed May 31, 2020, https://www.arcgis.com/apps/MapSeries/index.html?appid=8dba65584072450ca8928a5f3408373f; "Fisk University," *The Cultural Landscape Foundation*," https://tclf.org/fisk-university.

5. Mitchell Jr., "Jefferson Street"; "Hadley Park," *Cultural Landscape Foundation*, https://tclf.org/hadley-park; Phillips, "Hadley Park's Name Is Already Subversive."

6. Historic American Buildings Survey, "Adolphus Heiman House, 900 Jefferson Street, Northwest, Nashville, Davidson County, TN," 1933, https://www.loc.gov/item/tn0020.

7. Historic American Building Survey, "Worker's House, 1724 North Jefferson Street, Nashville, Davidson County, TN," Survey HABS TN-26, November 1971, https://www.loc.gov/resource/hhh.tn0045.photos; Mitchell Jr., "Jefferson Street."

8. Mitchell Jr., "Jefferson Street."

9. Ghianni, "Rekindling the Flame"; "Etta James—Rocks the House," *Chitlins, Catfish and Deep Southern Fried Soul* (blog), February 27, 2014, http://deepsouthernsoul.blogspot.com/2014/02; Joan Brasher, "Vanderbilt Students Help Preserve Jefferson Street's Musical History," *Vanderbilt News*, February 7, 2018, https://news.vanderbilt.edu/2018/02/07/vanderbilt-students-help-preserve-jefferson-streets-musical-history; Learotha Williams Jr., interview with the author, Farmer's Market, Nashville, TN, February 11, 2020.

10. Ghianni, "Rekindling the Flame"; Bill Kerby and David Thompson, "Spanish Galleons off Jersey Coast or 'We Live off Excess Volume,'" in *Hendrix on Hendrix: Interviews and Encounters with Jimi Hendrix*, Steven Roby, ed. (Chicago: Chicago Review Press, 2012): 56–57.

11. Interview with Learotha Williams Jr.

12. Dwight D. Eisenhower, "State of the Union, 1955," http://www.vlib.us/amdocs/texts/dde1955.htm.

13. "Highway History," US Department of Transportation, Federal Highway Administration," December 18, 2018, https://www.fhwa.dot.gov/interstate/faq.cfm#questions5; David Karas, "Highway to Inequity: The Disparate Impact of the Interstate Highway System on Poor and Minority Communities in American Cities, *New Visions for Public Affairs*, 7 (April 2015): 10.

14. "Ousted Firms Help Sought," *Nashville Tennessean*, April 10, 1964; "US Studying Reports I-40 Isolating Area," *Nashville Tennessean*, October 12, 1967.

15. "I-40 Delay Hearing Today," *Nashville Tennessean*, October 30, 1967.

16. "Ousted Firms Help Sought," *Nashville Tennessean*, April 10, 1964.

17. "Housing Authority to Mark 25 Years," *Nashville Tennessean*, June 28, 1964.

18. Eugene Dietz, "Council Acts Tuesday on 2200-Acre Project," *Nashville Tennessean*, June 28, 1956; Eugene Dietz, "What Other Areas Will Be Renewed?" *Nashville Tennessean*, July 1, 1956.

19. Davidson County, Tennessee, Death certificate no. 60-31219 (1960), Alphonso Prince, Tennessee Department of Public Health, Nashville; *Marshall-Bruce-Polk Co.'s Nashville City Directory, 1960*, (Nashville, TN: Marshall-Bruce-Polk Company, 1960), 1071; *Marshall-Bruce-Polk Co.'s Nashville City Directory, 1962*, (Nashville, TN: Marshall-Bruce-Polk Company, 1962), 982; *Marshall-Bruce-Polk Co.'s Nashville City Directory, 1963*, (Nashville, TN: Marshall-Bruce-Polk Company, 1963), 941; *Marshall-Bruce-Polk Co.'s Nashville City Directory, 1964*, (Nashville, TN: Marshall-Bruce-Polk Company, 1964), 154, 927.

20. 1900 US Census, Williamson County, Tennessee, population schedule, p. 158 (stamped), dwelling 68, family 68, Porter Epps, digital image, Ancestry.com, accessed September 25, 2019, http://ancestry.com; 1910 US Census, Williamson County, Tennessee, population schedule, p. 84 (stamped), dwelling 125, family 158, Wesley Epps, digital image, ancestry.com, accessed November 12, 2019, http://ancestry.com; Williamson County, Tennessee, Marriage License, no. 2019 (1919); 1920 US Census, Davidson County, Tennessee, population schedule, p. 490 (written), dwelling 884, family 956, William P. Winters, digital image, Ancestry.com, accessed November 12, 2019, http://ancestry.com; 1920 US Census, Williamson County, Tennessee, population schedule, p. 770 (written), dwelling 73, family 77, Ness Eps, digital image, Ancestry.com, accessed November 12, 2019, http://ancestry.com; Prince-Epps, Tennessee Department of Vital Statistics, Nashville; Williamson County, Tennessee, Chancery Court records, Prince, Will vs. Prince, Eula, 1924, Tennessee State Library and Archives, Nashville.

21. Williamson County, Tennessee, Chancery Court records, Prince, Will.

22. "Marriage Licenses," *Nashville Tennessean*, December 16, 1922; 1930 US Census, Davidson County, Tennessee, population schedule, p. 0058 (written), dwelling

243, family 250, William B. Prince, digital image, Ancestry.com, accessed November 12, 2019, http://ancestry.com; "Real Estate Transfers," *Tennessean*, November 18, 1939; 1940 US Census, Davidson County, Tennessee, population schedule, p. 188 (stamped), dwelling 186, William Prince, digital image, Ancestry.com; accessed November 12, 2019, http://ancestry.com.

23. 1910 US Census, Davidson County, Tennessee, population schedule, p. 9034 (written), dwelling 377, family 389, Charlie Peden, digital image, Ancestry.com, accessed November 12, 2019, http://ancestry.com; *Marshall-Bruce-Polk Co.'s Nashville City Directory, 1918*, (Nashville, TN: Marshall-Bruce-Polk Company, 1918), 482, "A. and I. State Normal Closes," *Nashville Globe*, May 31, 1918; *Marshall-Bruce-Polk 1920*, 456; 1920 US Census, Davidson County, Tennessee, population schedule, p. 25 (stamped), dwelling 217, family 227, Charles P. Peden, digital image, Ancestry.com, accessed November 12, 2019, http://ancestry.com; Nashville Public Schools, *Annual Report of the Public Schools of Nashville, Tennessee, 1924–1925* (Nashville: Ambrose Printing, 1925) 13; "8 Cadet Teachers Given Promotion," *Nashville Tennessean*, July 11, 1924; *Marshall-Bruce-Polk 1924*, 635; "Education Board Adds 54 to List of City Teachers," *Nashville Tennessean*, June 25, 1929; "36 Graduate in A. and I. Normal Exercises Today," *Nashville Tennessean*, June 6, 1932

24. 1930 US Census, Davidson County, Tennessee, population schedule, p. 0058 (written), dwelling 243, family 250, William B. Prince, digital image, Ancestry.com, accessed November 12, 2019, http://ancestry.com; "Real Estate Transfers," *Tennessean*, November 18, 1939; 1940 US Census, Davidson County, Tennessee, population schedule, p. 188 (stamped), dwelling 186, William Prince, digital image, Ancestry.com; accessed November 12, 2019, http://ancestry.com; Williamson County, Tennessee, Chancery Court records, Prince, Will.

25. Williamson County, Tennessee, Chancery Court records, Prince, Will.

26. Williamson County, Tennessee, Chancery Court records, Prince, Will; Thelma Battle, *Natchez Street Revisited*, vol. 1 (Franklin, TN: Williamson County Historical Society, 2016), 193.

27. Sylvia Woods and Family, with Melissa Clark, *Sylvia's Family Soul Food Cookbook: From Hemingway, South Carolina, to Harlem* (New York: William Morrow and Company, 1999) 7–8, 36–37.

28. "US Studying Reports I-40 Isolating Area," *Nashville Tennessean*, October 12, 1967; "Council to Ask I-40 Delay," *Nashville Tennessean*, October 18, 1967.

29. "US Studying Reports I-40 Isolating Area," *Nashville Tennessean*, October 12, 1967; Frank Sutherland, "Group Asks I-40 Delay," *Nashville Tennessean*, October 17, 1967.

30. Sutherland, "Group Asks I-40 Delay;" "Council to Ask I-40 Delay," *Nashville Tennessean*, October 18, 1967; Frank Sutherland, "Suit Threatened to Stall I-40," *Nashville Tennessean*, October 25, 1967; Nelly Kenyon, "Suit to Stop I-40 Filed,"

Nashville Tennessean, October 27, 1940; Frank Ritter, "I-40 Delay Hearing Today," *Nashville Tennessean*, October 30, 1967; Nellie Kenyon, "US Judge Refuses to Enjoy State From Awarding I-40 Pact," *Nashville Tennessean*, November 2, 1967.

31. Tom Ingram, "NAACP Fund Joins Fight to Stall I-40," *Nashville Tennessean*, November 5, 1967; Frank Sutherland and Craven Crowell, *"Nashville Tennessean*, November 10, 1967 ; Jaan Kangilaski, "Court Hears I-40 Case," *Nashville Tennessean*, December 9, 1967; Nashville I-40 Steering Committee v. Buford Ellington, US Court of Appeals for the Sixth Circuit, December 18, 1967, As Amended December 26, 1967; Dolores Smith, "I-40 Work Set to Start in '68," *Nashville Tennessean*, December 19, 1967; Edmund Willingham, "I-40 Approval Stipulates 5 Modifications," *Nashville Tennessean*, February 27, 1968; Rob Elder, "US Aide Says Altering I-40 Would Only Do More Harm," *Nashville Tennessean*, April 12, 1968; Rob Elder, "Shop Deck Over I-40 Urged," *Nashville Tennessean*, May 22, 1968; Lowell K. Bridwell to Flournoy [*sic*] Coles, in *Urban Highways: Hearings Before the Subcommittee on Roads of the Committee on Public Works, United States Senate* (Washington: US Government Printing Office, 1969) 563–64.

32. David Halberstam, "Widow Who'll Lose Home to X-Way Doesn't Like to Think about Moving," *Nashville Tennessean*, March 9, 1958.

33. Reginald Stuart, "Grapevine Talk Not Enough for Uneasy Residents," *Nashville Tennessean*, March 29, 1969.

34. Bill Carey, "Other Side of Revitalization," *Tennessean*, February 19, 1995.

35. Raymond A. Mohl, "Citizen Activism and Freeway Revolts in Memphis and Nashville: The Road to Litigation," *Journal of Urban History* 40, no. 5 (2014): 880.

36. The Otey family raised an additional $1 million in capital to launch a new phase of one arm of their businesses, the Otey Development Company. The purpose of the company was to use capital from African American business leaders to support new African American businesses in Nashville. The family hoped that the company would spur inventive entrepreneurship and keep talented kids in the community. They also planned to build better housing in North Nashville including new apartment complexes in both North and East Nashville, a middle-class subdivision in North Nashville and shopping centers in North Nashville and Edgehill, and all before 1971. The initiative was led by Inman Otey, Flem Otey III's uncle. Inman was Nashville's first Black real estate agent. He'd also helped launch the Community Federal Savings and Loan Association and fought for the establishment of the Phyllis Wheatley Home for the Aged, an eighty-five-unit apartment complex for the older Nashvillians being displaced by urban renewal and highway construction; Frank Sutherland, "Otey Sets Program to Cost $68 million," *Nashville Tennessean*, August 23, 1968; "House Resolution 369: A Resolution to Recognize Inman

Otey Sr. on the Occasion of His Retirement," http://www.legislature.state. tn.us/bills/105/Bill/HR0369.PDF; William T. Robinson Jr., "Tribute to Rev. Inman Otey Sr.," *PRIDE Publishing Group*, December 8, 2016, https://www. pridepublishinggroup.com/pride/2016/12/08/25373; Pat Welch, "Private Housing for Poor Voted," *Nashville Tennessean*, March 29, 1967.

37. Frank Ritter, "Negro Firms' Aid Need Cited," *Nashville Tennessean*, March 8, 1968.

38. Middle Tennessee Business Association, *Operation Northtown* (Nashville: Middle Tennessee Business Association, 1969); Reginald Stuart, "Battered by Sixties, Black Businessmen Hope for Brighter Days," *Nashville Tennessean*, January 11, 1970.

39. Ritter, "Negro Firms' Aid Need"; Rob Elder, "5 Banks Start Negro Loan Plan," *Nashville Tennessean*, March 30, 1968; Rob Elder, "Study Temporal Trinity, Lent Speaker Urges," *Nashville Tennessean*, April 2, 1968.

40. Charles L. Fontenay, "Interstate Highways: From Paper to Concrete," *Nashville Tennessean*, January 10, 1971.

CHAPTER 6

1. *Marshall-Bruce-Polk Co.'s Nashville City Directory, 1965*, (Nashville, TN: Marshall-Bruce Polk Company, 1965), 940; Kevin Alexander, *Burn the Ice: The American Culinary Revolution and Its End* (New York: Penguin, 2019), 93.

2. "Teacher Honored Twice in 3 Months," *Nashville Tennessean*, August 27, 1964; W. H. Shackleford, "Progressive Club to Choose Queen," *Nashville Tennessean*, November 1, 1953; Alexander, *Burn the Ice*, 93–94.

3. "Nashville Tops Crime List," *Nashville Tennessean*, July 24, 1963; Sarah Taylor, "Pearl Forum Sifts Youth Problems," *Nashville Tennessean*, August 3, 1963.

4. André E. Prince, "Purge This Juvenile Society Blot," *Nashville Tennessean*, July 28, 1963.

5. Alexander, *Burn the Ice*, 94; Evelyn Brooks Higginbotham, *Righteous Discontent: The Women's Movement in the Black Baptist Church, 1880–1920* (Boston, Harvard University Press, 1994), 14–15.

6. "Urban Renewal Cost Cut Seen," *Nashville Tennessean*, December 22, 1960.

7. "Historic Background Research and Ground Penetrating Radar, 26–40; Lizzie Porter Elliott, *Early History of Nashville* (Nashville: Board of Education, 1911), 12.

8. William Keel, "Housing Push Urged by West," *Nashville Tennessean*, December 13, 1950; "NAACP Charges 'Ghettos' Here," *Nashville Tennessean*, March 5, 1962.

9. Keel, "Housing Push Urged by West."

10. William Keel, "Council to Ask Renewal Funds," *Nashville Tennessean*, August 16, 1961; William Keel, "Planning Loan for Downtown Gets Go Ahead," *Nashville Tennessean*, September 20, 1961.

11. Nick Sullivan, "Metro Units Deny Racial Unfairness," *Nashville Tennessean*, June 14, 1966.

12. "5 Units Protest Relocation of Displaced," *Nashville Tennessean*, September 1, 1966; "Edgehill Project Citizens Meet Set," *Nashville Tennessean*, September 10, 1966; "Don't Sell, Edgehill Homeowners Told," *Nashville Tennessean*, September 12, 1966; Frank Ritter, "NHA Vows Edgehill Help," *Nashville Tennessean*, September 14, 1966; W. A. Reed Jr., "Edgehill Group Seeks US Aid," *Nashville Tennessean*, September 20, 1966.

13. Frank Ritter and Pat Welch, "For Greatness, What Does Nashville Need?" *Nashville Tennessean*, August 21, 1966.

14. "5 Units Protest Relocation of Displaced," *Nashville Tennessean*, September 1, 1966; "NHA to Hear Edgehill Urban Renewal Complaints," *Nashville Tennessean*, September 8, 1966.

15. Frank Ritter, "NHA Vows Edgehill Help," *Nashville Tennessean*, September 14, 1966; "University Project Meets Delayed until Election," *Nashville Tennessean*, September 22, 1966.

16. Frank Ritter, "Elderly Pair's Plea Stays NHA Action," August 31, 1967.

17. Rob Elder, "Housing Progress? Yes, But Does It Help the People Who Live There?" *Nashville Tennessean*, November 12, 1967.

18. Edwin H. Mitchell, "'You Did Not Speak for Us . . .'" *Nashville Tennessean*, October 12, 1967.

19. Rob Elder, "Study Temporal Trinity, Lent Speaker Urges," *Nashville Tennessean*, April 2, 1968.

20. "Scouts, School Share Bequests," *Nashville Tennessean*, October 1, 1960.

21. Frank Ritter, "Slum Residents' Cultural Tour Set in 'Silk Stocking District,'" *Nashville Tennessean*, July 12, 1968.

22. "Edgehill Unit Raps Housing," *Nashville Tennessean*, November 6, 1966.

23. Edmund Willingham, "Civil Rights Unit Asks Metro Open Housing," *Nashville Tennessean*, April 11, 1967.

24. Nellie Kenyon and Rob Elder, "Integration Not Goal: NHA," *Nashville Tennessean*, December 10, 1966.

25. "State Unit to Study Open Housing at Meet," *Nashville Tennessean*, December 9, 1966; Frank Ritter, "US Officials Due Here to Discuss Edgehill Problems," *Nashville Tennessean*, March 1, 1967.

26. Bill Preston Jr., "NHA Advised to Revamp Edgehill Plan," *Nashville Tennessean*, July 19, 1967.

27. Elisabeth M. Herlihy, Gerald S. Gimre, and L. Segoe, "The Administration of a Planning Office," National Conference on Planning, (Chicago: American Society of Planning Officials, 1938), 126–27, http://www.archive.org/stream/ proceedingsofconomatirich/proceedingsofconomatirich_djvu.txt.

28. Rob Elder, "Edgehill Project Shift Approved," *Nashville Tennessean*, December 7, 1967; Frank Ritter, "Sherri Myers to Coordinate NHA Project," *Nashville Tennessean*, December 13, 1969.

29. Wayne Whitt, "War Cost Putting Squeeze on Cities," *Nashville Tennessean*, January 21, 1968.

30. Nellie Kenyon, "Eminent Domain Power Abuse Charged to NHA," *Nashville Tennessean*, October 8, 1969; Frank Ritter, "NHA, Mayor's Group at Odds," *Nashville Tennessean*, October 9, 1969; Elain Shannon, "Urban Renewal Results Disastrous: Douglas," *Nashville Tennessean*, November 20, 1969.

31. Elain Shannon, "PAC Petitions for Edgehill Transportation," *Nashville Tennessean*, January 10, 1970; Reginald Stuart, "Battered by Sixties, Black Businessmen Hope for Brighter Days," *Nashville Tennessean*, January 11, 1970; Doug Hall, "Free 3-Day Bus Service Arranged for Edgehill," *Nashville Tennessean*, January 24, 1970; Mike Korpan, "70 Ride Free Buses from Edgehill," *Nashville Tennessean*, January 26, 1970; Doug Hall, "Metro Funds to be Asked for Edgehill Bus Service," *Nashville Tennessean*, February 2, 1970; "NHA Sets Renewal Area Meet," *Nashville Tennessean*, February 11, 1970; Wayne Whit, "Council Should Take Another Look at Edgehill Problems," February 22, 1970.

32. Office of Community Development Evaluation Division, Department of Housing and Urban Development, *The Model Cities Program, A Comparative Analysis of City Response Patterns and Their Relation to Future Urban Policy*, (Washington, DC: Government Printing Office, 1973) 6–10, 80.

33. US Department of Housing and Urban Development, *Citizen Participation in the Model Cities Program* (Washington, DC: US Government Printing Office, 1972), i.

34. US HUD, *Citizen Participation in the Model Cities Program*, 2; Rob Elder, "Model City Office Opens; Aid Urged," *Nashville Tennessean*, March 21, 1968.

35. Rob Elder, "Study Temporal Trinity, Lent Speaker Urges," *Nashville Tennessean*, April 2, 1968.

36. Tom Ingram and Keel Hunt, "Model Cities Director Fired," *Nashville Tennessean*, August 7, 1969.

37. Tom Ingram, "Model Cities Delay Sought," *Nashville Tennessean*, August 12, 1969.

38. Ingram, "Model Cities Delay Sought."

39. Sherry R. Arnstein, "A Ladder of Citizen Participation," *Journal of the American Institute of Planners* 35, no. 4 (July 1969), 216.

40. Doug Hall, "NHA Says Goodby [*sic*] to Retiring Gimre," *Nashville Tennessean*, July 1, 1970.
41. 1930 census; 1940 census.
42. "Mrs. Tucker Rites Today," *Tennessean*, May 22, 1974.
43. "Divorces Filed," *Tennessean*, November 3, 1966; "Death Notices," *Tennessean*, April 28, 1971.
44. Williamson County, Tennessee, Marriage Record, p. 425 (1967), Prince-Satterfield, Tennessee County Marriages 1790–1950, Nashville..
45. *Marshall-Bruce-Polk 1946*, 729; *Marshall-Bruce-Polk 1953*, 712; *Marshall-Bruce-Polk 1958*, 758, 821; *Marshall-Bruce-Polk 1959*, 745, 807.
46. *Polk's Nashville (Davidson County, Tenn.) City Directory 1966* (Detroit: RL Polk and Company, 1966), 968; "Card of Thanks," *Tennessean*, July 22, 1973; "Maudie Prince," *Tennessean*, February 18, 2011.
47. "Prince," *Tennessean*, May 27, 1974; "Prince," *Tennessean*, May 25, 1981; "Prince," *Tennessean*, May 27, 1985.

CHAPTER 7

1. Interview with Dollye Matthews.
2. Gail Williams O'Brien, *The Color of the Law: Race, Violence and Justice in the Post-World War II South* (Chapel Hill: University of North Carolina Press, 1999), 75; US Social Security Applications and Claims Index, no. 410303443, Bolton Francis Polk, digital image, Ancestry.com, accessed December 3, 2019, http://ancesstry.com.
3. O'Brien, *The Color of the Law*, 76–77.
4. O'Brien, *The Color of the Law*, 78–79.
5. Davidson County, Tennessee, Registration card no. 462 (1943), Bolton Francis Polk, United States World War II Draft Registration card, 1943, Ancestry.com, accessed December 3, 2019, http://ancestry.com; National Cemetery Administration, *Nationwide Gravesite Locator*; Social Security Applications and Claims, 1936–2007.
6. *Marshall-Bruce-Polk Co.'s Nashville City Directory, 1950*, (Nashville, TN: Marshall-Bruce-Polk Company, 1950), 739; *Marshall-Bruce-Polk 1951*, 747; *Marshall-Bruce-Polk 1959*, 734; *Polk's Nashville (Davidson County, Tenn.) City Directory 1971* (Detroit: RL Polk and Company, 1971), 784; *Polk's Nashville (Davidson County, Tenn.) City Directory 1972* (Detroit: RL Polk and Company, 1972, 785; *Polk's Nashville (Davidson County, Tenn.) City Directory 1973* (Detroit: RL Polk and Company, 1973), 766.
7. *Polk's Nashville (Davidson County, Tenn.) City Directory 1974* (Detroit: RL Polk and Company, 1974), 633–34; *Polk's Nashville (Davidson County, Tenn.) City Directory*

1975 (Detroit: RL Polk and Company, 1975) 641; *Polk's Nashville (Davidson County, Tenn.) City Directory 1976* (Detroit: RL Polk and Company, 1976), 609, 618.

8. *Polk's Nashville (Davidson County, Tenn.) City Directory 1978* (Detroit: RL Polk and Company, 1978), 125.

9. Interview with André Prince Jeffries; *Polk's 1978*, 115; *Polk's Nashville (Davidson County, Tenn.) City Directory 1979* (Detroit: RL Polk and Company, 1979), 119; Alexander, *Burn the Ice*, 99.

10. "Visitors' Tour Is Our Gain," *Nashville Tennessean*, May 14, 1957.

11. "Dynamic Urban Renewal Urged to Prevent Drab," *Nashville Tennessean*, February 26, 1958; Gene Graham, "Census Figure Perplexing," *Nashville Tennessean*, June 5, 1960.

12. Graham, "Census Figure Perplexing."

13. Graham, "Census Figure Perplexing."

14. Interview with André Prince Jeffries; Alexander, *Burn the Ice*, 98–99.

15. Interview with André Prince Jeffries; "All Tuckered Out," *Tennessean*, November 5, 1978.

16. Interview with André Prince Jeffries; "Prince, Mrs. Wilhelmina Martin," *Tennessean*, August 7, 1980; Alexander, *Burn the Ice*, 98–99; Dave Hoekstra, "Nashville's Original Hot Chicken," *Chicago Sun-Times*, September 10, 2006.

17. *Polk's Nashville (Davidson County, Tenn.) City Directory 1982* (Detroit: RL Polk and Company, 1982), 422, 660; *1983 Nashville (Davidson County, Tenn.) City Directory* (Taylor, MI: R.L. Polk and Company, 1983), 703; Alexander, *Burn the Ice*, 100–101.

18. Interview with André Prince Jeffries; *Polk's 1983*, 153; *1984 Nashville (Davidson County, Tenn.) City Directory* (Taylor, MI: R.L. Polk and Company, 1984), 172.

19. Interview with André Prince Jeffries; *1983 Nashville*, 153; *1984 Nashville*, 172; Eric Babcock and Page La Grone Babcock, "HNC: Nevermind Hot New Country, Here's Nashville Hot Chicken," *No Depression: The Journal of Roots Music*, 42 (October 2002), accessed on March 12, 2020, http://54.214.24.122/article/hnc-nevermind-hot-new-country-heres-hot-nashville-chicken.

20. Interview with André Prince Jeffries; interview with Dollye Matthews.

21. Dave Hoekstra, "Nashville's Original Hot Chicken," *Chicago Sun-Times*, September 10, 2006.

22. Mark Crawford, "The Attraction of Enterprise Zones: Tax Benefits and Incentives for Businesses," *Area Development* (November 2008), February 12, 2020, https://www.areadevelopment.com/siteSelection/nov08/enterprise-zones-cost-effective.shtml.

23. "1980 Ronald Reagan and Jimmy Carter Presidential Debate," Ronald Reagan Presidential Library, Oct. 28, 1980, https://www.reaganlibrary.gov/archives/speech/1980-ronald-reagan-and-jimmy-carter-presidential-debate; Robert

W. Benjamin, "The Kemp-Garcia Enterprise Zone Bill: A New, Less Costly Approach to Urban Redevelopment," *Fordham Law Journal* 9, no. 3 (1981): 659–95.

24. Department of Housing and Urban Development, *The President's National Urban Policy Report*, Washington, DC, 1982, 2.

25. Marsha Vandeberg, "Horton Seeks Downtown Enterprise Zone to Get Federal Urban Aid," *Nashville Tennessean*, December 2, 1980.

26. Vandeberg, "Horton Seeks Downtown Enterprise Zone."

27. Carolyn Shoulders, "Bill Hurts Residents, Citizens' Group Says," *Tennessean*, April 16, 1984; US Congress, House of Representatives, Committee on Banking, Finance and Urban Affairs, *Hearing before the Subcommittee on Housing and Community Development*, 97th Cong., 2nd sess., 1982, 269.

28. "House Backs Limit on Public Housing," *Nashville Tennessean*, June 13, 1986.

29. "Christ Church Vestry Minutes 1976," Christ Church Vestry Minutes, Christ Church Archives, Nashville, TN, May 17, 1971–January 16, 1977, https://954b6047-a-663e912c-s-sites.googlegroups.com/a/christcathedral.org/archives/vestry/1976-VestryMinutes.pdf; "Christ Church Vestry Minutes 1980," Christ Church Vestry Minutes, February 18, 1977–December 30, 1980, Christ Church Archives, Nashville, TN, https://954b6047-a-663e912c-s-sites.googlegroups.com/a/christcathedral.org/archives/vestry/1980-VestryMinutes.pdf; "Christ Church Vestry Minutes 1980," Christ Church Vestry Minutes, Feb. 18, 1977–Dec. 30, 1980, Christ Church Archives, Nashville, Tennessee, https://954b6047-a-663e912c-s-sites.googlegroups.com/a/christcathedral.org/archives/vestry/1980-VestryMinutes.pdf; "Christ Church Vestry Minutes 1976," Christ Church Vestry Minutes, Christ Church Archives, Nashville, TN, May 17, 1971–January 16, 1977, https://954b6047-a-663e912c-s-sites.googlegroups.com/a/christcathedral.org/archives/vestry/1976-VestryMinutes.pdf; "Christ Church Vestry Minutes 1980," Christ Church Vestry Minutes, February 18, 1977–December 30, 1980, Christ Church Archives, Nashville, TN, https://954b6047-a-663e912c-s-sites.googlegroups.com/a/christcathedral.org/archives/vestry/1980-VestryMinutes.pdf.

30. "Christ Church Vestry Minutes 1980," Christ Church Vestry Minutes, February 18, 1977–December 30, 1980, Christ Church Archives, Nashville, TN, https://954b6047-a-663e912c-s-sites.googlegroups.com/a/christcathedral.org/archives/vestry/1980-VestryMinutes.pdf.

31. "Gerald Gimre," *Des Moines Register*, August 15, 1991; "Deaths," *Des Moines Register*, June 6, 1986; "Deaths," *Des Moines Register*, January 19, 1988; "Christ Church Vestry Minutes 1991," April 19, 1991–April 16, 1993, Christ Church Archives, Nashville, TN, https://954b6047-a-663e912c-s-sites.googlegroups.com/a/christcathedral.org/archives/vestry/1991-VestryMinutes.pdf.

32. *Polk's 1982*, 9, 10, 156–651; interview with Dollye Matthews; interview with Bill Purcell.

33. Alan Bostick, "At Night, Lower Broadway's a Stage," *Tennessean*, January 5, 1987.

34. Interview with Bill Purcell.

35. Interview with Bill Purcell.

36. Bernie W. Arnold, *Nashville Cuisine: A Sampling of Restaurants and Their Recipes* (Kansas City, MO: Two Lane Press, 1992), x

37. Gail Kerr, "In Politics, Sometimes Courage Is a Matter of Finishing What You Started," *Tennessean*, March 14, 2001.

38. Conversation with André Prince Jeffries.

39. Gail Kerr, "In Politics, Sometimes Courage."

40. Dave Hoekstra, "Nashville's Original Hot Chicken," *Chicago Sun-Times*, September 10, 2006.

41. Hoekstra, "Nashville's Original Hot Chicken."

42. Gail Kerr, "In Politics, Sometimes Courage."

43. Interview with Bill Purcell; interview with André Prince Jeffries.

44. Thayer Wine, "Hot Chicken!" *Tennessean*, October 28, 2002.

45. Mark Ippolito, "Edgefield Wants Out of Enterprise," *Tennessean*, October 21, 1997.

46. Warren Duzak, "As People Move Back to City, Neighborhoods Plan for Future," *Tennessean*, April 18, 1984.

47. Marsha Vandeberg, "Edgefield Bill Advances," *Tennessean*, May 3, 1978; Renee Elder, "E. Nashville Finds a New Popularity," *Tennessean*, November 3, 1990; Renee Elder, "In with the Old, Out with the Poor?" *Tennessean*, November 11, 1990.

48. Elder, "E. Nashville Finds a New Popularity."

49. Adam Tanner, "Lifestyle Change May Have Sparked Fires," *Tennessean*, July 31, 1991.

50. Ted Rutland, *Displacing Blackness: Planning, Power and Race in Twentieth-Century Halifax* (Toronto: University of Toronto Press, 2018), 4.

51. White low-income neighborhoods housed 11.2 percent of the county's families, and they received 5.8 percent of the mortgages; Lacrisha Butherl, "Lending Practice Binds the Black Economically," *Tennessean*, February 26, 1989. By 1990, Davidson county had twenty-one historic districts, but only two were in North Nashville and two in East; "TENNESSEE—Davidson County—Historic Districts," *National Register of Historic Places*, https://nationalregisterofhistoricplaces.com/tn/davidson/districts.html.

52. Renee Elder, "Extending Edgefield Historic Area to Hurt Poor, Pastor Says," *Tennessean*, October 31, 1990.

53. Keith Snider, "East Community Fights for Funds," *Nashville Tennessean*, August 20, 1998.

54. Interview with André Prince Jeffries.

CHAPTER 8

1. Steve Younes, interview by the author, Living Waters Brewing, Nashville, TN, February 11, 2020.

2. Timothy P. Marshall and Tim Troutman, "Damage and Radar Analysis of the Nashville, TN, Tornado," Conference: 20th Conference on Severe Local Storms, January 2000, in Orlando, FL; Ricky Rogers, "Tornadoes Slammed into Nashville in 1998: 5 Things to Know," *Tennessean*, April 15, 2018; Nate Rau, "1998 Tornado Traumatized, then Sparked Revitalization in East Nashville," *Tennessean*, April 15, 2018; Jake Reed, "The 'Forgotten F5' Tornado of April 16, 1998," *WHNT19 News*, April 16, 2017, https://whnt.com/weather/valleywx-blog/the-forgotten-f5-tornado-of-april-16-1998.

3. Rogers, "Tornadoes Slammed into Nashville"; Rau, "1998 Tornado Traumatized"; Marshall and Troutman, "Damage and Radar Analysis."

4. Christine Kreyling, "R/UDAT: What's That?" *Nashville Scene*, January 14, 1999, https://www.nashvillescene.com/news/article/13002931/rudat-whats-that; Dan Heller, "If You Build It . . . How a Tornado Sparked East Nashville's Economic Resurrection," *East Nashvillian*, March 1, 2013, https://www.theeastnashvillian.com/15-years-later.

5. Christine Kreyling, "R/UDAT: What's That?" *Nashville Scene*, January 14, 1999, https://www.nashvillescene.com/news/article/13002931/rudat-whats-that; Dan Heller, "If You Build It . . . How a Tornado Sparked East Nashville's Economic Resurrection," *East Nashvillian*, March 1, 2013, https://www.theeastnashvillian.com/15-years-later.

6. Bill Purcell, "What Makes Us Stronger: A Reflection," *East Nashvillian*, March 1, 2013, https://www.theeastnashvillian.com/15-years-later.

7. Interview with Dollye Matthews.

8. Interview with Dollye Matthews.

9. Babcock and Babcock, "HNC"; Kay West, "Fried and True," *Nashville Scene*, April 19, 2001, https://www.nashvillescene.com/news/features/article/13005640/fried-and-tru.

10. Interview with Dollye Matthews; Kay West, "On a Roll," *Nashville Scene*, March 1, 2001, https://www.nashvillescene.com/news/features/article/13005446/on-a-roll; West, "Fried and True"; Babcock and Babcock, "HNC."

11. Edge, *Fried Chicken*, 132.

12. Babcock and Babcock, "HNC."

13. Chris Chamberlain, "Hot Chicken's World Domination," *Nashville Scene*, January 17, 2019, https://www.nashvillescene.com/food-drink/features/article/21041562/hot-chickens-world-domination.

14. David Burke, "Multifaceted Morgan Living in Limbo," *Quad-City Times*, April 8, 2010, https://qctimes.com/entertainment/music/multifaceted-morgan-

living-in-limbo/article_6c76c010-4198-11df-a9ab-001cc4c03286.html.

15. Interview with André Prince Jeffries.

16. Interview with Bill Purcell.

17. Jamie McGee, "Great Recession: Nashville's Opportunities, Challenges 10 Years Later," *Tennessean*, August 28, 2018, https://www.tennessean.com/story/money/2018/08/28/great-recession-nashville-10-years-later/824196002.

18. McGee, "Great Recession."

19. Interview with André Prince Jeffries.

20. Jane and Michael Stern, *Roadfood: An Eater's Guide to More Than 1,000 of the Best Local Hot Spots and Hidden Gems Across American* 10th edition (New York: Clarkson/Potter Publishers, 2017), 149.

21. Dan Angell, "Hattie B.'s Hot Chicken, Nashville, Tenn.," *Dan vs. Food* (March 26, 2013), accessed June 1, 2020, https://danvfood.wordpress.com/2013/03/26/hattie-bs-hot-chicken-nashville-tenn.

22. Interview with André Prince Jeffries.

23. Interview with Dollye Matthews.

24. Egerton, *Southern Food*, 16.

25. Witt, *Black Hunger*, 4–6; Frank Cullin, Florence Hackman and Donald McNeilly, *Vaudeville Old and New*, vol. 1 (New York: Routledge, 2007), 47.

CONCLUSION

1. Jamie Winders, *Nashville in the New Millennium: Immigrant Settlement, Urban Transformation and Social Belonging* (New York: Russel Sage Foundation, 2013), xix, 232; "Who Are the Kurds, and Why Are They in Nashville?" *Nashville Tennessean*, June 22, 2017; "Nashville, Tennessee Population 2020," *World Population Review*, http://worldpopulationreview.com/us-cities/nashville-population.

2. "'Community Statesmen' Need of City, Dr. Mims Says," *Nashville Tennessean*, April 27, 1949.

3. Witt, "Soul Food," 259.

EPILOGUE

1. Matthew Cappucci, "Tornado/Tornado Family May Have Been on Ground for More Than 50 Miles," March 3, 2020, https://twitter.com/Matthew Cappucci/status/1234833499867271175; Javier Zarracina and Janet Loehrke, "Mapping the Toll of Tuesday's Storms and Tornadoes in Nashville," *USA Today*, March 4, 2020, https://www.usatoday.com/in-depth/news/2020/03/03/nashville-tornadoes-mapping-storms-destruction/4937753002.

2. "Airport Sign Lands in Mt. Juliet Yard," *WKRN News*, March 4, 2020, https://www.wkrn.com/news/nashville-tornado/airport-sign-lands-in-mt-juliet-yard; Putnum County was hit even harder than Nashville. Eighteen of the people who died lived there, and two days after the storm, over a dozen people were still missing; Frances Stead Sellers, Meryl Kornfield, Kim Bellware and Brandon Gee, "Tennessee Tornado: Dozens Still Missing After Storms that Killed at Least 24 People," *Washington Post*, March 4, 2020, https://www.washingtonpost.com/weather/2020/03/04/nashville-tennessee-tornado-death-toll; Phil Helsel, Ben Kesslen and David K. Li, "At Least 24 Dead after Tornado Rips Through Nashville and Central Tennessee," *CBS News*, March 4, 2020, https://www.washingtonpost.com/weather/2020/03/04/nashville-tennessee-tornado-death-toll; Nicole Chavez, Jason Hanna and Chuck Johnston, "24 People Are Dead After a Tornado Ripped Through Tennessee and Destroyed Numerous Homes," CNN, March 4, 2020, https://www.cnn.com/2020/03/03/weather/nashville-tornado-tuesday/index.html.

3. Steve Hale, "After the Tornado, Vultures Descend on North Nashville," *Nashville Scene*, March 6, 2020, https://www.nashvillescene.com/news/pith-in-the-wind/article/21120560/after-the-tornado-vultures-descend-on-north-nashville; Travis Loller, "Tornado Clobbered Historically Black Neighborhood in Nashville," *Portland Press Herald*, March 7, 2020.

4. Interview with Dollye Matthews.

5. Interview with Learotha Williams.

6. Randy Fox, "Friday News Letter, March 6," *East Nashvillian*, March 6, 2020, https://www.theeastnashvillian.com/tornado-edition.

Bibliography

ARCHIVES

Davidson County Chancery Court
Davidson County Metro Nashville Archives
Tennessee State Library and Archives
Williamson County Archives and Museum

CENSUS RECORDS & VITAL RECORDS

Iowa. Marshalltown. United States World War I Draft Registration Cards,
      1917–1918. May 31, 2020. http://ancestry.com.
Tennessee. Davidson County. 1920 US Census, population schedule. Digital
      images. Ancestry.com. November 12, 2019. http://ancestry.com.
Tennessee. Davidson County. Death certificates. Tennessee Department of
      Public Health. Nashville.
Tennessee. Davidson County. United States World War I Draft Registration
      Cards, 1917–1918. November 12, 2019. http://ancestry.com.
Tennessee. Williamson County. 1850 US Census, slave schedule. Digital im-
      ages. Ancestry.com. May 31, 2020. http://ancestry.com.

Tennessee. Williamson County. 1860 US Census, slave schedule. Digital images. Ancestry.com. May 31, 2020. http://ancestry.com.

Tennessee. Williamson County. 1880 US Census, population schedule. Digital images. Ancestry.com. September 25, 2019. http://ancestry.com.

Tennessee. Williamson County. 1891 Enumeration of Male Voters. Digital images. Ancestry.com. October 4, 2019. http://ancestry.com.

Tennessee. Williamson County. 1900 US Census, population schedule. Digital images. Ancestry.com. September 25, 2019. http://ancestry.com.

Tennessee. Williamson County. 1910 US Census, population schedule. Digital images. Ancestry.com. November 12, 2019. http://ancestry.com.

Tennessee. Williamson County. 1920 US Census, population schedule. Digital images. Ancestry.com. November 12, 2019. http://ancestry.com.

Tennessee. Williamson County. World War II Draft Registration Cards, 1940–1947. Ancestry.com. November 12, 2019. http://ancestry.com.

Tennessee. Williamson County. Marriage certificates. Tennessee County Marriages 1790–1950. Nashville.

United States Social Security Applications and Claims Index, 1936–2007.

CITY DIRECTORIES

1983 Nashville (Davidson County, Tenn.) City Directory. Taylor, MI: R.L. Polk and Company, 1983.

1984 Nashville (Davidson County, Tenn.) City Directory. Taylor, MI: R.L. Polk and Company, 1984.

Caron's Directory of the City of Louisville for 1925. Louisville, KY: Caron Directory Company, 1925.

Caron's Directory of the City of Louisville for 1926. Louisville, KY: Caron Directory Company, 1926.

Caron's Directory of the City of Louisville for 1927. Louisville, KY: Caron Directory Company, 1927.

Caron's Directory of the City of Louisville for 1928. Louisville, KY: Caron Directory Company, 1929.

Caron's Directory of the City of Louisville for 1928. Louisville, KY: Caron Directory Company, 1928.

Marshall-Bruce-Polk Co.'s Nashville City Directory, 1918. Nashville, TN: Marshall-Bruce-Polk Company, 1918.

Marshall-Bruce-Polk Co.'s Nashville City Directory, 1920. Nashville, TN: Marshall-Bruce-Polk Company, 1920.

Marshall-Bruce-Polk Co.'s Nashville City Directory, 1920–21. Nashville, TN: Marshall-Bruce-Polk Company, 1921.

Marshall-Bruce-Polk Co.'s Nashville City Directory, 1922. Nashville, TN: Marshall-Bruce-Polk Company, 1922.

Marshall-Bruce-Polk Co.'s Nashville City Directory, 1924. Nashville, TN: Marshall-Bruce-Polk Company, 1924.

Marshall-Bruce-Polk Co.'s Nashville City Directory, 1928. Nashville, TN: Marshall-Bruce-Polk Company, 1928.

Marshall-Bruce-Polk Co.'s Nashville City Directory, 1931. Nashville, TN: Marshall-Bruce-Polk Company, 1931.

Marshall Bruce Polk Co.'s Nashville City Directory, 1933. Nashville, TN: Marshall-Bruce-Polk Company, 1933.

Marshall-Bruce-Polk Co.'s Nashville City Directory, 1940. Nashville, TN: Marshall-Bruce-Polk Company, 1940.

Marshall-Bruce-Polk Co.'s Nashville City Directory, 1942. Nashville, TN: Marshall-Bruce-Polk Company, 1942.

Marshall-Bruce-Polk Co.'s Nashville City Directory, 1943. Nashville, TN: Marshall-Bruce-Polk Company, 1943.

Marshall-Bruce-Polk Co.'s Nashville City Directory, 1946. Nashville, TN: Marshall-Bruce-Polk Company, 1946.

Marshall-Bruce-Polk Co.'s Nashville City Directory, 1947. Nashville, TN: Marshall-Bruce-Polk Company, 1947.

Marshall-Bruce-Polk Co.'s Nashville City Directory, 1950. Nashville, TN: Marshall-Bruce-Polk Company, 1950.

Marshall-Bruce-Polk Co.'s Nashville City Directory, 1951. Nashville, TN: Marshall-Bruce-Polk Company, 1951.

Marshall-Bruce-Polk Co.'s Nashville City Directory, 1953. Nashville, TN: Marshall-Bruce-Polk Company, 1953.

Marshall-Bruce-Polk Co.'s Nashville City Directory, 1956. Nashville, TN: Marshall-Bruce-Polk Company, 1956.

Marshall-Bruce-Polk Co.'s Nashville City Directory, 1958. Nashville, TN: Marshall-Bruce-Polk Company, 1958.

Marshall-Bruce-Polk Co.'s Nashville City Directory, 1959. Nashville, TN: Marshall-Bruce-Polk Company, 1959.

Marshall-Bruce-Polk Co.'s Nashville City Directory, 1960. Nashville, TN: Marshall-Bruce-Polk Company, 1960.

Marshall-Bruce-Polk Co.'s Nashville City Directory, 1961. Nashville, TN: Marshall-Bruce-Polk Company, 1961.

Marshall-Bruce-Polk Co.'s Nashville City Directory, 1962. Nashville, TN: Marshall-Bruce-Polk Company, 1962.

Marshall-Bruce-Polk Co.'s Nashville City Directory, 1963. Nashville, TN: Marshall-Bruce-Polk Company, 1963.

Marshall-Bruce-Polk Co.'s Nashville City Directory, 1964. Nashville, TN: Marshall-Bruce-Polk Company, 1964.

Marshall-Bruce-Polk Co.'s Nashville City Directory, 1965. Nashville, TN: Marshall-Bruce-Polk Company, 1965.

Polk's Nashville (Davidson County, Tenn.) City Directory 1966. Detroit: RL Polk and Company, 1966.

Polk's Nashville (Davidson County, Tenn.) City Directory 1971. Detroit: RL Polk and Company, 1971.

Polk's Nashville (Davidson County, Tenn.) City Directory 1972. Detroit: RL Polk and Company, 1972.

Polk's Nashville (Davidson County, Tenn.) City Directory 1973. Detroit: RL Polk and Company, 1973.

Polk's Nashville (Davidson County, Tenn.) City Directory 1974. Detroit: RL Polk and Company, 1974.

Polk's Nashville (Davidson County, Tenn.) City Directory 1975. Detroit: RL Polk and Company, 1975.

Polk's Nashville (Davidson County, Tenn.) City Directory 1974. Detroit: RL Polk and Company, 1974.

Polk's Nashville (Davidson County, Tenn.) City Directory 1976. Detroit: RL Polk and Company, 1976.

Polk's Nashville (Davidson County, Tenn.) City Directory 1978. Detroit: RL Polk and Company, 1978.

Polk's Nashville (Davidson County, Tenn.) City Directory 1979. Detroit: RL Polk and Company, 1979.

Polk's Nashville (Davidson County, Tenn.) City Directory 1982. Detroit: RL Polk and Company, 1982.

Register of Commissioned and Warrant Officers of the United States Naval Reserve. Washington: United States Government Printing Office, 1944.

Register of Commissioned and Warrant Officers of the United States Naval Reserve. Washington: United States Government Printing Office, 1951.

INTERVIEWS

Jeffries, André Prince. Interview by the author. Prince's Hot Chicken Shack, Nashville, TN. March 18, 2015.

Matthews, Dollye. Interview by the author. Bolton's Spicy Chicken and Fish, Nashville, TN. February 20, 2020.

———. Interview by Amy C. Evans. Southern Foodways Alliance. Nashville, TN. May 31, 2008.

Purcell, Bill. Interview by the author. Belcher, Sykes, Harrington LLC, Nashville, TN. March 2015.

Swett, David, Jr. Interview with John Egerton. Nashville, TN. July 17, 2006.

Townes, Hap. Interview with John Egerton. Southern Foodways Alliance. Nashville, TN. July 17, 2006.

Williams, Learotha, Jr. Interview with the author. Farmer's Market, Nashville, TN. February 11, 2020.

Younes, Steve. Interview by the author. Living Waters Brewing, Nashville, TN. February 11, 2020.

NEWSPAPERS, MAGAZINES, & TELEVISION STATIONS

ABC 2

CNN

Des Moines Register

East Nashvillian

Fox 17

Nashville American

Nashville Banner

Nashville Globe

Nashville Scene

NBC 4

Portland Press Herald

Tennessean

Times-Republican

Today

USA Today

Washington Post

BOOKS & ARTICLES

Adams, Luther. "'Headed for Louisville': Rethinking Rural to Urban Migration in the South, 1930–1950." *Journal of Social History* (Winter 2006): 407–30.

Alexander, Kevin. *Burn the Ice: The American Culinary Revolution and Its End.* New York: Penguin, 2019.

Arnold, Bernie W. *Nashville Cuisine: A Sampling of Restaurants and Their Recipes.* Kansas City, MO: Two Lane Press, 1992.

Arnstein, Sherry R. "A Ladder of Citizen Participation." *Journal of the American Institute of Planners* 35, no. 4 (July 1969): 216–26.

Babcock, Eric, and Page La Grone Babcock. "HNC: Nevermind Hot New Country, Here's Nashville Hot Chicken." *No Depression: The Journal of Roots Music* 42 (October 2002). Accessed February 23, 2020. https://www.nodepression.com/hnc-nevermind-hot-new-country-heres-hot-nashville-chicken.

Barnhart, Kenneth. "Negro Homicides in the United States." *Opportunity: Journal of Negro Life.* 10–11 (July 1932): 212–14.

Battle, Thelma. *Natchez Street Revisited*, vol. 1. Franklin, TN: Williamson County Historical Society, 2016.

———. *We Ran until Who Lasted the Longest: A Local Collection of True Ghost Stories and Other Miscellaneous Testimonies*. Franklin, TN: Williams County Historical Society, 2007.

Benjamin, Robert W. "The Kemp-Garcia Enterprise Zone Bill: A New, Less Costly Approach to Urban Redevelopment." *Fordham Law Journal* 9, no. 3 (1981): 659–95.

Berlin, Ira and Leslie S. Rowland, eds., *Families and Freedom: A Documentary History of African American Kinship in the Civil War*. New York: New Press, 1997.

Bobrow-Strain, Aaron. *White Bread: A Social History of the Store-Bought Loaf*. Boston: Beacon Press, 2012.

Bock, Sheila. "'I Know You Got Soul': Traditionalizing a Contested Cuisine." In *Comfort Food: Meanings and Memories*, edited by Michael Owen Jones and Lucy M. Long, 163–81. Oxford: University Press of Mississippi, 2017.

Boxwell, Leslie G. "Necessity of a State Highway Department." *Tennessee Agriculture* 3, no. 1 (January 1914).

Brearley, Harrington Cooper. *Homicide in the United States*. Chapel Hill: University of North Carolina Press, 1932.

Briggs, Gabriel A. *The New Negro in the Old South*. New Brunswick, NJ: Rutgers University Press, 2015.

Christenson, Mason K. "The Saloon in Nashville and the Coming of Prohibition in Tennessee." MA thesis, Middle Tennessee State University, Murfreesboro, 2013. Accessed January 14, 2020. https://jewlscholar.mtsu.edu/bitstream/handle/mtsu/3578/Christensen_mtsu_0170N_10152.pdf.

Cimprich, John. *Slavery's End in Tennessee: 1861–1865*. Tuscaloosa: University of Alabama Press, 2002.

Cooper, Abigail. "Interactive Map of Contraband Camps." *History Digital Projects* (2014). https://repository.upenn.edu/hist_digital/1.

Cullin, Frank, Florence Hackman, and Donald McNeilly. *Vaudeville Old and New*, vol. 1. New York: Routledge, 2007.

Deetz, Kelley Fanto. *Bound to the Fire: How Virginia's Enslaved Cooks Helped Invent American Cuisine.* Lexington: University Press of Kentucky, 2017.

Downs, Jim. *Sick from Freedom: African American Illness and Suffering during the Civil War and Reconstruction.* New York: Oxford University Press, 2012.

Dolzall, Gary W. "The Tennessee Central Story, Part 1." *Trains.* (September 1987).

Edge, John T., ed., *Foodways*, vol. 7. Chapel Hill: University of North Carolina Press, 2007.

————. *Fried Chicken: An American Story.* New York: G.P. Putnam's Sons, 2004.

Egerton, John. *Southern Food: At Home, on the Road, in History.* New York: Alfred A. Knopf, 1987.

Elliott, Lizzie Porter. *Early History of Nashville.* Nashville: Board of Education, 1911.

Geraldton, William W. *Nashville Social Directory.* Nashville: Cumberland Press, 1911.

Glenn, Evelyn Nakano. *Unequal Freedom: How Race and Gender Shaped American Citizenship and Labor.* Cambridge, MA: Harvard University Press, 2002.

Goldin, Claudia. "Female Labor Force Participation: The Origin of Black and White Differences, 1870 and 1880." *Journal of Economic History* 37, no. 1 (1977): 87–108.

Hadley, Lois Meguiar. *Garnered Memories: Journals by Elizabeth Lois Meguiar Hadley.* Nashville Metro Archives, http://www.nashvillearchives.org/documents/garnered-memories.pdf.

Harcourt, Edward John. "'That Mystic Cloud': Civil War Memory in the Tennessee Heartland, 1865–1920." PhD Diss., Vanderbilt University, 2008.

Harrison, William Henry. *Colored Girls' and Boys' Inspiring United States History and a Heart to Heart Talk about White Folks.* Self-published, 1921. Accessed February 2, 2020. https://www.gutenberg.org/files/57181/57181-h/57181-h.htm.

Hemdahl, Reuel. *Urban Renewal.* New York: Scarecrow Press, 1959.

Higginbotham, Evelyn Brooks. *Righteous Discontent: The Women's Movement in the Black Baptist Church, 1880–1920.* Boston: Harvard University Press, 1994.

Hoobler, James A. *A Guide to Historic Nashville, Tennessee.* Charleston: History Press, 2008.

Hopewell, P. C. "Tuberculosis in the United States before, during and after World War II." *Tuberculosis and War: Lessons Learned from World War II* 43 (2018): 179–87.

Hubbard, Theodora Kimball and Katherine McNamara. *Planning Information Up-To-Date: A Supplement, 1923–1928.* London: Oxford University Press, 1928. https://doi.org/10.1002/ncr.4110180511.

Karas, David. "Highway to Inequity: The Disparate Impact of the Interstate Highway System on Poor and Minority Communities in American Cities. *New Visions for Public Affairs*, no. 7 (April 2015): 9–21.

Kerby, Bill and David Thompson. "Spanish Galleons off Jersey Coast or 'We Live Off Excess Volume.'" In *Hendrix on Hendrix: Interviews and Encounters with Jimi Hendrix*, edited by Steven Roby, 55–60. Chicago: Chicago Review Press, 2012.

Kyriakoudes, Louis M. "Southern Black Rural-Urban Migration in the Era of the Great Migration: Nashville and Middle Tennessee, 1890–1930." *Agricultural History* 72, no. 2 (Spring 1998): 341–51.

Lam, Francis. "Edna Lewis and the Black Roots of American Cooking." In *Edna Lewis: At the Table with an American Original*, edited by Sara B. Franklin, 58–69. Chapel Hill: University of North Carolina Press, 2018.

Lewis, Edna. *The Taste of Country Cooking*, 30th Anniversary Edition. New York: Alfred A. Knopf, 2006.

Lovett, Bobby L. *The African-American History of Nashville Tennessee, 1780–1930: Elites and Dilemmas*. Fayetteville: University of Arkansas Press, 1999.

Mandelker, Daniel R. "The Comprehensive Planning Requirement in Urban Renewal," *University of Pennsylvania Law Review* 116, no. 1 (November 1967): 25–73.

Manning, Chandra. "Working for Citizenship in Civil War Contraband Camps." *Journal of the Civil War* 4, no. 2 (June 2014): 172–204.

McBride, William D. and S. Darrell Mundy. "Farrow-to-Finish Swine Production in Ten Counties of West Tennessee." Research Report, University of Tennessee Agricultural Experiment Station (1987) http://trace.tennessee.edu/utk_agresreport/90.

Middle Tennessee Business Association. *Operation Northtown*. Nashville: Middle Tennessee Business Association, 1969.

Mohl, Raymond A. "Citizen Activism and Freeway Revolts in Memphis and Nashville: The Road to Litigation." *Journal of Urban History* 40, no. 5 (2014): 870–93.

Nashville Public Schools. *Annual Report of the Public Schools of Nashville, Tennessee, 1924–1925*. Nashville: Ambrose Printing, 1925.

Nelson, Robert K. LaDale Winling, Richard Marciano, Nathan Connolly, et al., "Mapping Inequality." *American Panorama*. Edited by Robert K. Nelson and Edward L. Ayers. Accessed March 20, 2020. https://dsl.richmond.edu/panorama/redlining/#loc=12/36.151/-86.888&city=nashville-tn.

O'Brien, Gail Williams. *The Color of the Law: Race, Violence and Justice in the Post-World War II South*. Chapel Hill: University of North Carolina Press, 1999.

Office of Community Development Evaluation Division, Department of Housing and Urban Development. *The Model Cities Program: A Comparative*

Analysis of City Response Patterns and Their Relation to Future Urban Policy. Washington, DC: Government Printing Office, 1973.

Opie, Frederick Douglass. *Hog and Hominy: Soul Food from Africa to America.* New York: Columbia University Press, 2008.

Randall, Alice, and Caroline Randall Williams. *Soul Food Love: Healthy Recipes Inspired by One Hundred Years of Cooking in a Black Family.* New York: Clarkson Potter, 2015.

Robert, Charles Edwin. *Nashville and Her Trade for 1870.* Nashville: Roberts and Purvis, Republican Banner Office, 1870.

Roediger, David R. *Seizing Freedom: Slave Emancipation and Liberty for All.* New York: Verso Books, 2014.

Rose, Dixie. "YWCA Blue Triangle Branch Collection." Nashville Public Library. (February 9, 2019). Accessed February 2, 2020. https://library. nashville.org/blog/2019/02/ywca-blue-triangle-branch-collection.

Rutland, Ted. *Displacing Blackness: Planning, Power and Race in Twentieth-Century Halifax.* Toronto: University of Toronto Press, 2018.

Smith, Eric Ledell. "Bijou Theater." In *African American Theater Buildings: An Illustrated Historical Directory, 1900–1955,* 198–202. New York: McFarland, 2011.

Spinney, Robert Guy. *World War II in Nashville: Transformation of the Homefront.* Knoxville: University of Tennessee Press, 1998.

Starr, Kevin. *Golden Dreams: California in an Age of Abundance, 1950–1963.* New York: Oxford University Press, 2009.

Stern, Jane, and Michael Stern. *Roadfood: An Eater's Guide to More than 1,000 of the Best Local Hot Spots and Hidden Gems across America.* 10th edition. New York: Clarkson/Potter Publishers, 2017.

Sula, Mike. "The First Family of Fried Chicken: How Harold's Chicken Shack Grew from a Mom-and-Pop Stand to a Chain 62 Strong and Still Expanding." *Chicago Reader* (April 13, 2006). Accessed May 19, 2020. https://www.chicagoreader.com/chicago/the-first-family-of-fried-chicken/Content?oid=921815.

Taylor, Amy Murrell. *Embattled Freedom: Journeys through the Civil War's Refugee Camps.* Chapel Hill: University of North Carolina Pres, 2018.

"Tennessee Central Railway Company: The Scenic Railway of the South," *The Official Guide of the Railways and Steam Navigation Lines of the United States, Porto Rico, Canada, Mexico and Cuba.* New York: National Railway Publication Company, 1923.

Tennessee State Library and Archives. "Nashville – Jefferson Street." *Mapping the Destruction of Tennessee's African-American Neighborhoods.* Accessed May 31, 2020. https://www.arcgis.com/apps/MapSeries/index. html?appid=8dba65584072450ca8928a5f3408373f.

Tennessee State Planning Commission. *Tennessee State Industrial School.* Nashville: Tennessee State Planning Commission, 1937.

Tennessee Valley Archaeological Research. "Historic Background Research and Ground Penetrating Radar Survey Associated with the Greer Stadium Redevelopment Project in Nashville, Davidson County, Tennessee." Nashville: Metro Parks and Recreation, 2018.

Tompkins, Kyla Wazana. *Racial Indigestion: Eating Bodies in the 19th Century.* New York: New York University Press, 2012.

Tomky, Naomi. "The Maker of Baton Rouge's Best Chicken Also Fought for Civil Rights." *Food and Wine* (December 17, 2018). Accessed May 19, 2020. https://www.foodandwine.com/travel/restaurants/chicken-shack-baton-rouge-civil-rights.

Twitty, Michael W. *The Cooking Gene: A Journey through African American Culinary History in the Old South.* New York: Amistad, 2017.

US Department of Housing and Urban Development. *Citizen Participation in the Model Cities Program.* Washington, DC: US Government Printing Office, 1972.

———. Department of Housing and Urban Development, *The President's National Urban Policy Report.* Washington, DC: US Government Printing Office, 1982

US Department of Labor Bureau of Labor Statistics, "Employment and Pay Rolls of the City of Nashville and Davidson County, Tennessee, 1929 through 1938," *State, County and Municipal Survey Employment Pay Rolls 1929 through 1938.* Washington, DC: Labor Statistics Bureau, 1939.

Websdale, Neil. *Policing the Poor: From Slave Plantation to Public Housing.* Boston: Northeastern University Press, 2001.

West, Kay. *Around the Opry Table: A Feast of Recipes and Stories from the Grand Ole Opry.* New York: Center Street, 2007.

Whitacre, Joseph A. and W. J. Moore. *Marshall County in the World War, 1917–1918.* Marshalltown, IA: Marshall Printing Company, 1919. Accessed May 12, 2020. https://hdl.handle.net/2027/wu.89072939655.

Wills, Eric. "The Forgotten: The Contraband of America and the Road to Freedom." *Saving Places,* June 19, 2017. https://savingplaces.org/stories/the-forgotten-the-contraband-of-america-and-the-road-to-freedom.

Winders, Jamie. *Nashville in the New Millennium: Immigrant Settlement, Urban Transformation and Social Belonging.* New York: Russel Sage Foundation, 2013.

Witt, Doris. "Soul Food: Where the Chitterling Hits the (Primal) Pan." In *Eating Culture,* edited by Ron Scapp and Brien Seitz, 258–87. New York: State University of New York Press, 1998.

Woods, Sylvia, and Family, with Melissa Clark. *Sylvia's Family Soul Food Cookbook: From Hemingway, South Carolina, to Harlem.* New York: William Morrow and Company, 1999.

Index

CPSIA information can be obtained
at www.ICGtesting.com
Printed in the USA
LVHW091936050221
678491LV00002B/267